"There are ideas here that will appeal to grandparents as well as to three-year-olds."
— **The Boston Phoenix**

"Still the definitive guidebook for exploring the area's cultural and recreational sites."
— **The Boston Globe**

"Bernice Chesler has summed up the city in 327 pages of colorful prose."
— **Travel-Holiday**

"Packed with more information than any tourist could ever digest, this book includes the brass tacks on the well-known historical sites, as well as more intriguing destinations."
— **San Francisco Chronicle**

"Going to Boston? Take this book!"
— **The News Chief, Winter Haven, Florida**

"My bible — a good overall view of the arts scene that includes lots of information and tips on other attractions as well."
— **Larry Murray, executive director, ARTS/Boston**

"An encyclopedia of the Boston area and a guide well worth owning."
— **Family Travel Times**

". . . Hundreds of ideas for day and weekend trips."
— **Boston Parents Paper**

in and out of
BOSTON
with (or without) children

in and out of
BOSTON
with (or without)
children
Fourth Edition

Bernice Chesler

Photography by Stan Grossfeld

The Globe Pequot Press

Chester, Connecticut

Library of Congress Catalogue Number: 81-86605

ISBN: 0-87106-968-7

BOOK DESIGN BY BARBARA BELL PITNOF
MAPS BY DEB PERUGI
COVER DESIGN BY PETER GOOD

Manufactured in the United States of America

Fourth Edition/Eighth Printing

To David

Introduction

The eight years since the publication of the third edition have brought many changes in Boston's skyline, shoreline, attractions, and activities. The city's world of arts is filled with new presentations and admission options. Museums have switched programs and, in some cases, emphasis. More harbor islands are open. Other factories give tours. Fitness trails have come to the area. Even the Freedom Trail has expanded. The completed Faneuil Hall Marketplace is within minutes of vantage points and architectural and historical treasures of interest to both casual and serious lookers. The presence of the National Park Service is a significant addition to Boston and nearby Lowell. Moreover, there have been changes in the way people spend their time . . . and money.

This book, too, has changed. What started almost two decades ago as a compilation of cultural, recreational, and historical resources for children now includes information sources for all ages along with special programs for young ones, teenagers, and older citizens. And there are details for groups and for handicapped persons.

Hundreds of visits, workshops, conversations, questionnaires, and letters have helped shape this fourth edition. Reactions and questions have been gathered from newcomers (students, singles, and families), empty-nesters who now tour with a new perspective, short-term visitors, and long-time residents. They ask for more combinations (what's near the observation tower, the historical site, the museum). They ask for a sampler (what to do with one, two, or three days in town), and a list of regularly scheduled free things to do. Reasonably priced restaurants are always in demand. In response to requests, the book now includes theater and sport arena seating plans, a directory of useful phone numbers, and more and completely updated maps.

So what's missing? A few overused small places don't want to be in print. Some nearby open spaces that are occasionally mentioned in the press aren't really open to the public. Some distant attractions that asked to be included are just too distant, sorry. Most out-of-town locations in the book are within an hour's drive or near some major destination. In any case, no one can pay to be included.

Almost all prices have doubled since the last edition. Figures were confirmed at press time, summer 1982, but it's always a good idea to check prices and hours.

To those who have asked, and to those who wonder, "Don't

you get tired of doing the same thing?"—there's only one response: Thank goodness for people! Bostonians have contagious zest, tenacity, curiosity, dedication, and imagination. And Boston experiences evoke strong opinions. Many shared impressions, joys, and even problems are interwoven in the text. Suggestions and ideas have come from seemingly everyone I know or have ever met: librarians, curators, historians, group leaders, tourists, teachers, counselors, television colleagues, friends, neighbors, children, foreign visitors, and family.

Thanks to my editor and designer, Barbara Pitnof, who has somehow maintained her sense of organization and humor during the year-long project. Thanks also to Linda Holmfred who spent one 90-degree month enthusiastically discovering and carefully observing the city.

There is always one more idea that surfaces from the diverse opportunities in this compact area. It's great to hear that readers are inspired to find, or are reminded of, other possibilities. Comments and suggestions are welcome. Please address them to me at The Globe Pequot Press, 138 West Main Street, Chester, Connecticut 06412.

Happy exploring.

Bernice Chesler

The information in this book has . . .

. . . **addresses** in Boston (and communities in Massachusetts) unless designated otherwise.

. . . **distances** and **directions** calculated from Boston.

. . . **admissions** and **fees** that are subject to change. (Permanence is hard to come by.)

. . . **hours** that may change, too. Check before you leave. It's a challenge to arrive and find there's a special reason for closed doors on a particular day.

. . . **area codes** whenever a particular exchange lies beyond the 617 area.

Group leaders know that . . .

. . . **reservations** are either necessary or preferred. They are mutually beneficial.

. . . **special rates** are often available with advance notice.

. . . it's a good idea to make an **advance visit.**

. . . **transportation** involves expense, insurance, and parental permission slips—all details that take time.

. . . **spring bookings** fill early in the school year.

. . . **rainy summer days** bring a deluge of requests to the larger institutions. The pages herein may help with the less obvious.

. . . **advance materials** may be available. Orientation creates interest. Follow-up is follow-through. (Those with young children sometimes role-play before an excursion.)

. . . **supervision** is essential. A recommended ratio: one adult for every ten children. (One for every six is even better.) Sometimes groups separate and then meet at a specified time.

. . . when **gravestone rubbing** is part of a field trip, they must check with the local city or town hall. (It's not allowed in Boston.)

. . . **Access to Boston** (page 270) has hundreds of exact architectural details to help people with special needs make plans.

. . . it's hard to plan every detail.

Contents

Maps and Seating Plans

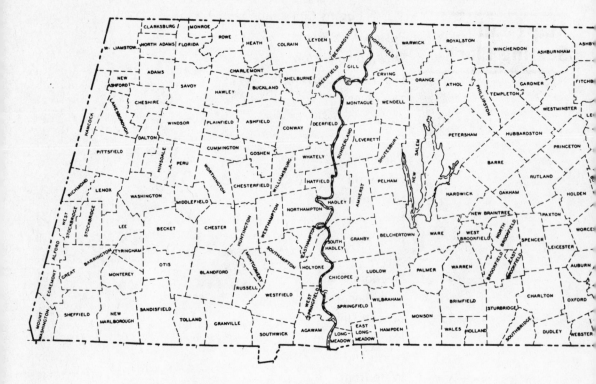

Massachusetts Cities and Towns

An Introduction
to the City

Boston Area Roads

One-Stop Introductions

- Where am I? How did Boston grow? The best introduction to the city: **John Hancock Observatory** (page 117).
- A good overview of today's Boston in a polished multimedia show: **Where's Boston** (page 133).
- The story of the city's landmarks and architecture shown with graphics and participatory displays: **Place Over Time.** For the current location of this popular exhibit — a filmed taxi ride and walk through Boston — call the Boston Landmarks Commission at 725-3850.

Information Centers

BOSTIX Page 34.

Cultural information about the performing arts, museums, and tourist attractions. And a good place for buying tickets.

Boston Common Information Booth Tremont Street (at West, opposite McDonald's)

Ⓣ: Park Street on the Red or Green Line.
OPEN: Year-round, 9-5 daily except Thanksgiving, Christmas, and New Year's.

In-person service only. Multilingual staff. Free brochures. Maps and guidebooks for sale.

Boston National Historical Park Visitor Center 15 State Street
PHONE: 223-0058.
DIRECTIONS: Opposite the Old State House, 1 block from Faneuil Hall (away from the waterfront).
Ⓣ: State on the Orange or Blue Line.
OPEN: Year-round, 9-5 daily except Thanksgiving, Christmas, and New Year's.

Helpful staff, free maps and plenty of printed information, and welcome rest rooms.

The National Park Service also runs the visitors' center at **Charlestown Navy Yard** (page 105). It's open 9 to 5 daily, and offers the same kind of information *and* free parking.

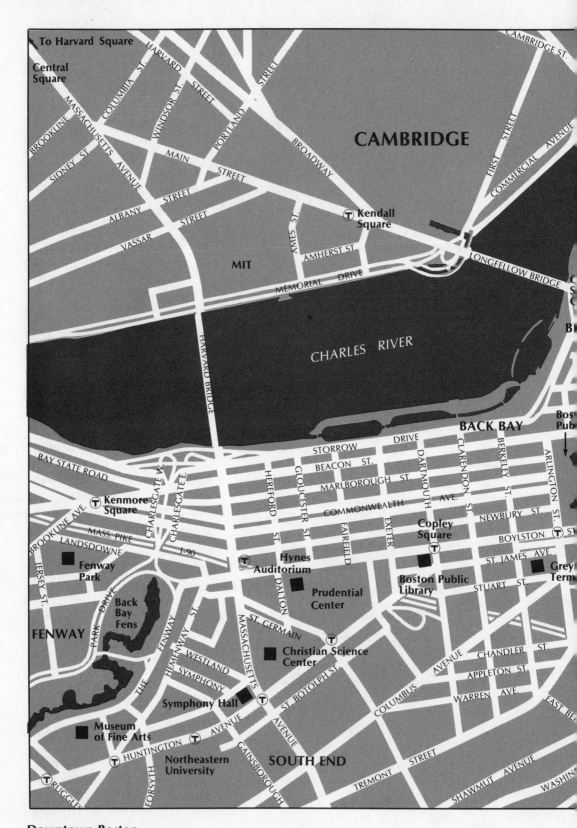

Downtown Boston

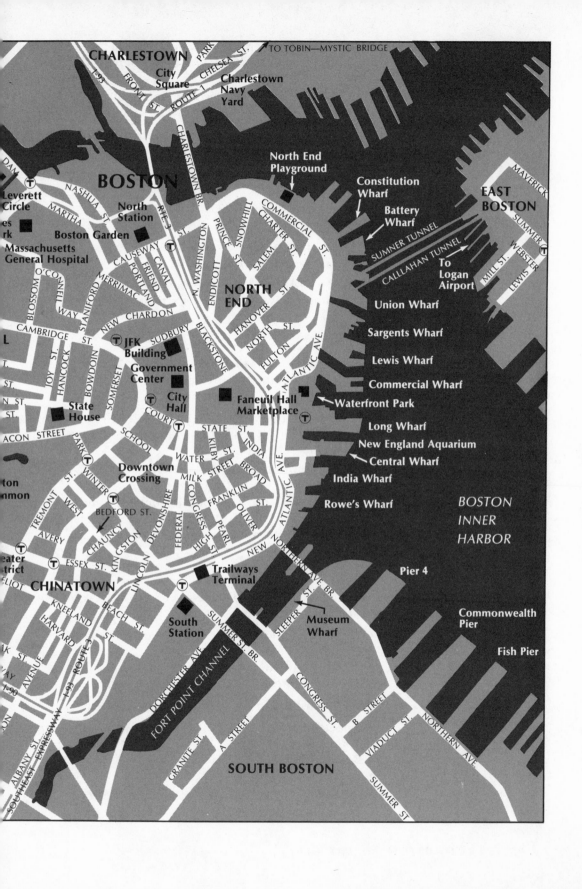

CHARLESTOWN

TO TOBIN—MYSTIC BRIDGE

City Square

Charlestown Navy Yard

North End Playground

Constitution Wharf

Battery Wharf

EAST BOSTON

MAVERICK

BOSTON

Leverett Circle

North Station

SUMNER TUNNEL

CALLLAHAN TUNNEL

To Logan Airport

Boston Garden

Massachusetts General Hospital

NORTH END

Union Wharf

Sargents Wharf

JFK Building

Government Center

Lewis Wharf

Commercial Wharf

Waterfront Park

City Hall

Faneuil Hall Marketplace

Long Wharf

New England Aquarium

State House

Central Wharf

India Wharf

Downtown Crossing

Rowe's Wharf

BOSTON INNER HARBOR

BEDFORD ST.

Trailways Terminal

Pier 4

CHINATOWN

South Station

Museum Wharf

Commonwealth Pier

Fish Pier

SOUTH BOSTON

Greater Boston Convention & Tourist Bureau 15 State Street (in the same building as the National Park Service visitors' center)

PHONE: 367-9275, 338-1976 (recorded information).
OPEN: Weekdays 9-5. Closed holidays.

In-person or phone information about hotels, restaurants, shopping, museums, and tourist sites.

Recorded Information

TIME AND TEMPERATURE: 637-1234.

LOCAL WEATHER: 936-1212.

NATIONAL WEATHER SERVICE: 567-4670.

MARINE WEATHER (SPRING-FALL): 569-3700.

SMITHSONIAN OBSERVATORY SATELLITE INFORMATION: 491-1497.

VOICE OF AUDUBON (WHAT BIRDS HAVE BEEN SEEN WHERE): 259-8805.

Help

For other services, see More (pages 267-273). Also see the community service numbers at the beginning of the Boston phone book.

EMERGENCY MEDICAL SERVICES: Call the Beth Israel Hospital Visitor Hotline at 735-3300. Calls about children are referred to Children's Hospital, 735-6000.

POISON INFORMATION: 232-2120. The Boston center is at 300 Longwood Avenue.

24-HOUR PHARMACY: The only one for miles around is Phillips Drug, 155 Charles Street, Boston, 523-1028. It's at Charles Street Circle, near Massachusetts General Hospital.

Events

Published listings are everywhere, but the most complete information can be found in

- **The Boston Globe:** All Thursday editions have Calendar, an event supplement.
- **The Boston Phoenix:** A weekly issued on Saturdays.
- **The Herald American:** The Sunday edition.

Recorded listings include

- **Selected Events:** 338-1976 (Greater Boston Convention & Tourist Bureau).
- **Boston Garden:** 227-3200.
- **Boston Jazz Line:** 262-1300.
- **Harvard University:** 495-1718 (during the school year), 495-2939 (summers).

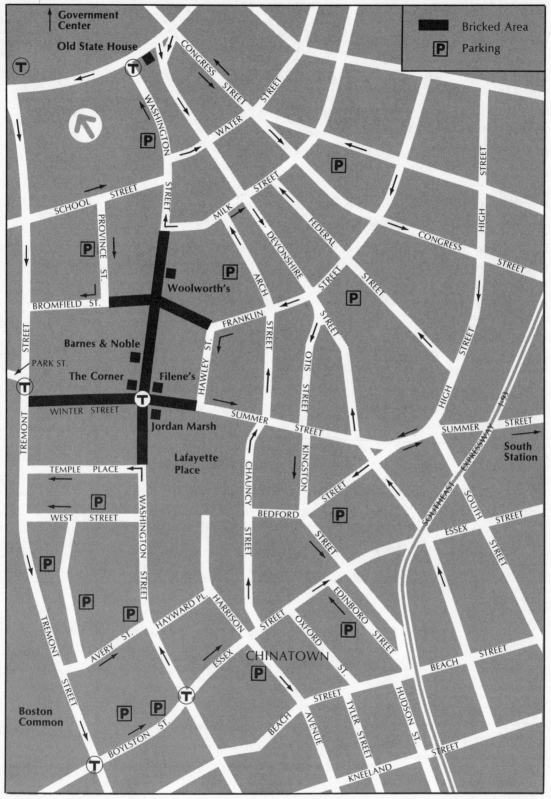

Downtown Crossing

One, Two, or Three Days in Boston

Even a compact city can be too much to cover all at once. The Market-place (page 131) is a magnet. The Freedom Trail (page 95) isn't arranged chronologically — each site stands on its own merit — so it doesn't have to be done all at once or in any order. Some visitors concentrate on major museums (a visit to any one can easily absorb a half day).

These suggestions should reduce a bountiful menu to edible size.

One Day, an Outside Overview with Inside Options
(to Swallow the City Whole, on Foot)

JOHN HANCOCK OBSERVATORY (PAGE 117): Orientation.
BACK BAY (PAGE 125): Commonwealth Avenue, the Public Garden and the swan boats.
BEACON HILL (PAGE 128): Historic district.
FANEUIL HALL MARKETPLACE (PAGE 131): Food, entertainment, shops, people watching *Where's Boston,* old street patterns, and, on Fridays and Satur-days, Haymarket pushcarts.
THE WATERFRONT (PAGE 140): Open space, views, the Aquarium.
NORTH END (PAGE 138): An ethnic neighborhood with inside Freedom Trail sites (Paul Revere House and Old North Church).

Two Days, Inside and Outside

Day 1:

CHARLESTOWN NAVY YARD (PAGE 105): Visitors' center, museum, tours, the USS *Constitution.*
NORTH END (PAGE 138): An ethnic neighborhood. Two inside Freedom Trail sites: Paul Revere House and Old North Church.

- **Museums:** See page 147 for a list of recorded-information numbers.
- **Zoo Information:** 438-3662.

Evening Hours

EVENTS: Check the listings above.
MUSEUMS: Which are open when? See pages 147–148.
OBSERVATION TOWERS: Open until 11 or 12. See page 117.

THE WATERFRONT (PAGE 140): Open space, views, the Aquarium.

FANEUIL HALL MARKETPLACE (PAGE 131): Food, entertainment, shops, people watching *Where's Boston,* old street patterns, and Haymarket pushcarts.

Day 2:

BACK BAY (PAGE 125): Newbury Street, Commonwealth Avenue, Copley Square, the Public Garden.

DOWNTOWN CROSSING (PAGE 7): Filene's Basement, people watching, benches on brick streets, fast foods, summer entertainment, discount books at Barnes & Noble.

INSIDE FREEDOM TRAIL SITES: Old South Meeting House and the Old State House (page 100).

HARVARD SQUARE (PAGE 135): Walking tours, museums (the glass flowers), shops, historic sights.

Three Days (to Savor)

Day 1: Follow the rough outline of Day 1 above.

Day 2: Recuperate with a change of pace.

A GUIDED WALK (PAGE 123): Concentrate on one area.

A MUSEUM (PAGE 145): See a program and exhibit. (Check the recorded-information numbers, page 147.) Youngsters may prefer the Children's Museum (page 151).

OR DRIVE TO CONCORD (PAGE 54): If you haven't seen anything that fits your idea of real New England.

Day 3: Try Day 2 of Two Days with renewed energy and enthusiasm.

Traveling In and Out of Boston

GETTING AROUND: Bus tours, horse-drawn rides, and the subway. See pages 120–125.

BICYCLING: For suggested routes, contact the Boston Area Bicycle Coalition (page 220).

COMMUTING: Rush hours are usually 7:30 to 9:30 in the morning and 4 to 6 in the afternoon. Most roads into the city — especially the Southeast Expressway — are bumper to bumper at these times. Many local radio and television stations carry traffic reports throughout the morning and late afternoon.

DRIVING: It's not a recommended method for the uninitiated. Streets are narrow and jammed with traffic; and one-way patterns keep drivers in circular motion. Signs are improving, but Boston can still be confusing. Friday afternoons deserve special mention. After 3 traffic is particularly heavy. And extra patience helps when there's the slightest precipitation.

MASS. PIKE: Winter weather and road conditions are on tape 24 hours a day at 237-5210.

PARKING: If you must drive into the city, plan to pay for parking. (Free parking is available in Charlestown, at the navy yard.) Garages and lots are sprinkled throughout the downtown area. The **Boston Common Underground Garage** (523-7395) is a good buy at night. Its free shuttle bus runs around the Common Monday through Saturday from 7:30 in the morning to midnight. Or walk on outside streets (not through the Common, please). The **Government Center Garage** (723-6623) has a coiled ramp, tightly wound, for getting to and from the eight levels. The **Prudential Center Garage** (267-2965) is mammoth; try to park near your destination.

WALKING: Recommended. Before taking the Ⓣ or a cab, check the distance to where you're going. Boston is a compact city.

THE SHUTTLE: A good way to see in-town attractions. The bus runs from June through mid-October. See page 120.

Ⓣ: The nation's oldest subway had its first run from Park to Boylston in 1897. The system isn't always dependable — and it's very crowded at rush hours — but, when everything works the way it's supposed to, the Ⓣ is an efficient way to travel.

- **RAPID TRANSIT SERVICE:** Depends on the lines. First trains leave for Boston about 5 a.m.; last trains leave the city about 12:30 a.m.
- **PHONE INFORMATION:** 722-3200 (weekdays), 722-5050 (recorded); 722-5657 (Park Street Information Center — keep ringing).

AIR TRAVEL: Logan International Airport is in East Boston. (Call 411 for airline numbers.) The best way to get here — particularly during rush hours or on Fridays before school vacation weeks — is the Ⓣ. (But allow extra time.) The stop is Airport on the Blue Line. From there it's a short bus ride (additional fare) to all terminals.

BOAT: See page 226.

BUS: If you don't know which company services a particular outlying community, call Greyhound, but plan to wait your turn for an answer.

- **Greyhound:** 10 St. James Avenue (near Park Square), Boston, 423-5810. Ⓣ: Arlington on the Green Line. Going to New York? Greyhound also stops at the Riverside Ⓣ sta-

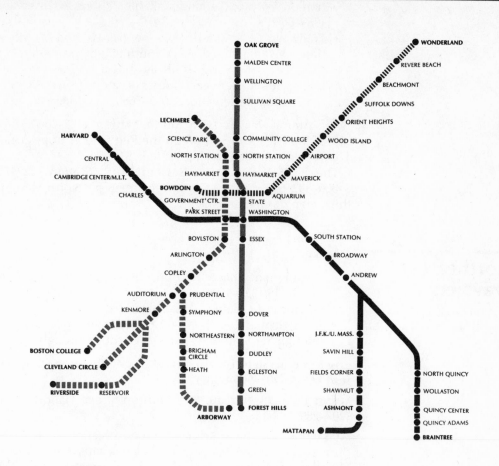

<img_1 contains the MBTA subway map with the following stations:>

OAK GROVE
MALDEN CENTER
WELLINGTON
SULLIVAN SQUARE
WONDERLAND
REVERE BEACH
BEACHMONT
SUFFOLK DOWNS
ORIENT HEIGHTS
LECHMERE
HARVARD
SCIENCE PARK
COMMUNITY COLLEGE
WOOD ISLAND
CENTRAL
NORTH STATION
NORTH STATION
AIRPORT
CAMBRIDGE CENTER/M.I.T.
HAYMARKET
HAYMARKET
MAVERICK
CHARLES
BOWDOIN
GOVERNMENT CTR.
AQUARIUM
PARK STREET
STATE
WASHINGTON
BOYLSTON
ESSEX
SOUTH STATION
ARLINGTON
BROADWAY
COPLEY
ANDREW
AUDITORIUM
PRUDENTIAL
KENMORE
SYMPHONY
DOVER
BOSTON COLLEGE
NORTHEASTERN
NORTHAMPTON
J.F.K./U. MASS.
BRIGHAM CIRCLE
DUDLEY
SAVIN HILL
CLEVELAND CIRCLE
HEATH
EGLESTON
FIELDS CORNER
NORTH QUINCY
RIVERSIDE
RESERVOIR
GREEN
SHAWMUT
WOLLASTON
FOREST HILLS
ASHMONT
QUINCY CENTER
ARBORWAY
QUINCY ADAMS
MATTAPAN
BRAINTREE

Orange Line: Oak Grove to Forest Hills.

Red Line: Harvard to Ashmont and Mattapan. Harvard to Braintree via Quincy. The Harvard extension to Alewife on the North Cambridge–Arlington border is scheduled to open in 1984.

Blue Line: Bowdoin to Wonderland. Connects with the Orange Line at State and with the Green Line at Government Center.

Green Lines: Lechmere to Riverside connects with the Blue Line at Government Center and the Red Line at Park Street. Park Street to Arborway. North Station to Boston College. Park Street to Cleveland Circle.
NOTE: Copley does not have a pedestrian walkway joining inbound and outbound areas. The necessary transfer can be made at Arlington.

The Ⓣ

tion in Newton. (Parking available.) Phone for reservations (969-8660).

- **Trailways:** 551 Atlantic Avenue (across from South Station), Boston, 482-6620. Ⓣ: South Station on the Red Line. Going to New York? Trailways has a Natick terminal on Speen Street, between Routes 9 and 30 (exit 13 on the Mass. Pike). Reservations: 653-5660, 235-5445 (Wellesley).

TRAIN: Amtrak leaves from **South Station** (482-3660, 1-800-523-5720). Ⓣ: South Station on the Red Line. It stops at Route 128 in Dedham too. Parking there is $1 a day.

The B&M Railroad leaves from **North Station** (227-5070, 1-800-392-6099) at 150 Causeway Street. Ⓣ: North Station on the Green or Orange Line.

Northeast Travelers Information

CANADA:

- Government Office of Tourism: 500 Boylston Street, Boston 02116 (536-1730).
- Province of Quebec: 426-2660.
- Nova Scotia: 1-800-341-6096. Open 9 to 5 daily April through September; weekdays October through March.

CONNECTICUT: State Tourist Office, 210 Washington Street, Hartford 06106 (203-566-3385).

MAINE: Publicity Bureau, 77 Winthrop Street, Hallowell 04347 (207-289-2423).

MASSACHUSETTS: The state has thirteen vacation areas. For addresses contact the Massachusetts Department of Commerce, Division of Tourism, 100 Cambridge Street, Boston 02202 (727-3201).

The Nantucket Information Bureau (1-800-642-7504) books "just for tonight" if there's an available space. For advance reservations call Nantucket Accommodations (508-228-9559), a clearinghouse for daily, weekly, or monthly stays in guest house and cottages.

NEW HAMPSHIRE: Office of Vacation Travel, Box 856, Concord 03301 (603-271-2343, 1-800-258-3608).

RHODE ISLAND: The Department of Economic Development, 7 Jackson Walkway, Providence 02903 (401-277-2601, 1-800-556-2484).

VERMONT: Travel Division, 61 Elm Street, Montpelier 05602 (802-828-3236).

Where to Stay

A full roster of places, complete with facilities and range of rates, is available from the Greater Boston Convention & Tourist Bureau (page 6). . . . In summer, many touring families find a

pool a practical asset, and, at times, the major attraction for children. . . . Hotels and inns outside Boston are often less expensive than those in town. Another alternative, in a style borrowed from Europe, is a paid home stay. Massachusetts could be called "the bed & breakfast capital of the country," with more than 500 personalized B&Bs located in the metropolitan Boston area alone. Full details are included in my 500-page book *Bed & Breakfast in New England,* published by The Globe Pequot Press.

Restaurants

This isn't intended as a gourmet guide. Most suggestions are moderately priced places where you'll feel comfortable with youngsters. . . . Children's menus may or may not be offered. Always ask. . . . Prices are hard to keep up with. . . . Hours too can change. Call before you travel any distance. Most Italian and Chinese restaurants are open daily.

BACK BAY
Prudential Center

Cardullo's Gourmet Shop, Prudential Shopping Plaza (Sheraton-Boston side). All kinds of sandwiches to take out and enjoy on the plaza (crowded at lunchtime). Phone: 536–8887. Open: Monday–Saturday.

Top of the Hub, Prudential Tower. A view and a popular, reasonably priced ($8.75, $5.95 under 13) Sunday brunch — all-you-can-eat eggs, meats, and pastries. No reservations (after 11 you could wait up to an hour). Phone: 536–1775. Open: Monday–Saturday 11:30–2:30, Sunday brunch 10:30–2. Dinner from 5:30 daily.

Copley Square

Ideal Diner, 21 Huntington Avenue (behind the library). Not really a diner, but a simple, neat little restaurant with a new menu daily. Good soups, burgers, steak, chicken, and fish. Homemade poppyseed cake and cheesecake too. Breakfast is a bargain; the rest is inexpensive. Phone: 247–8249. Open: Monday–Thursday 7 a.m.–10 p.m., Friday–Saturday 7 a.m.–11 p.m., Sundays 9 a.m.–10 p.m.

Copley Seafood, 565 Boylston Street (between Clarendon and Dartmouth). Simple decor and menu. Fish chowder, broiled and fried fish, burgers, and salads. Lunchtime is always busy. Phone: 266–7990. Open: 11:30–9 daily.

Ken's Deli, 549 Boylston Street (across from Trinity Church). A big place, on two floors, for dessert, a bite, or a full meal.

Lost? Neighborhood street maps are in Looking Around (pages 115–143).

There's a wait at lunchtime and after 11 at night. Phone: 266-6149. Open: 7 a.m.–3 a.m. daily.

Fridays, 26 Exeter Street (corner Newbury). Very decorated, right to the sidewalk greenhouse (you can eat here too). Taped music (not quiet). A large assortment, including sandwiches, seafood, and full meals — all invitingly served. Children's menu. Come as you are. On average, a half-hour wait. Phone: 266-9040. Open: Monday–Thursday 11:30 a.m.–1 a.m., Friday–Sunday 11 a.m.–1 a.m.

Nearer the Public Garden

Malben's Gourmet, 378 Boylston Street (corner Arlington and Berkeley). Sandwiches to go. Phone: 267-1646. Open: Monday–Saturday 7–6.

Magic Pan, 47 Newbury Street (at Berkeley). Crepes are a specialty. Children's menu. A waiting line at 1 and again about 6:30. Phone: 267-9315. Open: Monday–Thursday 11–11, Friday–Saturday 11 a.m.–midnight, Sundays 11–10.

Legal Sea Foods, Boston Park Plaza Hotel, Columbus Avenue and Arlington Street (1 block from Boylston). The freshest fish. Almost always an hour's wait (except Sundays about 3 and daily about 5). There's a shorter wait in the less formal fish market restaurant. Best buys are the weekday lunch specials for about $3.50. Children's specials are on the menu. Phone: 426-4444. Open: Monday–Saturday 11–10, Sundays noon–10.

BEACON HILL

There are usually half a dozen reasonably priced restaurants along Charles Street. (Several seem to change management, name, and menu annually.) You could walk a 4-block stretch, look at the menus (all posted in windows), and choose one.

Beacon Hill Pancake House, 30 Charles Street (corner of Chestnut). Reasonable prices for all-day breakfasts, sandwiches, and omelettes. Phone: 523-8554.

Rebecca's, 21 Charles Street. A not-too-formal setting, but gourmet food. Dill soup, stuffed grape leaves, chicken breast with watercress, and croissants. Phone: 742-9747. Open: Monday 7:30 a.m.–10 p.m., Tuesday–Saturday 7:30 a.m.–midnight, Sundays 11–10.

Primo's, 28 Myrtle Street. Good pizza, subs, veal and other Italian dishes, cannoli, and more — all to eat in or take out. From Charles Street it's a climb up Revere to Myrtle, but worth it. Phone: 742-5458. Open: Weekdays 10 a.m.–11 p.m., weekends 10–9.

CHINATOWN

Every other doorway seems to lead to a restaurant. Most are open daily from late morning to past midnight.

Pak Nin, 84 Harrison Street (corner Kneeland). A half-dozen tables in a family-run place. Simple and inexpensive (specials are posted). Phone: 482-6168.

Yee Hong Guey, 34 Oxford Street (corner Beach). A comfortable place with booths and air-conditioning. The lunch specials are a good buy. Phone: 426-6738.

Bo-Shek Coffee House, 63 Beach Street. Informal (a counter and some tables), inexpensive, and good. Take-out is particularly busy. Phone: 482-4441.

Imperial Teahouse, 70 Beach Street (next to the official gate). A big place, on two floors. Good (some say the best) dim-sum. From 9 to 3 daily about twenty different items, including steamed pastries filled with meats and vegetables, are wheeled to your table. They start at a dollar. A regular menu too. There's usually a wait at lunch. Phone: 426-8439.

China Pavilion, 14 Hudson Street. Good dim-sum here too, from 9 to 3 daily. A regular menu is always available. All served amid lanterns and mirrors. Phone: 338-7234.

FANEUIL HALL MARKETPLACE

In addition to seventy-five fast-food places, there are twelve fine restaurants — all relatively expensive — in the celebrated complex.

But there's only one **Durgin Park,** 30 North Market. An old-timer, no longer off the beaten path, but still serving the same traditional cooking (even the corn bread) and heaping helpings at big long or round tables with checked cloths. Not great for private conversations — it's noisy and you share tables — but kids fit right in and you may meet someone interesting. The only way to avoid at least a half-hour wait at lunch and after 7 is to buy a drink at the Gaslight Pub. From there you're ushered up a private stairway for almost immediate seating. Reasonable prices (lunch specials, until 3, start at $2). One drawback: no air-conditioning. Phone: 227-2038. Open: Monday–Saturday 11:30–10, Sundays noon–9.

HARVARD SQUARE

Dozens of ethnic restaurants tucked in alleys and converted buildings. Some feel there's a certain style to most Cambridge restaurants . . . slow service.

Grendel's Den, 89 Winthrop Street. The upstairs dining room feels traditional and comfortable, and the patio's in use in good weather. On the menu: a salad bar, omelettes, sandwiches, and kabobs. Downstairs, pita sandwiches and burgers to go. Phone: 491-1160. Open: Daily from 11. Downstairs is closed Sundays.

Ahmed's, 96 Winthrop Street. White cloths and flowers in a converted wood-frame house, a good place for a leisurely meal (not really for children). French and Moroccan (Middle Eastern) dishes. Lunch prices are reasonable. Phone: 876-5200. Open: Monday–Saturday 11:30–2:30, Sunday brunch 11–3. Dinner from 5 daily.

Elsie's (the original), 71 Mt. Auburn Street. Sit at the counter or take out, and enjoy one of the huge, reasonably priced

Lost? Neighborhood street maps are in Looking Around (pages 115–143).

sandwiches (roast beef is a specialty). Homemade soups, salads, giant cookies, and brownies. People and posted notices provide the decor. Phone: 354-8362. Open: Monday–Saturday 7 a.m.–1 a.m., Sundays 10 a.m.–1 a.m.

Regina Pizzeria, 9 Holyoke Street (two doors in from Massachusetts Avenue). Booths and good pizza. Phone: 864-9279. Open: Monday–Saturday 11 a.m.–midnight, Sundays 3–11.

Cafe at the Atrium, 50 Church Street. The setting — lots of plants and vertical space, and a waterfall — is as important as the food. (It can be noisy when it's crowded.) Interesting light meals, salads, coffees, and desserts. Phone: 491-3745. Open: Monday–Saturday 11 a.m.–midnight, Sundays from noon.

NORTH END

Italian menus abound. Many good buys and pizza places are open daily.

European, 218 Hanover Street. All kinds of Italian dishes, although some come just for the pizza. A huge place (hardly ever a wait) and fast service. Reasonable prices and a children's menu. Phone: 523-5694. Open: 11 a.m.–12:30 a.m. daily.

Piccolo Venezia, 63 Salem Street. Plain, functional, and tiny. Reasonable prices. Long lines after 6. Phone: 523-9802. Open: Monday–Saturday 11:30–9:30.

Villa Francesca, 150 Richmond Street. Enlarged, but seating is still close, with a wait on Fridays and Saturdays. Sunday's special is lasagna and salad. Air-conditioned. Phone: 367-2948. Open: 5–10:30 daily. Reservations accepted Sunday through Thursday.

Daily Catch, 323 Hanover Street. A hole in the wall that features squid prepared in half a dozen ways. Phone: 523-8567. Open: Tuesdays and summer Sundays 5:30–10, Wednesday–Saturday 11:30–10:30.

Regina Pizzeria (the original), 11½ Thatcher Street (between Prince and North Washington). Just pizza. Devotees say the crust here is better than that in the branches around town. It's popular, and there's usually a line. Phone: 227-0765. Open: Monday–Saturday 11 a.m.–midnight, Sundays 3–midnight.

THE WATERFRONT

Boston's waterfront is lined with award-winning restaurants. Most feature seafood. Expect an hour's wait after 6:30; 2 hours', on weekends.

The Chart House, 60 Long Wharf. Not especially for families, but crayons and color-in menus for kids while they wait, waiters who sing for birthdays, and family-style salads. A traditional menu for adults ($8 to $18 for dinner) and a children's menu ($2 to $5), offered in the oldest commercial building in Boston. Phone: 227-1576. Open: Monday–Thursday 5–11, Fridays 5–midnight, Saturdays 4:30–midnight, Sundays 3–10.

The Winery, Lewis Wharf. Entertainment nightly, and an all-you-can-eat salad bar and a carafe of wine with every meal. Between $7.50 and $14 for dinner. Phone: 523-3994. Open: Monday–Thursday 11:30–4 and 5–10, Friday–Saturday 11:30–4 and 5–midnight, Sundays 5–10.

Jimbo's Fish Shanty, 245 Northern Avenue (across from Jimmy's Harborside). Casual and reasonable. Good service once you're seated. Not specifically for children but busy enough and noisy enough so that youngsters don't have to sit perfectly still. Railroad memorabilia everywhere (three working model trains are suspended from the ceiling). Burgers, salads, fish, chicken, lobsters, and steak. The hobo fish stew is hot and tasty — a meal in itself. Phone: 542-5600. Open: Monday–Thursday 11:30–9:30, Friday–Saturday 11:30 a.m.–midnight, Sundays 1–8 (until 9 in summer).

No Name, 15½ Fish Pier. No sign. No number. But it's here, in the middle of the pier. (Turn left just before Jimmy's Harborside parking area.) In the back room, a view of fishing boats; in the small dining room, a counter where fishermen used to come for breakfast. Soon to open, a windowed second story overlooking the waterfront. For thirty years Nick Contos has been carrying on the family tradition. No batter (bread crumbs only on fried foods), no seasoning. Just plain fresh fish (the stew has almost a pound of fish in it) and homemade pies. Phone: 338-7539. Open: Monday–Thursday 11–9:30, Friday–Saturday 11–10.

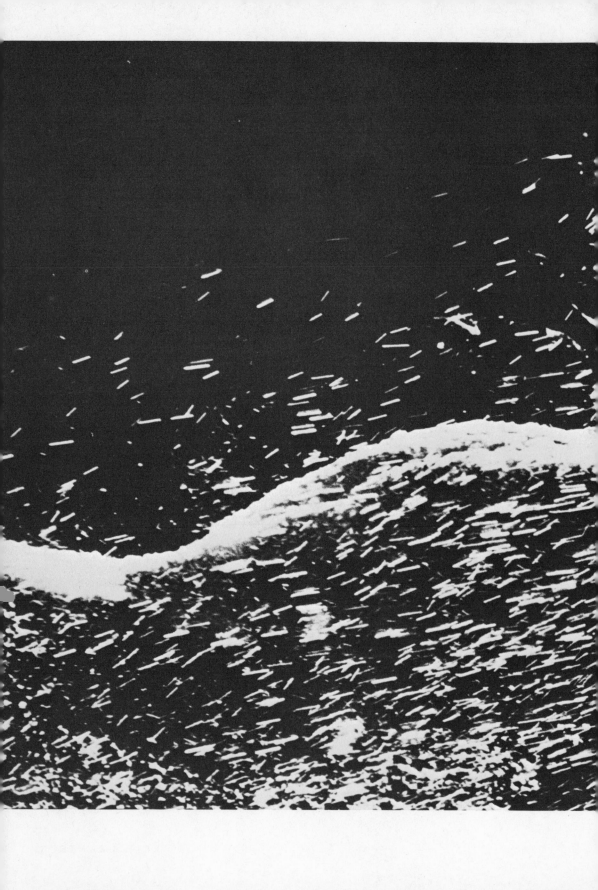

Animals

Parks and Zoos

Benson's Animal Farm Hudson, New Hampshire

PHONE: 603–882–2481.

LOCATION: 45 miles northwest of Boston, 3 miles from Nashua.

DIRECTIONS: I-93 north to New Hampshire exit 3 (Route 111). Follow Route 111 west, 8 miles.

OPEN: Daily April–mid-September, weekends until early November. Memorial Day–Labor Day, 10–6:30; at other times, 10–4:30. The ticket booths close 1½ hours before the park. Christmas in New England (hayrides and lights), mid-November–early January, daily, except Christmas and New Year's Eve, 4–9.

AVERAGE STAY: Hours; many spend all day. Mondays and Fridays are less crowded.

ADMISSION: $6.50 adults, $5 ages 3–11, free under 3. Includes all shows, exhibits, and amusements; extra charge for animal rides.

EATING: Large picnic areas. Barbecuing allowed. Snack bars and cafeteria.

SHOWS: 26 scheduled daily, weather permitting, throughout the park. Live-animal demonstrations (touching allowed) and wildlife films are the well-received educational programming; other programs are for entertainment. Parade at 2 every day, with animals, costumed characters, and an antique fire engine.

"If they eat that in the wild, what do you feed them?"

—ANN, AGE 11

Generations return to North America's oldest (sixty years) animal park to find lions, giraffes, penguins, flamingos, macaws, cockatoos, spotted deer, monkeys, baboons, and more — at least a thousand animals — many in their natural environments. Donkeys, chickens, sheep, goats, and llamas are in the petting zoo.

Put on your walking shoes for this big place with its manicured lawns and flowers. The shores of the lake are once again serene because the amusements, a quarter of the park's attractions, have moved from there to a different part of the 350-acre site. Waiting lines are routine for the whirling, twirling rides.

Does the park get "zooey" at times? It depends on your point of view. There's so much to see and do that its fans consider Benson's a one-day vacation.

Capron Park Zoo County Street (Route 123), Attleboro

PHONE: 508–222–3047

LOCATION: 35 miles south of Boston.

DIRECTIONS: I-93 south to Route 128 north, to exit 63 (I-95 south), to exit 5 (Route 152). Take Route 152 south, toward downtown Attleboro, to Route 123 west, toward Providence, 1 mile.

OPEN: Year-round, 8 a.m.–dark daily.

ADMISSION: Free.

EATING: A picnic area with tables and grills.

A family place. Small. Usually well kept. The tropical rain forest — where the only divider between you and birds (there aren't many now) is a thin mist of water — is still here. The rest of the zoo's collection includes fourteen large felines, monkeys, bears, and hoofed animals. A children's playground is on the grounds.

Capron Park is also home to the **Attleboro Museum** and its exhibits of contemporary artists and printmakers, and handcrafts. Collections include a furnished 1700s kitchen and dining room. Admission is free. Open Tuesday through Friday, 12:30 to 4:30; weekends from 2 to 5. Closed holidays. Phone: 508–222–2644.

From here it's a 4-mile drive to the **National Fish Hatchery** on Bunday Road, North Attleboro, off Route 152. Hatchery troughs are filled with all different sizes of "this big" brook, brown, and rainbow trout. Pick up a leaflet at the adjacent nature trail, and find the twenty numbered observation points around the swampy pond. Benches, too, at several spots. Admission is free. Open weekdays, except holidays, from 7:30 to 3:30.

Drumlin Farm Nature Center South Great Road (Route 117), South Lincoln

PHONE: 259–9807.

LOCATION: 22 miles west of Boston.

DIRECTIONS: Mass. Pike to Route 128 (I-95) north to exit 49 (Route 20). Follow the signs to Route 117 west. Or Route 2 west to Route 126 south (toward Walden Pond). Left at the lights onto Route 117.

TRAIN: 35-minute ride from North Station (227–5070); 10 minutes less from Porter Square, Cambridge. It's possible to walk to the farm from the station, but not with very young children in tow.

OPEN: Year-round, Tuesday–Sunday 9–5. Closed Mondays except holidays; also closed Thanksgiving, Christmas Eve and Day, and New Year's.

AVERAGE STAY: 1½ hours or longer, depending on programming.

ADMISSION: $2 adults, $1 senior citizens and ages 3–16, free under 3. Hayrides or sleigh rides (most Sunday afternoons), $.50.

TOURS: For schools and other organized groups, and for special needs youngsters. Reserve early; spring bookings fill quickly.

RULES: No picnicking. And please, no dogs.

STROLLERS: Paths can accommodate them.

HANDICAPPED: Some buildings are accessible.

This large demonstration farm, also headquarters for the Massachusetts Audubon Society, is one of those places that you and the children will want to go back to again and again. It's particularly good for youngsters up to 12. Visitors see a typical New England farm garden, grapevines, horses, pigs, cows, owls, night animals, and chickens (see if you can find a freshly laid egg). There are fields to run in, tall grass to hide in, short trails to follow, and ponds to explore. Sunday afternoons there's usually a hands-on activity, maybe milking.

WHAT ELSE? Plenty. Public workshops, clinics, forums, classes for all ages (preschoolers to adults), a day camp, and a library. There's also a great gift shop with something for everyone.

Audubon Ark is a traveling live-animal program. A staff that likes and knows animals — and young people — brings a screech owl, a skunk or woodchuck, and a snake named Slim to schools and other groups. Flexible programming. For scheduling and fees, contact Drumlin Farm, 259-9807.

Franklin Park Zoo Franklin Park, Dorchester

PHONE: 442-2002 (Boston Zoological Society).

The Boston Zoological Society is working with the Metropolitan District Commission to turn Greater Boston's zoos into recreational, educational, and research facilities. The most active place at the moment is Stone Zoo (page 28), but major reconstruction is under way at Franklin Park. Eventually visitors will find an extensive series of environments here — tropical forest, bush forest, desert, and savanna — and a brand-new children's zoo, all designed to encourage looking. A sample of what's to come is the small Bird's World exhibit with its elevated outdoor walkway and indoor environments. The range area with moated exhibits is also open.

A 45-minute drive from Boston

Macomber Farm 450 Salem End Road, Framingham

PHONE: 508-879-5345, 237-0543 (Wellesley).

LOCATION: 25 miles west of Boston.

DIRECTIONS: Mass. Pike to exit 12 (Route 9). Travel east on Route 9 for 2 miles to Temple Street (at the second light). Turn right onto Temple, then right onto Salem End Road.

OPEN: May–October, weekdays 9:30–5, weekends 10–6.

AVERAGE STAY: At least 2 hours, depending on the number of demonstrations you linger over.

ADMISSION: $5 adults, $4 senior citizens, $2.50 ages 4–12 (most appealing to this group), free under 4.

EATING: Plenty of unshaded picnic tables inside the grounds; shaded tables are near the parking lot.

HANDICAPPED: Fully accessible.

Macomber is not a working farm; it has no cages and no rides. But it does have six beautiful new barns, the ultimate in animal housing and demonstration sites. The 1800s barn, moved here board by board, with old tools and sleigh, stands in contrast to the solar-heated visitors' center overlooking a man-made pond.

"When I walked in the footprints, they made me sound like a clomping horse!"
— RACHEL, AGE 6

The exhibits educate through interaction — with staff members, with domestic animals, with electronic games and learning devices. You put on a mask and adjust the lens to see how a horse or sheep sees. A videotape helps you compare your gait on a treadmill to a horse's. A wagon waiting to be pulled gives you an idea of what it's like to "work like a horse." Electronic games let you join a flock of sheep to learn about their social organization. Other exhibits explain what henpecking is, and how clean and intelligent pigs and piglets are.

The farm, opened in 1981 by the Massachusetts Society for the Prevention of Cruelty to Animals, looks as though someone waved a magic wand over the estate once used to raise Thoroughbreds. It's landscaped (the trees are still too new for shade) and tranquil. And the size is just right.

Southwick's Wild Animal Farm Off Route 16, Mendon

PHONE: 508–883–9182.

LOCATION: 35 miles southwest of Boston.

DIRECTIONS: Mass. Pike to exit 11A (I-495 south), to exit 20 (Milford), to Route 16 west, toward Mendon. Then follow the signs.

OPEN: May–October, 10–5 daily.

AVERAGE STAY: 1½–2 hours. Picnickers tend to be here longer.

ADMISSION: $4 adults, $3 ages 3–12, free under 3. Rides (offered on weekends) are extra.

EATING: Picnicking in the oak grove. Barbecuing allowed, but bring your own grill.

The farm supplies zoos all over the country, so the population is constantly changing. An antelope here today may be traded tomorrow. The basics — chimpanzees, zebras, lions, and tigers — are usually among the hundreds of animals in the wooded area. Every continent except Antarctica is represented.

For young children there's a walk-in kiddie zoo where they can pet and feed sheep and goats. On weekends there are animal rides (ponies, camels, even elephants from time to time), and a merry-go-round too. Under its new management, Southwick's has been freshly painted and cleaned.

About 15 minutes from Boston

Walter D. Stone Memorial Zoo 149 Pond Street (next to Spot Pond Reservoir), Stoneham

PHONE: 438–3662 (full recorded information).
LOCATION: 7 miles north of Boston.
DIRECTIONS: I-93 north to exit 8 (Stoneham-Melrose). Then follow signs to the zoo.
BUS: Hudson Line (395–8080). No service Sundays or holidays.
OPEN: Year-round, daily except Christmas and New Year's. Winter, 9–4; summer, 9–5.
AVERAGE STAY: 1–1½ hours. On Sundays come before 11; not as crowded Monday through Saturday.
ADMISSION: Free. (This may change soon.) Suggested contribution: $1 adults, $.50 children.
EATING: A picnic grove. Sorry, no fires allowed.
TOURS: Available with reservations. Call 442–2005.
RULES: Please, no pets.

A highlight is the four-story aviary where over a hundred tropical birds are perched or flying around you. Some blend with the foliage; others are vividly colored. A panel of photographs is the key to identification. The simulated natural environment is complete with pools, plantings, and a waterfall.

This comparatively small zoo has a circular layout, good for a see-all visit. Swans, ducks, and geese are in the lovely central pond; giraffes, elephants, penguins, sea lions, baboons, and gorillas — one or two of each — are in the surrounding areas.

Duck Feeding

Not too far from downtown Boston is **Larz Anderson Park** (page 184). A little farther away, but home to hundreds of ducks, is the MDC area on **Norumbega Road,** along the Charles River in Newton, near Routes 30 and 128. To get here, drive west on Commonwealth Avenue (Route 30) past the Marriott Hotel. Take the first right after the MDC police station and the next right (down the ramp), and follow the "Duck Feeding" signs. Some families make a special trip here in winter, when the ducks are likely to give a pretty noisy welcome. Nearby: Canoeing on the Charles (page 223). Or it's less than a mile uphill along Norumbega Road to Norumbega Tower, where there's a small park with a few fireplaces and picnic tables. For an open-air look out over the Charles, climb the tower's narrow circular stone steps.

Fish

State hatcheries are open 9 to 4 every day of the year. They grow trout to stock Massachusetts streams, ponds, and lakes for recreational fishing.

Hatcheries are located in Sandwich on Route 6A (see page 88 for other local attractions), and in Sunderland on Route 16 and Montague on Turners Fall Road (combine with maple sugaring, page 278). The state's most modern facility, McLaughlin Trout Hatchery, is in Belchertown. Write to the chief culturist there for special tours.

National Fish Hatchery Page 24.

New England Aquarium Page 160.

Pet Adoptions and Tours

If these major resources aren't convenient, they can recommend other humane societies or shelters in the area.

Animal Rescue League of Boston 10 Chandler Street (corner Arlington and Tremont), Boston

PHONE: 426-9170.
PARKING: Lot available.
Ⓣ: Arlington on the Green Line; then an 8-minute walk. Cross over the turnpike via the bridge.
OPEN: Weekdays 10–4, Saturdays 9–3.
TOURS: By appointment, weekdays fall through late spring, for ages 6 up.

Visitors see the clinic, a pet-care movie, and the feeding and exercise areas before the most popular part — the adoption kennel — where hundreds of dogs and cats are waiting in cages. It's a noisy, but educational, visit.

Massachusetts Society for the Prevention of Cruelty to Animals American Humane Education Society, 350 Huntington Avenue, Boston

PHONE: 522-5055.
PARKING: Lot available.
Ⓣ: Copley on the Green Line; then Arborway bus.
OPEN: Tuesday–Saturday 10:30–3:30, Friday nights 6–8:30, Sundays noon–5.
TOURS: By appointment, weekdays, for 10 to 30 people, ages 8 up.

People come here to both give up and adopt cats and dogs. If you'd like to adopt, call before you come to check availability, fees, and identification requirements.

Arts

Tickets by Phone

Specific phone services are listed in event ads; ticket agencies, in the Yellow Pages. The service charge through a phone service or agency is usually $2 a ticket.

Bargains

How to see performances — less expensively, inexpensively, or free:

- **SHOP BOSTIX:** Half-price arrangements (page 34).
- **SUBSCRIBE TO A SERIES.**
- **JOIN A MUSEUM.**
- **USE YOUR STUDENT ID.**

Or be on the lookout for

- **RUSH SEATS:** Practices vary: Watch the ads or call. The Boston Symphony Orchestra sells a ticket per person ($4.50), on the day of performance only, for Friday afternoon and Saturday evening concerts. Tickets go on sale at the Huntington Avenue entrance Friday mornings at 9 and Saturday afternoons at 5.
- **USHERING:** Resident theater companies often exchange free admission for ushering at a single performance or series. Minimum-age requirements vary, but some companies do accept high-schoolers.
- **OUTSIDE THE THEATER DISTRICT:** There's lots of reasonably priced, good theater outside Boston's theater district, at schools and area theaters. And the intimacy of a setting like the Alley Theatre in Cambridge or Nucleo Eclettico in the North End can add to the appeal.

Newspaper listings (page 6) and mailing lists are full of information about the many marvelous cultural bargains offered at area universities, schools, museums, and churches.

- **UNIVERSITIES:** Special performances and lectures at Boston University, Northeastern, MIT, and other schools are open to the public. Call the public information or cultural events office at the institution for a schedule. Sometimes a place on the mailing list costs $5 yearly. Harvard has recorded information at 495-1718 during the school year, and at 495-2939 over the summer. There's no charge for many of the events listed in the *Harvard Gazette*'s weekly calendar. And those could keep you busy eight days a

Best known for its half-price tickets, **Arts/Boston** is a nonprofit organization that makes live performances available to the public at low cost through two services:

- **Arts/Mail:** Advance tickets for music, theater, and dance — taking a chance on seat location — all at a large discount. For an application (no charge) to be put on the mailing list, write 100 Boylston Street, Suite 735, Boston 02116.
- **BOSTIX:** The octagonally shaped ticket and information booth next to Faneuil Hall (Ⓣ: State Street on the Orange or Blue Line, or Government Center on the Green or Blue Line) is open Monday through Saturday from 11 to 6. (There's usually a line when the booth opens.) On Sundays (open noon to 6) generally more tickets are available, especially for classical concerts. Recorded information: 723–5181.

    HALF-PRICE TICKETS: Availability is posted at the booth on the day of performance. (There's no way of knowing the list without going there.) When the allotment sells out, that's it. Occasionally other tickets become available during the day. (BOSTIX seldom has tickets for a family show like *Nutcracker*, which usually sells out on its own.) The service charge ranges from $1 to $2 depending on face value. Cash sales only; no credit cards accepted.

    FULL-PRICE TICKETS: These are sold in advance, with a $1 to $2 service charge. In-state checks accepted; but again, no credit cards.

    DISCOUNT PACKETS: Usually a dozen coupons for museums and tourist attractions (contents change from time to time) for about $1.

    PRINTED MATERIAL: *Panorama*, an annotated list of performances, museums, and tourist attractions — and brochures about performing groups, museums, and historic sites. All free; just ask.

week! The newspaper is available free at the information center (page 137) or by subscription (call 495-4743).

- SCHOOLS, COLLEGES, AND ARTS CENTERS: The New England Conservatory of Music offers more than three hundred free concerts each year. Berklee College of Music has student and faculty recitals. The Longy School of Music in Cambridge and the All Newton Music School in Newton have full schedules too. Arts centers, sometimes in recycled churches, firehouses, or schools, often have professional presentations with reasonable or free admission.

- **MUSEUMS:** Most museums have regularly scheduled programs (see the recorded-information list on page 147). The auditorium at the Museum of Fine Arts (page 156) is heavily booked. The Gardner Museum (page 153) presents concerts (suggested donation $1) three times a week. The Museum of Our National Heritage (page 173) offers programs for a nominal charge.
- **CHURCHES:** Churches are often a home for theater and more frequently a source of classical music. Concert listings usually include Boston's Emmanuel Church, King's Chapel, Old West Church, and Trinity.

Regularly Scheduled Presentations

FOR FAMILIES AND
YOUNG PEOPLE

Adventures in Music Box 59, Concord 01742

PHONE: 508–369–1984.
HELD: Weekends throughout the school year.
ADMISSION: $8.75, series of four concerts; $3–$3.50, single performances. Tickets sold through schools or by mail.
AGE APPEAL: 5–12, and families.

Performances include classical, opera, folk, and popular music, with dance, drama, and an orchestra. Audience participation is often encouraged. The nonprofit educational corporation, founded in 1959 with five participating towns, now involves thirty-six communities. Four programs, all open to the public, are given weekends each year at various locations.

Alternative Family Cinema Off the Wall, 15 Pearl Street, Cambridge

PHONE: 547–5255, 354–5678 (recorded information).
Ⓣ: Central on the Red Line; then just around the corner.
HELD: October–mid-April, weekends and school vacations.
ADMISSION: $1.25.

Hour-long animated and live-action films from all over the world in a coffeehouse-style screening room that seats eighty. Beverages and pastries sold.

Boston Ballet 553 Tremont Street, Boston

PERFORMANCES AT: Metropolitan Center, 270 Tremont Street (opposite the Shubert Theatre), Boston.
PHONE: 542–3945.
GROUP RATES: Available for 20 or more.

Formed in 1965 through a Ford Foundation grant, the company has achieved international acclaim. Programs include world premieres of works by distinguished choreographers. BOSTIX (page 34) carries tickets for most performances. Annual productions of *Sleeping Beauty* and *Nutcracker* attract family audiences. Classes are offered for preschoolers through adults.

Theater Seating Plans

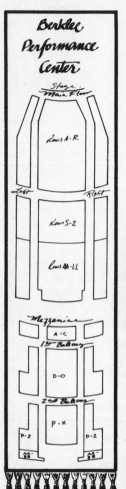

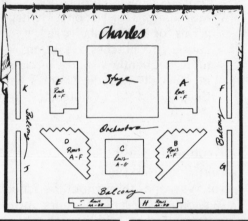

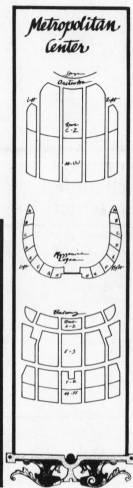

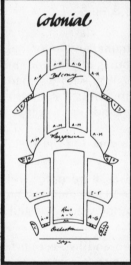

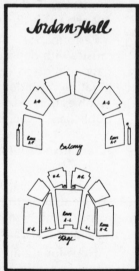

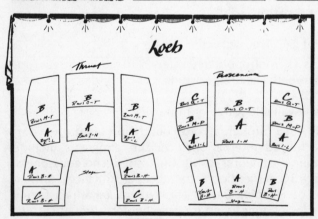

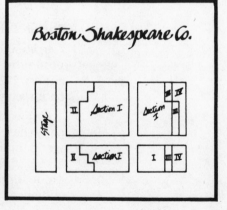

RENEE KLEIN

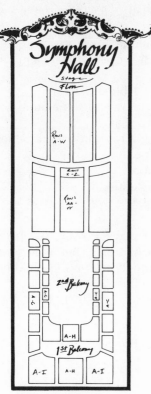

Symphony Hall

Stage
Floor

Rows A-W

Rows X-Z

Rows AA-rr

2nd Balcony

1st Balcony

A-I   A-H   A-I

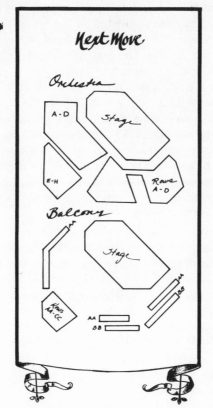

Next Move

Orchestra

A-D

Stage

E-H

Rows A-D

Balcony

Stage

Rows AA-CC

AA

BB

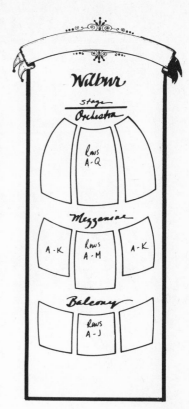

Wilbur

Stage
Orchestra

Rows A-Q

Mezzanine

A-K   Rows A-M   A-K

Balcony

Rows A-J

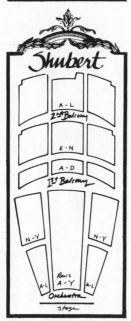

Shubert

A-L
2nd Balcony

E-N

A-D
1st Balcony

N-Y   N-Y

Rows A-Y
A-L   A-L
Orchestra
Stage

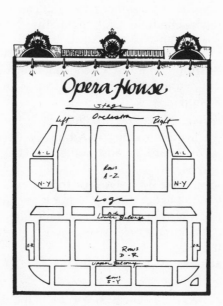

Opera House

Stage
Left   Orchestra   Right

A-L   Rows A-Z   A-L
N-Y   N-Y

Loge

Lower Balcony
Rows D-R

Upper Balcony
Rows S-Y

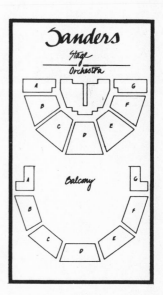

Sanders

Stage
Orchestra

A   G
B   F
C   E
D

Balcony

A   G
B   F
C   E
D

Boston Children's Theatre 124 Holland Road, Brookline

PERFORMANCES AT: New England Life Hall, 225 Clarendon Street (at Boylston), Boston.

PHONE: 277-3277 (school office, schedule, reservations, and mailing list). The box office (266-7262) is open after 10 a.m. on days of performance only.

Ⓣ: Copley on the Green Line; then a 1-block walk.

HELD: During the school year on Saturdays and some Sundays, and weekdays during school vacations.

ADMISSION: $3-$5. Reservations strongly recommended. Series subscriptions and group rates available.

AGE APPEAL: Depends on the production.

TOURING COMPANY: January–April, weekends.

STAGEMOBILE: A summer touring company, with stage, at area outdoor locations.

Casts for the annual series of four plays are selected from students (ages 8 to 17) at the Boston Children's Theatre School. Because the theater is fairly wide and deep, young children prefer the close seats in the center section.

NEARBY: John Hancock Observatory (page 117), Back Bay (page 125), swan boats (page 228).

Boston Public Library Copley Square, Boston

PHONE: 536-5400.

Ⓣ: Copley on the Green Line.

ADMISSION: Free.

Regularly scheduled children's programs include films, musicians, and storytellers. For adults there are films and author visits; for senior citizens, programs planned weekly. The library does not mail notices, but you can pick up a flyer or call for the day's schedule. A fall highlight: Children's Books International (page 289).

Boston Symphony Orchestra Youth Concerts Symphony Hall, 251 Huntington Avenue (corner of Massachusetts Avenue), Boston

PHONE: 266-1492, 267-0656.

Ⓣ: Symphony on the Arborway-Green Line.

HELD: Saturdays and some weekdays in November, January, and March.

ADMISSION: $12, series of three concerts; $9, series of two. Advance tickets through schools, or by sending a stamped self-addressed envelope to Anita Kurland, Symphony Hall, Boston 02115. Single tickets ($4.50) are sold the morning of concerts at the box office.

AGE APPEAL: One series for Grades 4-7; two series for Grades 8-12.

Harry Ellis Dickson conducts the Boston Symphony Orches-

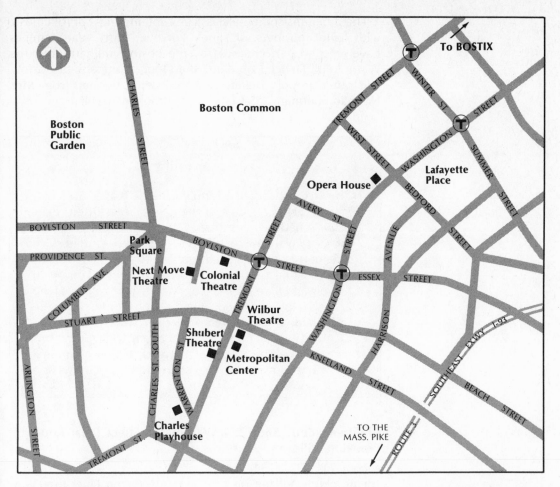

Theater District

tra in 1-hour concerts especially prepared for young people. Each concert has a specific theme, and often includes dance, opera, narration, or other art media. Sometimes the audience learns about a single instrument, perhaps the harp or even the harmonica.

BEFORE AND AFTER: Reservations are required for lectures about and demonstrations of the orchestra's collection of ancient instruments, and the half-hour behind-the-scenes tour. It's all free.

Brookline Youth Concerts Roberts Auditorium, Brookline High School, Tappan Street, Brookline

PHONE: 566–7694.

Ⓣ: Brookline Hills on the Riverside–Green Line.

HELD: Three Saturday afternoons during the school year.

ADMISSION: Single tickets: $2.50 adults, $1.50 children. Series: $5 adults, $3 children. No reserved seats.

AGE APPEAL: Grades K–8.

The programs combine classical, contemporary, or folk music with ballet, puppets, or slides. For over thirty years families have enjoyed performances by the Boston Philharmonic, the Walnut Hill Dance Company, the Opera Company of Boston, and other groups. Tickets can be ordered by mail from Mrs. Norman Sherman, 255 Clark Road, Brookline 02146.

Films for Children

- THEATER: **Alternative Family Cinema** (page 35).
- PUBLIC LIBRARIES: One of the best places. Often regularly scheduled and free.
- LOANS: Available for all ages from many sources. Two major resources (each publishes a catalog of its broad collection) are the **Boston Public Library** in Copley Square (536–5400), which loans films at no charge to registered organizations only, and the **Abraham Krasker Memorial Film Library** at Boston University's School of Education, 765 Commonwealth Avenue (353–3272), which charges nominal fees but is available to everyone.

Children's Book Shop 237 Washington Street (near Route 9), Brookline Village

PHONE: 734–7323 (734–READ).

Ⓣ: Brookline Village on the Riverside–Green Line; then a 5-minute walk.

HELD: Sunday Special Events, September–mid-December and late January–May, Sunday afternoons at 4.

ADMISSION: Free, but seating is limited.

AGE APPEAL: 5 up.

Audiences sit on the floor for the programs, which feature children's book authors, illustrators, and storytellers. The format varies according to the guest, but it's always family oriented. Call to check who's coming. (This is a special place that understands browsers, shoppers, and creators — of all ages — in the world of children's books.) A delightful combination with the Puppet Show Place (page 44)!

Children's Museum Friday Night Performance Series

MUSEUM PHONE AND INFORMATION: Page 151.

ADMISSION: $2.50 (includes museum admission).

Every Friday night, year-round, two half-hour performances of mime, theater, music, magic, puppets, or storytelling.

The Children's Workshop 1963 Massachusetts Avenue, Cambridge

PHONE: 354-1633.

HELD: Afternoon Performances, September–June (and sometimes into the summer), Wednesdays and Saturdays at 3:30.

ADMISSION: $1.50.

AGE APPEAL: Check when you call for information. Usually ages 3 up.

Sit on a rug for a 45-minute performance by puppeteer, mime, singer, or storyteller. The shop is a toy store with space and imagination, cubbies filled with touch possibilities, and recycle materials from the Children's Museum (page 151). Single and series workshops for kids and adults in everything from creative movement to magic.

The Loon and the Heron Theater for Children 7 Eliot Street (1 block from the former site of the Children's Museum), Jamaica Plain

PHONE: 524-7611.

Ⓣ: Eliot Street on the Arborway–Green Line. Or a 10-minute walk from Forest Hills on the Orange Line.

HELD: Weekends fall through spring; weekdays by arrangement.

ADMISSION: $2–$5. Group rates available.

AGE APPEAL: Grades 1 up.

HANDICAPPED: Many performances are planned for audiences that include hearing and sight impaired.

Since 1977 the adult company has been performing — with imaginative sets and exquisite costumes — all over the country. Programs often include puppets and audience participation. The Eliot Street building is a traditional theater, so younger children should sit as close as possible. The company tours, and offers classes for all ages.

Mandala Folk Dance Ensemble Box 246, Cambridge 02138

PHONE: 868-3641.

HELD: Call for a schedule.

ADMISSION: Free or whatever the sponsoring organization is charging. Tickets for the spring series in John Hancock Hall, $5–$9.

Museums often schedule weekend or vacation performances by resident or touring organizations. Check newspapers or call the recorded-information numbers (page 147) for current events.

AGE APPEAL: Everybody.

Go around the world through folk dance and music with this troupe of thirty-five talented dancers, singers, and musicians. The group has an esprit de corps that's contagious. Members do most of their own research and make most of the authentic costumes.

Marco the Magi's Production of "Le Grand David and His Own Spectacular Magic Company" Cabot Street Cinema Theatre, 286 Cabot Street, Beverly 01915

PHONE: 508–927–3677.
LOCATION: 20 miles north of Boston.
DIRECTIONS: Tobin-Mystic Bridge to Route 1 north, to Route 128 north, to exit 22E (Route 62). Follow Route 62 2.5 miles to Cabot Street. Turn right onto Cabot for 2 blocks. From Salem take Route 1A over Salem-Beverly Bridge, go up Cabot Street for 1 mile.
HELD: Year-round, Sundays at 3 and 8:15. First-come, first-served seating begins 45 minutes before performances. Even the waiting time is filled with showmanship — by jugglers and puppeteers in the lobby.
ADMISSION: $5.50 adults, $3.75 under 12. Box office open daily 9 to 9. For mail orders add $1 and a self-addressed stamped envelope, but call first to see what's available. Often sold out weeks in advance.
AGE APPEAL: 5 all the way up.
RESTAURANTS: Nearby, driving toward Salem, is Capri, a family-run Italian restaurant. Just over the bridge, on the water, is Stromberg's.

This is worth a special trip at least once, and many return. In an ornate restored theater, built for vaudeville in 1920, you'll see disappearing and reappearing performers and birds, trumpet players, tap dancers, and barbershop singers, with yards of banners, scarves, ruffles, and brocaded costumes — all against endlessly changing, gorgeous backdrops. Constant surprises keep the interest of all ages through the 2½-hour program. Make sure you leave through the lobby for a close-up performance — the perfect end to a unique theatrical experience.

Another form of magic is the strong ensemble spirit and freshness of the company — seventy people who obviously love what they're doing. Performances, started in 1977, are still led by originator Cesareo Pelaez (Marco the Magi), a middle-aged professor of psychology.

Opera Company of Boston Opera House, 539 Washington Street, Boston

PHONE: 426-5300.
ADMISSION: Subscriptions and group rates available. Single tickets sold 2 weeks before performances.

Under the artistic direction of Sarah Caldwell the company has received international recognition. Plans for young people vary from season to season, but may include day performances, in-school programs, dress rehearsals, a New England tour, and *Hansel and Gretel* at Christmastime.

Plays for Children

At this very moment there are at least a half dozen fantastic, energetic, creative groups performing in the Boston area. They may be multiracial, educational, issue oriented, bilingual, or participatory. Some are part of regional professional theater; others are independent. Alas, they change from year to year. Economic survival is the major factor. For information about scheduled performances, check the newspapers (page 6); for information about specific groups, check with the New England Theatre Conference (page 48) or other organizations (page 46).

Colleges also offer programming. For years Emerson and Wheelock have had touring groups. Lesley College, Boston University, and Northeastern are among others that usually perform during the school year too.

Puppet Show Place 32–33 Station Street, Brookline Village
PHONE: 731–6400.
Ⓣ: Brookline Village on the Riverside–Green Line, and you're there.
HELD: Year-round, weekends at 1 and 3; weekdays by appointment.
ADMISSION: $2.50 for weekend shows. Reservations accepted. Group rates (5 or more) and subscriptions available.
AGE APPEAL: 5 up.

The home for all the puppet activity in the region has a theater that holds 120 people, half of whom are usually adults. It's almost as much fun to watch the children as it is the 45-minute performances given by rotating puppeteers who write their own scripts, and make their own sets and costumes. The intimate setting, brick walls, graduated seats, and effective lighting make this a very special place.

Workshops are held here for children and adults. Displays of puppets are on loan from all over the country. And the charming theater can be rented.

The Puppet Show Place, headquarters for the Boston Area Guild of Puppetry, acts as a referral center for touring puppe-

"I was amazed that they could do all those things at the same time."
— BENJY, AGE 7

teers and maintains a reference library open to the public.

WHAT'S AROUND? A neighborhood with enough to fill an afternoon. Next door is Tuesday's Ice Cream Parlor. Around the corner is the Children's Book Shop, one of the best of its kind in the area, with comfortable reading areas and free Sunday programs (page 40). There are natural food stores, antique shops, a century-old tin-ceilinged Woolworth's that carries everything from house dresses to crayons, and the Village Coach House Restaurant, a pub where families are welcome.

Storytelling

Traditional storytellers—family, friends, and neighbors —have learned to share a tale through generations. Modern-day storytellers, or revivalists, use published or original material from many cultures in programs that often incorporate drama, music, and mime.

For accessible quickies, call **Dial-a-Story:**

- Newton Public Library, 552–7148.
- Quincy Public Library, 471–2405.

Toy Cupboard Theatre and Museums 57 East George Hill Road, South Lancaster

PHONE: 508–365–9519.

LOCATION: 57 miles northwest of Boston.

DIRECTIONS: I-495 to Route 117 west, to Route 110 south, 1 mile. At Five Corners, take Boston Road to East George Hill Road.

HELD: July–August, Wednesdays and Thursdays at 2 and 3:30; September–June, the first Saturday of the month at 10:45.

ADMISSION: $.75.

AGE APPEAL: 4–6.

PICNICKING: Allowed on the grounds. Simple, please.

Step through one of the three archways into the small, seventy-five-seat theater, take your place on a pine bench, and see a children's classic adapted to the puppet stage. For over forty years Herbert Hosmer has been presenting 45-minute puppet and marionette programs in the two-hundred-year-old building, once a woodshed. After each performance the audience is invited to take a closer look at the puppets. Punch and cookies are served, and lollipops and balloons are "on the house."

Most people spend a half hour looking at the jam-packed museums in Mr. Hosmer's yard. There are collections of puppets, marionettes, dollhouses — and more dollhouses — and pop-up books (some for touching).

NEARBY: You're in apple country (page 288), a couple of miles from Bolton Orchards (page 286).

Where's Boston Page 133.

Organizations and Clearinghouses

Action for Children's Television 20 University Road, Cambridge 02138

PHONE: 876-6620.

There's no better clearinghouse in the field of children's television. ACT is a national nonprofit consumer organization working to encourage diversity in and to eliminate commercial abuses from the medium. The library, open to the public by appointment, has a unique collection of information and includes subscriptions to over a hundred journals.

Cultural Education Collaborative 164 Newbury Street, Boston 02116

PHONE: 267-6254.

This curriculum-oriented service is designed primarily for teachers who want to locate programs, materials, and resource people from the more than 350 cultural institutions throughout the state. Fees depend on the technical service offered. CEC sells a directory of resources.

Folk Arts Center of New England Page 232.

Folksong Society of Greater Boston Box 492, Somerville 02143

PHONE: 326-0443.

A very active organization that schedules concerts, workshops, singing parties, and family picnics. It is the Boston area's central source for information about traditional folksinging.

Massachusetts Council on the Arts and Humanities 80 Boylston Street, 10TH Floor, Boston 02116

PHONE: 727-3668.

The council "stimulates and encourages the practice, study and appreciation of arts and humanities in the public interest." Its grants and programs vary according to its funding. Although the council does not provide lists of the more than fifteen hundred cultural organizations in the state, its public information office can act as a referral center.

The Adaptive Environments Center Massachusetts College of Art, 26 Overland Street (not far from Sears), Boston 02215

PHONE: 266-2666 (weekdays 9-5).

Ⓣ: Kenmore on the Green Line (except Arborway); then a 10-minute walk. Buses from Allston and Chestnut Hill stop on Brookline Avenue close to Overland Street.

HANDICAPPED: Accessible.

Staffers with art and human services backgrounds have developed a unique model site with a full array of services for interior design and accessibility planning:

- The **Access Hot Line,** live and free, offers information about ramps, playgrounds, and home needs. Ask where to buy or how to make, and about legislation. Someone will call you back with details. (There is a fee for in-depth consultations.)
- The **Open Shop,** open by appointment, supplies tools and help for $5 an hour.
- The **Lifespace Open Studio** incorporates textiles and wood in courses for designing and making.
- The **Library** is a study in storage space with pullout shelves, all books facing front, and a color-coded catalog system in large print. No charge for use as a reference, but circulation is limited to members (who also receive discounts on all fees).

Massachusetts Cultural Alliance 33 Harrison Avenue, Boston 02110

PHONE: 423-0260.

Originally formed as a service organization for nonprofit cultural institutions in Greater Boston, MCA now helps hundreds of organizations in the state with management, collaboration, and communications. The annual annotated directory ($2) lists over 160 area members. The job-listings board is open to anyone, as is MCA's distribution service (fee charged) for sending resumes to its member organizations.

New England Foundation for the Arts 26 Mt. Auburn Street, Cambridge 02138

PHONE: 492-2914.

Its free book of selected performing groups (mostly Boston based) includes descriptions and fees. Organizations can apply for a subsidy (one-third) for specific performances.

New England Theatre Conference Executive Secretary Marie L. Philips, 50 Exchange Street, Waltham 02154

PHONE: 893–3120 (after 5:30 p.m.).

A nonprofit association of individuals and theater groups that are working in a particular area — children's, secondary school, college, university, community, or professional — of theater. Although the conference does not act as a clearinghouse for specific performances, it can lead you to professionals who offer a wide variety of programs related to children's theater.

Puppet Show Place Page 44.

A referral center for touring puppeteers.

Simmons College Center for the Study of Children's Literature 300 The Fenway, Boston 02115

PHONE: 738–2258.

In addition to courses and a full master's program for students, the center offers programs for the public. It serves the community as a referral and information center in the field of children's literature. If a children's book author or illustrator is scheduled to appear in the area, the center is sure to know.

Theater Access for the Deaf c/o Barbara Levitov, Commission on the Physically Handicapped, Boston City Hall, Boston 02201

PHONE: 923–0911 (voice/TTY-TDD).

The group makes arrangements with performing companies for sign language–interpreted performances. Call to check which theater presentations (national and local) have scheduled Greater Boston interpreted performances for hearing-impaired theater-goers of all ages.

Booking a touring company? The chemistry between audience and performers can vary from one location to another. It's an interesting phenomenon. Often the setting, orientation, and mood of the receiving group make a difference.

The West Suburban Creative Arts Council 80 Dean Road, Weston 02193

Forty school systems south and west of Boston are served by this group. Members (mostly parents) are interested in the visual and performing arts as part of school curriculums, and will share their experiences and information about the resources constantly being reviewed. Visitors are welcome to the meetings, held every other month between September and May, for an exchange about artists, programs, and planning procedures.

Young Audiences of Massachusetts 74 Joy Street, Boston 02114 PHONE: 742–8520.

This national nonprofit organization offers programs of fine music, theater, and dance. Audience participation is part of most presentations. Although concerts are usually at schools, arrangements can be made by other groups.

Day Trips

There's always more to see than time allows. Start early. . . . Some readers are very energetic and go far afield for day trips. Others find that automobile confinement has its limitations. Survival suggestions (there's no magic formula): Pack snacks, books, or wrapped surprises for youngsters. Start a story and let others finish it. Count categories of things you see en route. Find signs that begin with every letter of the alphabet. Stop at a playground along the way. . . . Picnic lunches save time and money. . . . Prefer to go with a group? Or let someone else do the planning? See day trip organizations (page 91). . . . Leading a group? See the suggestions on page xi.

Battleship Cove

KNOW YOUR INTERESTS
— AND THOSE OF
YOUR YOUNGSTERS

PHONE: 508–678–1100.
LOCATION: Fall River, 50 miles southeast of Boston.
DIRECTIONS: I-93 south to Route 128 north, to Route 24, to I-195 west, to exit 5.
PARKING: Free, in a central lot. Then walk to all attractions.
OPEN: Year-round, daily except Thanksgiving and Christmas. May–June and September–October, 9–5; July–August, 9–6; November–April, 9–4:30.
AVERAGE STAY: About 2½ hours on the ships, 1 hour at the museum.
ADMISSION (TO ALL THREE SHIPS AND THE MUSEUM): $4 adults, $2 ages 6–13, $.75 ages 2–5, free under 2.
EATING: Snack bar in the USS *Massachusetts,* open daily during the summer and weekends throughout the year.
COMBINATION IDEAS: New Bedford (page 71), Lincoln Park (page 205), Horseneck State Beach (page 216), or a visit to one of the many factory outlets in the area (most are open Monday through Saturday; a brochure is available at the cove).

Tour the **USS Lionfish** first. It's a quick down-and-out walk through the submarine. Young children and people who don't like close spaces should stay on the main deck. The **USS Joseph P. Kennedy, Jr.** is a destroyer that saw service during the Korean and Vietnamese conflicts. The **USS Massachusetts** is a World War II battleship with a main deck twice the size of a football field. It has knobs and wheels to turn, guns to aim, and turrets to climb. There's plenty of up and down and back and forth to see the forecastle, the stern, the ward room (the snack bar's here), the open bridge, the conning tower, and the galleys where meals were prepared for over twenty-three hundred officers and men. Taped information and sound effects at each of the thirty-eight stations give an idea of what life on board was like.

One block from the ships is the **Marine Museum,** where ship models are at children's eye level. Many different crafts are represented, but steamships dominate. The most spectacular of them all is the 14-foot builder's model of the Fall River Line steamer *Puritan.*

Concord

LOCATION: 20 miles northwest of Boston.

DIRECTIONS: Route 2 west. Or the Mass. Pike to Route 128 (I-95) north, to exit 46 (Route 2 west).

TRAIN: 41-minute ride from North Station (227–5070); 10 minutes less from Porter Square, Cambridge.

RESTAURANTS: The Colonial Inn serves a traditional menu. October is extremely busy. The 99 Restaurant, less than a mile west of Concord Center on Route 62, serves $1.99 specials.

PICNICKING: At Fiske Hill (page 66), 5.5 miles down Route 2A. Or at the riverside by Nashoba Valley Winery (page 56).

FARMS (PICK-YOUR-OWN PLACES): See page 283.

Where to begin?

Old North Bridge Monument Street

PARKING AND ADMISSION: Free.

TALKS: 20-minute presentations by National Park Service rangers near the bridge daily June to September, on weekends in the spring and fall, and by request at other times.

HIKERS: You can enter (foot access only) Great Meadows National Wildlife Refuge (page 195) from the parking area across the street from the bridge.

HANDICAPPED: About 200 yards from the parking area over a dirt and gravel surface.

This seems the perfect setting for an introduction to the history of this charming New England town. The bridge, the fourth reproduction at the scene of "the shot heard round the world," is beautiful anytime of the day (especially at dusk), and all seasons of the year. It's a 10-minute walk, in part along the road the patriots marched in 1775, to the visitors' center.

A view and the story in the side garden

North Bridge Visitor Center 171 Liberty Street

PHONE: 508–369–6993.

DIRECTIONS: Driving from Concord Center follow the signs out

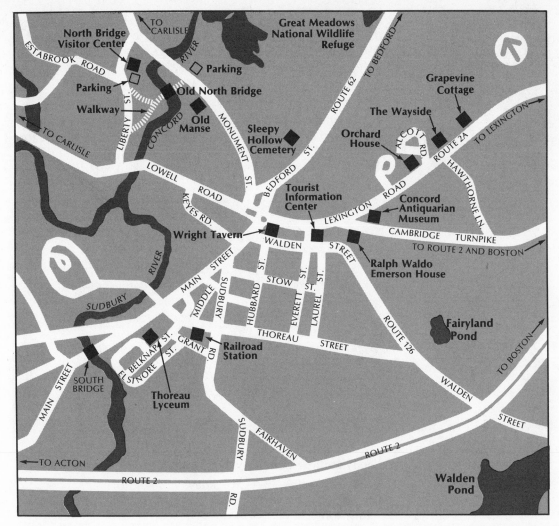

Concord

Lowell Road to Liberty Street. Or walk from Old North Bridge.
PARKING AND ADMISSION: Free.
OPEN: Year-round 8:30–5 daily, summers until 6.

Audiovisual programs in the beautifully landscaped Buttrick mansion (1911). But the surprise is the second-floor try-on room, where kids can see how they look in eighteenth-century fashions — three-cornered hats, bonnets, and weskits.

The National Park Service is here year-round. Special programs can be arranged by reservation. Write Box 160, Concord 01742, for information. The park is actually located in Lincoln, Lexington (page 66), and Concord.

Next to Old North Bridge

The Old Manse Monument Street
PHONE: 508–369–3909.
OPEN: Mid-April–May, Saturdays 10–4:30, Sundays 1–4:30, and

by appointment; June–October, Thursday–Saturday and Mondays 10–4:30, Sundays and holidays 1–4:30.

ADMISSION: $2.50 adults, $1 ages 11–16, $.75 under 11. Educational group rates available. (Recommended for students in Grades 7 up who are studying American literature.)

The house, built in 1769–1770 by Ralph Waldo Emerson's grandfather, remained in the family except for the three years it was rented to Nathaniel Hawthorne. During the 30-minute tour you'll see Hawthorne's writing on the windowpanes, and original wallpaper and furnishings dating back to 1769.

The **Nashoba Valley Winery** is located at 100 Wattaquaboc Hill Road in Bolton. (From Route 495, take Exit 27 to Route 117 west; proceed 1 mile and take left at yellow blinking light; the winery is ¾ mile up the hill on the left.) The winery is open seven days a week from 11 to 6. No appointments necessary for tours Friday through Sunday; for those Monday through Thursday, call 779–5521. Wines are made here year-round from fresh New England fruits. You'll see fermenting and storage tanks, oak wine barrels, and bottling equipment — and end with a taste of the product.

Out-of-towners see and many area residents miss

Sleepy Hollow Cemetery Bedford Street (off Monument)

PHONE: 508–369–7526 (weekdays 8:30–4:30).

GRAVESTONE RUBBING: Allowed. Groups should call ahead for permission.

HANDICAPPED: Some areas are very hilly.

The second entrance leads you to Author's Ridge, and the graves of Emerson, Thoreau, the Alcotts, Hawthorne, and Margaret Sidney. The setting is beautiful, and the tombstones make interesting reading.

If you're only going into one house

Orchard House Louisa May Alcott Memorial Association, 399 Lexington Road (Route 2A)

PHONE: 508–369–4118.

OPEN: Mid-April–mid-November, Monday–Saturday 10–4:30, Sundays 1–4:30. Closed Easter.

ADMISSION: $2 adults, $1 under 12. Group rates available weekdays only. (Not recommended for children under 7.)

HANDICAPPED: The first floor is accessible.

Rave reviews come from many adults and adolescent girls (in particular) for the half-hour tour through the home of Louisa

"Kids who haven't read Alcott want to; others want to reread."

— TOUR LEADER

May Alcott and her philosopher father Bronson. Because nothing is roped off, you feel like a guest, not just a tourist. Readers of *Little Women* will recognize the mood pillow and other items from the book.

Special children's programs are offered Monday mornings during the summer. These may include hoop rolling, storytelling, or acting. Registration is required.

Near Orchard House

The Wayside Lexington Road (Route 2A)

PHONE: 508–369–6975.
DIRECTIONS: 1 mile east of Concord Center on Route 2A.
OPEN: April–June and September–October, Thursday–Monday, 10–5:30; summer, 10–5:30 daily.
ADMISSION: $.75 adults, free under 16.
HANDICAPPED: Not accessible.

You'll see the Alcotts' piano and Nathaniel Hawthorne's tower study in the home that's decorated as it was when Margaret Sidney, author of the Five Little Peppers books, lived here from 1883 to 1924. The 12-minute audiovisual presentation in the barn fills you in.

Also near Orchard House

Grapevine Cottage 491 Lexington Road (Route 2A)

Step into the yard of one of Concord's oldest houses and see the original Concord grapevine, which bears in September. The plaque on the fence tells how Ephraim Wales Bull started it all.

A famous lantern, seen in the Old North Church steeple in 1775

The Concord Antiquarian Museum 200 Lexington Road (Route 2A), Box 146

PHONE: 508–369–9609.
OPEN: Year-round, Monday–Saturday 10–4:30, Sundays 2–4:30. Closed New Year's, Easter, Thanksgiving, and December 24.
ADMISSION: $3 adults, $2 senior citizens, $1 under 15. Group rates available.
GROUPS: Special programs by reservation.
HANDICAPPED: Access ramp.

The Thoreau Room has the bed he slept in at Walden, and his flute and surveying instruments. And there's a replica of Emerson's study with its original furnishings. The guided tour through the seventeen rooms of antiques from the seventeenth through nineteenth centuries takes about 45 minutes.

The oldest flag in the country, the only minuteman flag carried at the Old North Bridge on April 19, 1775, is on display weekdays from 10 to 4 at the Bedford Public Library, Mudge Way (off Great Road), 275-9440.

Ralph Waldo Emerson House 28 Cambridge Turnpike (at Lexington Road)

PHONE: 508–369–2236.

OPEN: Mid-April–October, Thursday–Saturday 10–4:30, Sundays and holidays 2–4:30.

ADMISSION: $2 adults, $1 ages 6–17, free under 6.

During the half-hour tour you see everything, even the battered hat on the hallway stand — just as Emerson left it.

Thoreau Lyceum 156 Belknap Street

PHONE: 508–369–5912.

OPEN: January–March, Tuesday–Saturday 10–5, Sundays 2–5; April–December, Monday–Saturday 10–5, Sundays 2–5. Closed New Year's, April 19, Memorial Day, July 4, Labor Day, and Christmas.

ADMISSION: $1 adults, $.50 Grades 1–12, free for preschoolers.

HANDICAPPED: Inaccessible.

Most visitors spend a half hour looking at survey maps, letters, pictures, and other belongings of the Concord naturalist-writer-philosopher and his family. Behind the lyceum is a replica of Thoreau's Walden House at Walden Pond.

Edaville Railroad

A TOUCH OF AMUSEMENT PARK AND NOSTALGIA — MIXED TOGETHER

PHONE: 508–866–4526.

LOCATION: South Carver, 40 miles south of Boston.

DIRECTIONS: I-93 south to Route 3 south, to Route 44, to Route 58 south. Or I-93 south to Route 3 south, to Route 18 south, to Route 58 south. Or I-93 south to Route 128 north, to Route 24, to Route 25, to Route 58 north. Then follow the signs.

OPEN: May–early June, Sundays and Memorial Day noon–5; mid-June–Labor Day, 10–5:30 daily; Labor Day–mid-October, weekdays 10:30–3 (diesel engine), weekends and holidays 10:30–5 (steam engine).

AVERAGE STAY: 3 hours. Bring bicycles for a 6-mile loop around the lake through cranberry bog country. Keep bearing right on the paved roads from the parking lot exit.

ADMISSION (INCLUDES TRAIN RIDE AND MUSEUM): $5 adults, $3 ages 3–12, free under 3. Rides like the carousel and model T are extra. Group rates (minimum 15) available. Discount coupons (at most McDonald's).

EATING: Picnic tables in a grove. Snack bar. Barbecued-chicken dinner ($4 adults, $3 children) served the last weekend in May, Sundays in June, daily in summer, and Sundays in fall.

The real draw is the half-hour ride (5.5 miles) through woods and cranberry bogs on the old-fashioned steam train built in 1907. A bonus in late summer and fall: seeing the bogs wet- or dry-picked, from the narrow-gauge train.

Plenty of touch possibilities for curious youngsters: exploring the Bridgton and Saco car with its wooden interior and seats that go either way; climbing on steamrollers or into the cab of a train. Surprises include a charming carousel, built in Amsterdam in 1858.

The indoor museum (no touching here) has large displays of antique autos, horse-drawn fire equipment, toy trains (the largest collection in America), Kentucky rifles, and all sorts of railroad memorabilia. While you're looking at the drugstore or barbershop in the re-created nineteenth-century village, youngsters may be reading the fine print on the toothache-gum label.

Gloucester

LOCATION: 35 miles north of Boston.

DIRECTIONS: Tobin-Mystic Bridge to Route 1 north, to Route 128 north.

TRAIN: 1-hour ride from North Station (227–5070).

INFORMATION: Booths are open Memorial Day through Columbus Day at Harbor Loop opposite the police station in Fitz Hugh Lane House (508–283–7376) and on the boulevard at the junction of Routes 133 and 127 (508–283–2651). The Cape Ann Chamber of Commerce is at 128 Main Street (508–283–1601).

RESTAURANTS: In town, the Gloucester House has a reasonably priced summer luncheon menu, served under a tent on the waterfront. Karvela's, near Fishermen's Memorial Statue, is a family-run place with family prices for pizza, seafood, and Greek specialties. Blackburn Tavern has sandwiches, full dinners, and Sunday brunch.

Essex, 7 miles away, has two popular places for fried clams (especially) on Main Street. The Village has service and quiet booths. Expect a half-hour wait on weekends. At Woodman's you order, pick up, and eat inside at picnic tables. It's plenty noisy, but the food is good and the portions are generous.

PICNICKING: At Stage Fort Park right in town, or at Dog Bar Breakwater (page 62) in East Gloucester.

COMBINATION IDEA: Whale watching (page 250).

Gloucester offers insights into the fishing industry, unique museums, ocean views, and open space. Perhaps you've heard about **Dogtown,** an eighteenth-century settlement, now a wilderness of ruined foundations along twisting paths. Unless you have a strong sense of direction or lots of time, go with a leader, or on a scheduled trip with the Appalachian Mountain Club (page 251) or the Sierra Club (page 201).

IN TOWN

If you come from Routes 128 and 133, turn right for Stage Fort Park, left for the harbor and town.

Stage Fort Park (page 210) has plenty of room for picnicking,

Cape Ann

climbing rocks, and throwing Frisbees. The site was used as a defense fort during the Revolution and the War of 1812. . . . There's nothing "to do" at **Fishermen's Statue,** but this memorial to those who have "gone down to the sea in ships" is important to the area. . . . Follow Western Avenue toward the Gloucester House Restaurant, and park in the public lot for the best view of fishing boats in the **harbor.** Foreign ships unload at Rose's Wharf. . . . There are four processing plants along **Commercial Street.** . . . On the Harbor Loop is the **Gloucester Marine Railways Corporation,** where work is done mostly on wooden boats, occasionally on steel. If an exterior is being repaired, you may be able to see rib cages and all.

A good introduction to the world of fish

Gloucester Fishermens Museum Rogers and Porter streets, Box 159

PHONE: 508–283–1940.
OPEN: Year-round, Monday–Saturday 10-4, Sundays 12:30-4. Closed national holidays.
ADMISSION: $2 adults, $1 under 13; $5.50 families.
GROUPS: Organized visits and orientation material, guided walks, and wharf tours — for all ages.

Taste salt cod, use hundred-year-old tools to caulk seams and shape a mast, speak with a retired fisherman while he mends a net, coil ropes, see a movie, learn with the popular touch-tank, and look over the recent hauls. In about an hour — without sophisticated displays — you come to understand a bit about fish and the life of a fisherman.

ALONG ROUTE 127

Ravenswood Park Western Avenue (Route 127)
ADMISSION: Free.
RULES: No cars and no picnicking.

Immense trees, mostly pine and hemlock, surround 5 miles of unpaved paths for walking and cycling. The sign may be overgrown; look for Ravenswood Community Chapel.

Hammond Castle Museum 80 Hesperus Avenue
PHONE: 508–283–2080.
DIRECTIONS: From Boston, Tobin-Mystic Bridge to Route 1 north, to Route 128 north, to exit 14 (Route 133). Follow Route 133 east to Route 127. Right on Route 127 for about 1 mile to Hesperus on the left.
OPEN: May–October, 10–4 daily; November–December and February–April, Thursday–Tuesday 10–4. Closed Thanksgiving and Christmas.
AVERAGE STAY: The guided tour — the only way to see the castle — lasts 45 minutes, but you'll be here at least an hour.
ADMISSION AND TOUR: $3 adults, $1 under 13.

EATING: The Roof Top Cafe serves sandwiches, salads, quiches, and pastries.

PROGRAMMING: Workshops for all ages, some for the entire family, are held throughout the year. Children may make gargoyles out of soapstone or act out plays from the Middle Ages. Call for a schedule of offerings.

A drawbridge over a moat leads to the castle, but you enter through a small iron door into a 100-foot hall filled with art and religious exhibits. The highlight for many, though, is the 10,000-pipe organ, many of its parts from ancient churches. (Make advance arrangements for a miniorgan concert.) Inventor John Hays Hammond, Jr., designed and built the castle (1926–1928) overlooking the Reef of Norman's Woe, described in Longfellow's "Wreck of the Hesperus." He used portions of houses and churches from abroad to resemble, not one particular castle, but the structures of Europe in medieval times.

EAST GLOUCESTER AND EASTERN POINT

Toward the tip of East Gloucester

From the end of Route 128 follow the "Scenic Shore Drive" signs. Rocky Neck, the oldest art colony in the country, has galleries, shops, and restaurants, open April through October.

Beauport Eastern Point Boulevard
PHONE: 508–283–0800.
OPEN: Mid-May–mid-September, weekdays 10–4; mid-September–October, weekdays 10–4, weekends 1–4.
ADMISSION: $4 adults, $1.50 ages 6–12, free under 6.

It's a 1-hour guided tour through what's been called the most fascinating house in America. Each of the twenty-five rooms has been designed and decorated to represent a different period of American life. (Some of the rooms were moved here from prerevolutionary houses.) Henry Davis Sleeper, a Boston architect and interior decorator, originally built Beauport as a small summer house, enlarging it over the first three decades of this century.

From Beauport turn right onto Farrington Avenue to Atlantic Road for a **scenic ride** toward Rockport. Spectacular views of the varied coastline along Bass Rocks, Good Harbor Beach, sandy Long Beach, and Pebble Beach (named for its smooth stones, once used as ballast on Gloucester fishing vessels). At the end of Eastern Point, just beyond Niles Beach, are **Dog Bar Breakwater** and **Eastern Point Light.** Both were built after the gale of '98 with granite from Rockport quarries. A favorite of many families, the breakwater is a half mile long. Fish for mackerel, flounder, pollock, or blues. Collect colorful sea anemones for saltwater-fish tanks. Watch your footing — and young children.

Lexington

LOCATION: 12 miles northwest of Boston.

DIRECTIONS: Route 2 west to Waltham Street. Then follow signs to Lexington Center.

Ⓣ: Harvard on the Red Line. Then bus to Arlington Heights, and bus to Lexington (no service on Sundays).

RESTAURANTS: In Lexington Center there are two Chinese restaurants that have strong followings: Peking Garden at 27 Waltham Street and Yangtze River at 21–25 Depot Square. Bel Canto at 1715 Massachusetts Avenue has great soups, salads, deep-dish pizza, entree turnovers, beers and wines, and cappuccino. Mario's at 1773 Massachusetts Avenue is a small, popular Italian restaurant. For ice cream plus sandwiches and salads: Chadwick's Ice Cream Parlour at 903 Waltham Street, at Concord Avenue, a purple building. It's an experience from 11 to 11, 363 days a year. Flocked wallpaper, a 1907 nickelodeon that works, a printed barbershop clock that runs backward, a high-wheeler that's ridden now and then by owner John Adams (his real name!), and an 1878 Lamson Cash Railway System — all part of the turn-of-the-century decor that'll keep you busy while you wait for a seat in this noisy bustling place. Chadwick's announces about a hundred birthdays each day (a free sundae for the celebrant) with bells and drums, hats, favors, candles, and chorus. Holidays? Lovers get free sundaes on Valentine's Day; menus are printed backward on April Fool's Day; Santa comes to a candle-lit dining room at Christmastime. To get here from Lexington Center, turn onto Waltham Street for 2 miles. From Boston, take the Waltham–Spring Street exit off Route 2 west, and bear right all the way. Question? Call 861–1166.

PICNICKING: At tables right outside the visitors' center (below), or at Fiske Hill (page 66) on Route 2A.

COMBINATION IDEA: Most day-trippers combine Lexington with Concord (page 54), just 5 miles away along Route 2A.

The **Museum of Our National Heritage** (page 173) has terrific programs (often free) and changing special exhibits (always free). . . . **Lexington Gardens,** 93 Hancock Street (862–7000), about a mile from the Green, is a huge nursery with hundreds of plants — bonsai, orchids, cacti, ferns, and herbs. Closed Sundays. Tours through the retail and propagation greenhouses can be arranged from July through March. . . . **Wilson Farm,** operated by the same family for almost a hundred years, has flowers, plants, and picture-book produce. And you don't have to be on a tour (page 264) to visit the chickens.

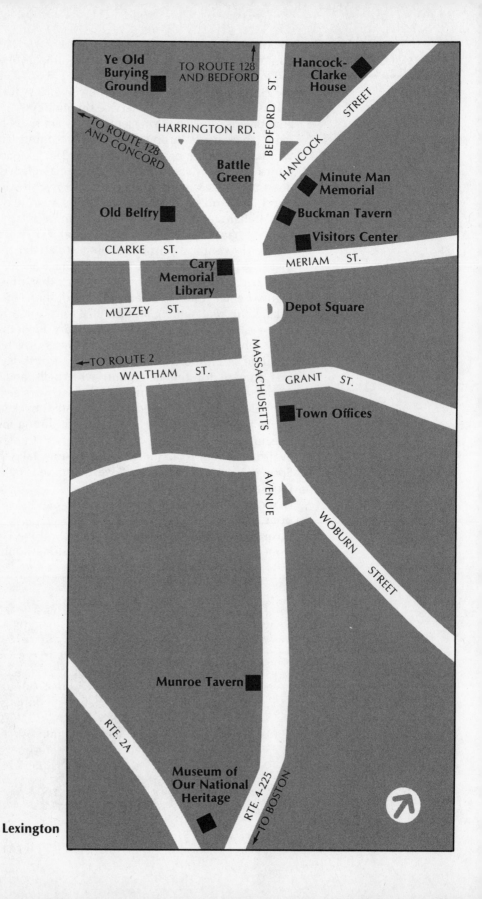

Lexington

Battle Green Lexington Center

The site of the first battle of the Revolution is a small, triangular-shaped area bordered with trees, monuments, and the prominent Minuteman Statue of Captain John Parker. The bench near the boulder inscribed with Parker's famous command is a popular resting place.

Across from Minuteman Statue

Visitors Center 1875 Massachusetts Avenue

PHONE: 862–1450.
OPEN: Year-round, daily. April–October 9–5, until 8 during the summer; November–March, 1–4.
ADMISSION: Free.

What to see? A diorama of the Battle of Lexington, and the hundreds of shards and artifacts found (many by children) in the 1960s, when the town's historical society unearthed the original foundation of the Hancock-Clarke House (below).

Just beyond the Green and the Unitarian church

Ye Old Burying Ground Harrington Road

GRAVESTONE RUBBING: No permit necessary, but please notify the Cemetery Commission at 862–0500.

The graves of Captain Parker, Governor Eustis, Reverend John Hancock, and Reverend Jonas Clarke. The oldest stone is dated 1690.

LEXINGTON HISTORICAL SOCIETY HOUSES

OPEN: April 15–October 31, Monday–Saturday 10–5, Sundays 1–5.
ADMISSION: Each house: $1 adults, $.25 under 12. Combination ticket: $2.25 adults.

Buckman Tavern 1 Bedford Street

PHONE: 861–0928.
HANDICAPPED: Two steps. Once in, you're fine.

Busiest because it's just across from the Green. This is where the minutemen met on April 19, 1775. It takes about 30 minutes for the guided tour through the seven rooms, built in 1690.

A 10-minute walk from the Green

Hancock-Clarke House 35 Hancock Street

PHONE: 862–5598.
HANDICAPPED: Two steps to get in, and two steps inside.

This is where John Hancock and Samuel Adams were sleeping when Paul Revere arrived the night of April 18, 1775. During the 20-minute tour, guides share anecdotes about the personal and political lives of famous residents. Furnishings in the eight rooms, built in 1698, include a rotisserie in the family room, a large chopping bowl Mrs. Clarke used to prepare food for her twelve children, and a trundle bed.

In the 1960s the original site across the street was excavated, and in 1974 the house was moved back to its first foundation.

Munroe Tavern 1332 Massachusetts Avenue
DIRECTIONS: 1 mile toward Arlington from the Green.
HANDICAPPED: A slight hill and two steps. Once in, you're fine.

The tavern, built in 1690, was used as a hospital on April 19, 1775. It's a 20-minute tour through the four furnished rooms.

MINUTE MAN NATIONAL HISTORICAL PARK

DIRECTIONS: About 2.5 miles from Battle Green, on Route 2A.
HEADQUARTERS: In North Bridge Visitor Center (page 54).
ADMISSION: Free.

Fiske Hill is a popular picnic area in a wooded glen, but few follow the 1-mile marked trail across fields and woods to the foundation remains of the eighteenth-century Fiske farmhouse.

About 2 blocks beyond Fiske Hill, off the road, is the **Battle Road Visitors Center** (862–7753), open 8:30 to 5 September through June, until 6 in the summer. Stop here for helpful staff, audiovisual programs, and printed information.

Lowell

SPECIAL AND MOSTLY FREE

LOCATION: 30 miles northwest of Boston.
DIRECTIONS: I-93 north to exit 11 (Route 128/I-95 south), to exit 43 (Route 3 north), to exit 30 (Lowell Connector), to exit 5N (Thorndike Street). Then follow "Lowell National and State Park Parking" signs.
PARKING: The one official lot is free; a nominal fee is charged at municipal lots.
TRAIN: 43-minute ride from North Station (227–5070); then a 15-minute walk.
RESTAURANTS: Exposed brick and hanging plants have arrived in Lowell. An alternative, an old-timer open 11 to 10 daily, is the Olympia at 452 Market Street, which has terrific Greek food. Eat in the original (twenty-five years old) section or in the addition with chandeliers and white cloths. The same moderate prices in both areas, and take-out is $1 less.

Much of what made up the nation's most significant planned industrial city is still here. Nothing is re-created. Although there are no working textile mills left, seven of ten mill complexes remain. Several of the seemingly endless brick structures that

A little lost? Check the map on page 2.

line the intricate network of canals now house the Lowell Museum and visitors' centers. Lowell Heritage State Park is involved with the educational and recreational aspects of the canal and river systems. Its administrative and waterpower exhibits are in the Mack Building at 25 Shattuck Street.

Since the National Park Service came to Lowell in 1978, to commemorate the role of the Spindle City in the Industrial Revolution, the city is revitalized. For visitors this means exciting programming in the midst of historic landmarks and diverse ethnic neighborhoods.

Start at

Lowell National Historical Park Visitors Center Market Mills, Market Street (corner of Dutton)

PHONE: 508–459–1000.

OPEN: Year-round, 8:30–5 daily. Closed Thanksgiving, Christmas, and New Year's.

PICNICKING: On benches in the park next to the center.

GUIDED TOURS: Free. Year-round, daily. In summer, the first tour starts at 9; the last, at 3:30. Reservations (accepted by phone) strongly recommended. Fall through spring, there's at least one tour a day. Call for a schedule. Tours are different from season to season, and from year to year. They may look at folk music or ethnic heritage or the labor movement.

SELF-GUIDED TOURS: 2½ hours, and include canal rides to sites.

TRANSPORTATION FOR TOURS: On foot (up to a mile), by trolley (one that's been in continuous use for almost a century), and boat. All free.

HANDICAPPED: All programs are accessible, but building and transportation systems vary. Call for details.

For tour reservations, orientation, and a program schedule, this is the place. The center is in the former home of the Lowell Manufacturing Company, maker of cotton and woolen goods, cloth, and handwoven carpets. The park service offerings here make tourists out of nontourists. Children seldom get restless.

"The working loom in the museum makes a deafening sound."
— TEACHER

(A day here may not be ideal for preschoolers, though.) The 1- to 3-hour tours weave through the Spindle City, highlighting the history of its people, mills, and over 5 miles of canals. Gatehouses have original hand- and water-propelled equipment, and costumed gatekeepers playing the part of 1850s residents. The ride on the canal gives a perspective on a city that's a monument to an era. You'll come away with a strong feeling for nineteenth-century life in what was the nation's largest producer of cotton cloth.

Lowell's Greek neighborhood

The Acres

Landmarks are St. Patrick's Church and Holy Trinity Church, about 2 blocks from the neighborhood shops on Market Street. World Cheese is at Number 302, at the corner of Worthen.

Giavis Market at Number 357 has ripe olives and feta cheese. Every morning at Number 503, the fillo dough is stretched to 7-foot squares in the Smyrna Lowell Confectionary Company, run by the same family since 1903. At 275 Dutton Street Ymittso Candle Manufacturing welcomes families (but no groups) from 8 to noon to see buckets of melted wax poured into a machine that makes thirteen dozen candles at a time.

> **Prince Company** is the largest pasta-making factory in the country, second largest in the world. Tours, by advance arrangement only, starting in late 1982. Call the Macaroni Division, at 508–458–4111 or 227–9425 (Boston), for information.

Marblehead

LOCATION: 17 miles north of Boston.

DIRECTIONS: Callahan Tunnel to Route 1A north, to Route 129 east.

Ⓣ: Haymarket on the Orange or Green Line; then a 55-minute bus ride (722–3200).

INFORMATION: June–August, daily, near the YMCA at Essex and Pleasant streets, and at Abbot Hall (page 69).

RESTAURANTS: An incredible variety of bustling places in this small community. Jacob Marley's, closed Mondays, serves huge portions; Dill's has quick service; Priscilla's, a small place, has good, reasonably priced vegetarian dishes; Nancy's Incredible Edibles, a tiny place, has soups and light meals; Miguel's is Mexican in food and decor; the Barnacle, on the harbor, has a relaxed atmosphere and a great view; and the Driftwood at 63 Front has an inexpensive menu, mostly fried foods.

PICNICKING: At Fort Sewall or Redd Pond in town. Chandler Hovey Park, at the tip of Marblehead Neck by the lighthouse, is a great vantage point. (Stop on the way to see the garden and English country cottage at Stowaway Sweets, on the corner of Beach Street and Atlantic Avenue.)

The entire town is 4 square miles in all. (If you're caught on a one-way street, you're not very far off course.) As a day-tripper you'll have plenty of company all summer long and on fall weekends. Fall weekdays are quieter.

Walkers find the town filled with charm as they amble along winding streets with hidden lanes, interesting doorways, and old-fashioned gardens. A 2-mile tour, described in the Chamber of Commerce booklet, includes the **Jeremiah Lee Mansion** (1768) and the **Hooper Mansion** (1728), both open to the pub-

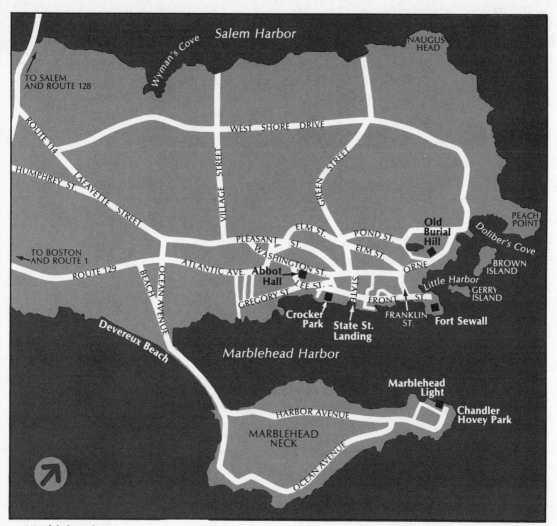

Marblehead

lic. In **Old Town,** parallel (sort of) to Washington Street and the shopping center, are Front Street and the harbor. If you can stay until dusk, you may be rewarded with silhouettes of masts and sails against the sunset.

State Street Landing is the best place for a close-up of harbor activity. (Band concerts here summer Thursdays from 7 to 9.) For more of an overview, walk to **Crocker Park,** a block toward the Boston Yacht Club, or look from the harbor entrance at **Fort Sewall** (1724) at the end of Front Street. Not too far from Fort Sewall, off Orne Street, is **Old Burial Hill,** with gravestones of revolutionary soldiers. Rubbing permits ($1) are issued at the Cemetery Department, Waterside Road off West Shore Drive, from 12:30 to 4 weekdays.

Town maps are available at the information booth and in **Abbot Hall,** the spired building with a clock in the tower. Bring the whole family in to see the original *Spirit of '76,* the painting given to Marblehead by General John Devereux, whose son was the model for the drummer boy. And open the chest on the wall to see the deed to the town, dated 1684. Abbot Hall is open year-round, weekdays from 8 a.m. to 9 p.m., and May 30 through October, Saturdays from 9 to 6, Sundays and holidays from 11 to 6.

Mystic Seaport

PHONE: 203-536-2631.

LOCATION: Mystic, Connecticut, 100 miles southwest of Boston.

DIRECTIONS: I-93 south to Route 128 north, to I-95 south, to Connecticut Route 27 south. If the distance is beyond your usual day trip, consider making a special effort.

OPEN: Year-round, daily except Christmas. May–October, 9–5; November–April, 9–4. The grounds and selected exhibits are open until 8 mid-May through mid-September. Busy in summer, particularly on weekends.

ADMISSION: Summer: $8 adults, $4 ages 5–15, free under 5. Winter: $7 adults, $3.50 ages 5–15, free under 5. Two-day tickets are available. Admission includes parking and all exhibits except the steamboat ride and the planetarium show.

EATING: Picnic areas, a snack bar, and a restaurant.

GROUPS: Arrangements must be made at least 3 weeks in advance for day trips, study tours, and overnight programs. There are no guided tours, but schools can arrange for self-guided tours integrated with classroom curriculum. The education department has a resource center.

PROGRAMMING: In summer, visitors can help make chafing gear and nets, or watch demonstrations of sail setting and furling, chantey singing, fish drying, and small boat sailing. Games on the green for children. All summer and spring and fall weekends there are whaleboat demonstrations (five oarsmen and one steerer) and rides on the *Sabino,* the nation's last coal-fired passenger-carrying steamboat, up the Mystic River.

HANDICAPPED: Wheelchairs available ($10 deposit, no charge for use).

REMINDER: Wear comfortable shoes and bring a jacket.

All ages enjoy this delightful nineteenth-century village, re-created with buildings and shops moved from other locations. The greatest attractions are the ships docked at the seaport. You can board the *Joseph Conrad,* a training ship built in 1882, or the *L. A. Dunton,* one of the last great Gloucester fishing schooners, with its nests of dories once used with long trawl lines. Or explore the *Charles W. Morgan,* the only American wooden whaler in existence, and see craftsmen using traditional and modern methods and tools to restore it.

The children's museum has an adult watch-walkway above

the cabin room where youngsters climb onto a quilt-covered bunk to see out a porthole, play with reproduction toys, or try on copies of period clothes — all in an elaborate setting that reproduces a child's life at sea.

Everywhere interpreters are happy to explain the activity. Walk the cobblestone street and stop in at the doctor's office, the apothecary shop, the tavern, the general store; step along the old ropewalk to see how rope was made; and smell the oakum used for caulking in the chandlery. The fires are burning in the shipsmith shop to make hoops for casks, or harpoons or lances or other tools. The Buckingham House has foods cooking in its fireplace made from recipes of the 1800s. And there are furnished homes of the period, and a large building filled with ship models, figureheads, paintings, and navigational equipment.

All maintenance and restoration work on the seaport's two hundred historic ships and boats is done on the premises. Craftsmen in the Henry B. duPont Shipyard may be replanking, reframing, caulking, or painting. Replicas of wooden boats are built to keep centuries-old skills and traditions alive, and to show visitors how they would have been sailed. The originals remain ashore on display.

New Bedford

LOCATION: 53 miles south of Boston.
DIRECTIONS: I-93 south to Route 128 north, to Route 24, to Route 140, to I-195 east, to exit 15 (downtown).
BUS: Trailways (482–6620), 1¼-hour ride.
INFORMATION: The Office of Tourism is at 1213 Purchase Street (508–997–6501). The Tourist Information Center at 4244 Water Street, between William and Union streets, is open Memorial Day to Labor Day, Monday through Saturday 9 to 5, Sundays 1 to 5.
RESTAURANTS: Several new places have opened along the waterfront. Candleworks, in a recycled building at 72 North Water Street, has good seafood and chocolate mousse. Down to Earth at 522 Pleasant Street, closed Sundays, has homemade natural foods for lunch and, on Thursdays, Fridays, and Saturdays, for dinner. An excuse to see the hurricane barrier and beaches in the south end of town: Davy's Locker, on the water at 1480 Rodney French Boulevard, has reasonably priced seafood. Me and Ed's is popular for good Italian food in an informal setting.
COMBINATION IDEA: A half-hour drive to Battleship Cove (page 53).

The **Whaling Museum** (page 72) is the main attraction. . . . Opposite the museum is the **Seamen's Bethel** with ship-shaped pulpit and wide-planked floor. . . . On the waterfront you can get a close look at the largest **fishing fleet** on the East Coast, take a **harbor tour,** or **sail** to Cuttyhunk or Martha's Vineyard (page 229). . . . The **Glass Museum** (not for young children) is in a restored mansion. . . . A fire engine takes you to the **Fire Museum**. . . . A brochure about the area's **factory outlets** (handbags, sportswear, bedspreads) is available at the information center (above.)

If you take a short drive west to Fairhaven for a picnic, on your right as you go over the bridge you'll see the **hurricane barrier** — the most formidable flood protection device in the country. From the state park at Fort Phoenix (parking $3 during the summer) in Fairhaven you can walk along the top of the barrier into the middle of the harbor.

Whaling Museum 18 Johnny Cake Hill

PHONE: 997-0046.
OPEN: Year-round, Monday–Saturday 9–5, Sundays 1–5. Closed Thanksgiving, Christmas, and New Year's.
AVERAGE STAY: 1½ hours.
ADMISSION: $2 adults, $1 ages 6–14, free under 6.
PROGRAMMING: In spring, whale-watching trips. In summer, a whaling voyage film, Monday through Saturday at 10:30 and 1:30, Sundays at 2. (The theater's air-conditioned.) Full outreach offerings too.
LIBRARY: There's a public access area in the climate-controlled facility that houses the world's largest collection of materials on whaling history.
HANDICAPPED: Elevator available.

Walk the decks of the half-scale whaling bark *Lagoda*, built in 1850. Touch harpoons, anchor chains, and blubber hooks; then climb to the balcony of the museum for a topside view. In the most comprehensive collection of artifacts from the American whaling industry are nineteenth-century tools and equipment, scrimshaw (intricate carvings on whalebone and teeth), ship models, paintings, dolls and toys, and early household items. In one gallery youngsters are encouraged to feel a piece of sailcloth or a sperm whale's tooth, hold a ropemaker's tool, or smell a jar of whale oil. And the museum is small enough to explore completely in one trip.

Two blocks away
Pairpoint Glass Works 47 North Second Street

OPEN: Weekdays 8:30–4:30, Saturdays 8:30–noon.
ADMISSION: Free.

Glassblowers at work. For a description, see page 90.

Not sure where the town is? Check the map on page 2.

Newport, Rhode Island

SUNDAY IS VERY BUSY;
COME EARLY

LOCATION: 80 miles southwest of Boston.

DIRECTIONS: I-93 south to Route 128 north, to Route 24. Then follow Route 138 or Route 114 into Newport.

INFORMATION: The booth next to Brick Market at Long Wharf and America's Cup Avenue is open 9 to 5 daily except Thanksgiving, Christmas, and New Year's. Tickets for all mansion, boat, and land tours are on sale here. Phone: 401–847–1600.

RESTAURANTS: Zillions. Black Pearl on Bowen's Wharf has one casual and one formal (French) dining room. The Pier, off Thames Street on West Howard, is one of several places that have patios overlooking the harbor. Chowder is the specialty in the coffee shop at Seamen's Institute in Market Square, closed Sunday evenings. From 4 to 10 Salas' Restaurant at 343 Thames, overlooking the harbor, features Oriental or Italian spaghetti by weight — an inexpensive way to feed a family. The menu also has conventional fare at reasonable prices.

The information booth is well supplied with details about historic sites, public beaches (First Beach has good surfing), and more estates than those mentioned below. . . . **Trinity Church,** the country's oldest Episcopal church, is open June through September, Monday through Saturday 10 to 4. . . . **Touro Synagogue,** America's oldest synagogue, is open during the summer, weekdays 10 to 5, Sundays 10 to 6; fall through spring, Sundays 2 to 4. . . . The **International Tennis Hall of Fame and Museum** is open daily May through October. . . . **Green Animals,** a sculptured privet, is in Portsmouth, 7 miles north of Newport on Route 138.

For a taste of Newport in a day, consider

- **The Wharf Area:** As you come into town, just beyond Brick Market, there's a semicircular road, America's Cup Avenue, that leads to cobblestone Bowen's and Bannister's wharves. Here are shops and restaurants in revitalized eighteenth- and nineteenth-century buildings. Ahead (south), along Thames Street, is Christie's (on the right), which offers a dockside view of yachts and fishing boats. Newport Shipyard is in the distance.

- **Ocean Drive:** This 10-mile drive (cyclists: along moderate terrain) is well signed. If you start from Thames Street, you'll come to Fort Adams State Park, a pier and small beach with a slide in the water — free. Then you'll travel by well-fenced estates, rocky beach areas with parking, and many spots for picnicking and exploring. Near the end of the drive is Brenton Point State Park, an overlook area with grass and sand. From here there's a radical change as you go along Bellevue Avenue to the mansions.

- **Newport Mansions:** All are sumptuous. Those open to the public by the Preservation Society have 1-hour guided tours. The Breakers, once the home of Cornelius Vander-

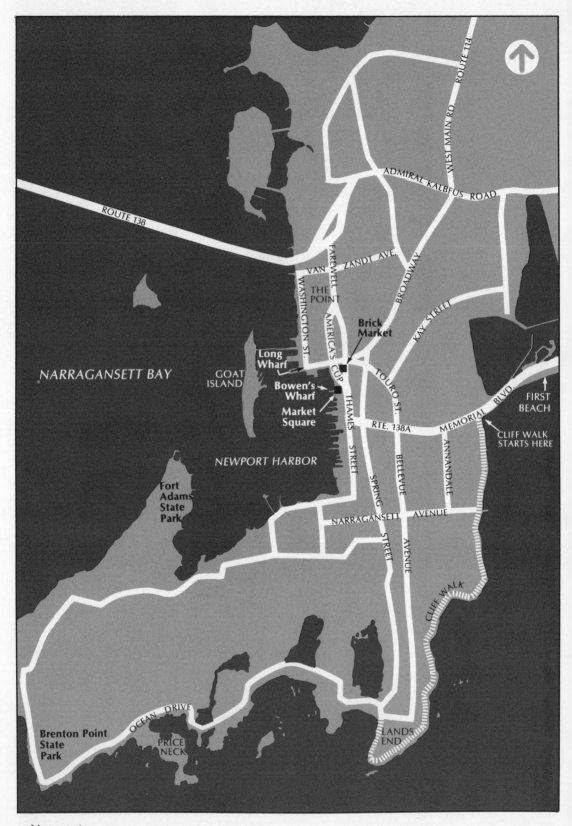

Newport

bilt, and Marble House are particularly popular. In April, the Breakers, Marble House, and Rosecliff are open 10 to 5 daily. All are open May through November, 10 to 5 daily. During the summer, a different one is open each night until 8. (Summer weekends are always busy; midweek there's hardly ever a wait.) In winter, Chateau-sur-Mer, the Elms (built for coal magnate Edward J. Berwind), and Marble House are open weekends from 10 to 4. Admission is $4.50 for the Breakers and Marble House; $3.50 for Chateau-sur-Mer, the Elms, Kingscote, and Rosecliff. Combination tickets are available. Children (ages 6 to 11) are $1.25 at all.

- **Cliff Walk:** A free walkway developed by estate owners during Newport's Gilded Age. It starts on Memorial Boulevard just after Cliff Walk Manor. The path goes for almost 3 miles between dozens of mansions, including the Breakers, and an uninterrupted view of sailboats and lobstermen. Height (and drop) may make you uncomfortable with young children.
- **The Point:** One of the oldest sections of Newport. Weave your way through the narrow streets where you can easily tell which colonial homes have been or are in the process of being restored. An "OC-Acorn" sign means the house is a private restoration; a "Newport Restoration Foundation" sign, the house was or is being restored (for rentals only) by Doris Duke's very active organization.

Old Sturbridge Village

PHONE: 508–347–3362.
LOCATION: Sturbridge, 60 miles west of Boston.
DIRECTIONS: Mass. Pike to exit 9. Follow signs to Route 20 west.
BUS: Trailways (482–6620), 1½-hour ride.
OPEN: Year-round, April–October, 9–5 daily; November–March 10–4. Closed Christmas, New Year's, and winter Mondays except during Christmas and Washington's Birthday school vacation weeks. Busiest in summer and on Columbus Day weekend.
ADMISSION: $7.50 adults, $3.50 ages 6–12, free under 6. Major credit cards accepted.
EATING: Picnic areas in a pine grove. Light snacks, cafeteria, and buffet.
PROGRAMMING: Check the signboard to find sheep shearing, maple sugaring, fife and drum concerts, kiln firing (a 24-foot-high reproduction), and sleigh rides (winter weekends and Washington's Birthday week).
THANKSGIVING DINNER: Reservations required. See page 290.
WORKSHOPS: Include hands-on possibilities for children and adults in energy and technology, fashion, blacksmithing, spin-

ning, and needlework — all in the wonderful custom-designed education building. There's a fee, and reservations are necessary. The village's education department also develops workshops, study guides, and resource materials for specific age groups.

STROLLERS: Not allowed in buildings.

REMINDER: Wear comfortable shoes and dress for outdoors.

Plan to arrive early: There's more than a day of fascination for everyone at this outdoor living-history museum of early New England life. Forty buildings of the 1790–1840 period have been moved from all over New England and reconstructed on 200 rolling acres of meadow and woodland.

The costumed staff brings the village to life. The miller, the candlemaker, the printer — all working craftsmen — eagerly explain what they're doing. The farmer, too, loves visitors, and animals (oxen, cows, and sheep). You can buy fresh warm cookies at the bakery in summer, rest on the village green, see a potter shape utensils from native clay, or ride through the covered bridge and around the mill pond on a horse-drawn carryall. And, if you're late for school, you'll hear about it from the teacher.

Plymouth

LOCATION: 41 miles southeast of Boston.

DIRECTIONS: I-93 south to Route 3 south, to exit 6 (Route 44) toward Plymouth. Turn right at the first lights to the center of town. Or take exit 5 to the new information center.

BUS: Greyhound (423–5810), 1⅓-hour ride.

INFORMATION: The booth on South Park Avenue, corner of Court, is open April 15 through November, 9 to 5 (508–746–4734). The Chamber of Commerce (508–746–3377) is at 85 Samoset Street.

RESTAURANTS: Inn for All Seasons, on the way to Pilgrim Village, cooks great vegetables and entrees. The appetizers alone are good enough to make a meal. In town the Lobster Hut has seafood, coleslaw, and french fries. Eat outside on picnic tables by boats and seagulls. Al's Subs has take-out and eat-in Greek salad, pita bread sandwiches, and subs. Arthur's, on Route 3A toward North Plymouth, has a family following for its Italian menu. Children 12 and under eat free fried foods or peanut butter and jelly sandwiches, dessert, and a beverage — as long as an adult orders a full dinner — September through June, Sundays noon to 9, at Bert's Restaurant on Route 3A just across from the entrance to Pilgrim Village.

Plimoth Plantation consists of Pilgrim Village and Wampanoag Summer Campsite, *Mayflower II* and the waterfront attractions in town, and two early houses.

On busy days you have to wait to step inside the portico to

see **Plymouth Rock,** a comparatively small treasure. The imagination has been at work, and the usual reaction is disappointment. Across from Plymouth Rock, climb **Cole's Hill,** where the Pilgrims buried their dead in unmarked graves. Vistascopes give a better view of the harbor.

Plymouth is filled with historical sites: "Is this the original parking lot?"
— CAROL, AGE 6

Across Leyden Street, the oldest street in the country, is **Brewster Gardens,** a small peaceful park often overlooked by tourists, where you're welcome to have a refreshing drink from the spring. Follow the posted map here for a short walking trail along Town Brook, over the wooden bridge, to **Jenney Grist Mill,** where you'll see a water-powered mill grinding corn, wheat, or rye, as the Pilgrims did over three hundred years ago. (Herring run time here is late April to early June.) The pretty pond is a good place for feeding ducks and geese.

> Too much to choose from? Begin at Pilgrim Village. Then drive to the public parking area (no charge) at Jenney Grist Mill, take the trolley to Cranberry World, and cover the waterfront on foot.

The highlight of Plimoth Plantation

Pilgrim Village and Wampanoag Summer Campsite Route 3A
PHONE: 508–746–1622.
DIRECTIONS: 3 miles south of Plymouth Rock, on Route 3A.
OPEN: The Village: April–November, 9–5 daily. Campsite: May–October.
AVERAGE STAY: Allow 2 hours for leisurely looking.
ADMISSION: $5 adults, $2.50 ages 5–13, free under 5.
GROUPS: Special rates and orientation materials available.
EATING: Cafeteria with hot and cold food. Picnic tables on a first-come basis.
SPECIAL PROGRAMMING: A midsummer celebration, a re-created wedding, a harvest festival, and Native American exhibits.
STROLLERS AND WHEELCHAIRS: Paths are rough.
REMINDER: This is an outdoor museum by the ocean; it can be cool in spring and fall. Wear comfortable shoes to cope with the paths.

It's worth a special trip to this replica community. After a brief, excellent orientation you're on your own among interpreters who portray (to the hilt) 1627 residents through personality, attitudes, mannerisms, and speech. They're happy to talk with you, to share a riddle, some personal history, or gossip, while they're cooking, building, and caring for animals and gardens. The trials and punishments are another effective way to turn the clock back for visitors. In the campsite modern-day Native Americans depict the life of an extended family

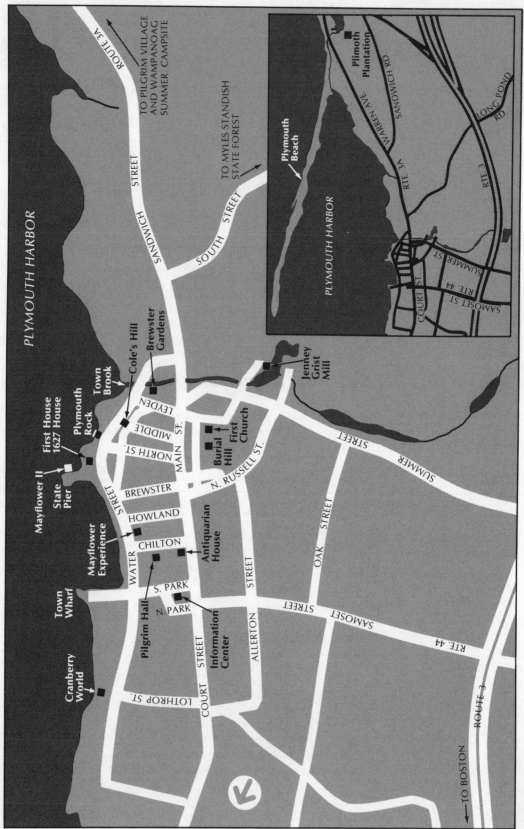

PLYMOUTH HARBOR

Cranberry World

Town Wharf

Mayflower Experience

Mayflower II
State Pier

First House
1627 House

Plymouth Rock

Town Brook

Cole's Hill

Brewster Gardens

Jenney Grist Mill

WATER STREET

HOWLAND

CHILTON

S. PARK

N. PARK

Pilgrim Hall

Information Center

LOTHROP ST.

COURT STREET

ALLERTON STREET

SAMOSET STREET

RTE. 44

ROUTE 3

TO BOSTON

LEYDEN

MIDDLE

NORTH ST.

MAIN ST.

BREWSTER

N. RUSSELL ST.

Burial Hill

First Church

OAK STREET

SUMMER STREET

SANDWICH STREET

SOUTH STREET

ROUTE 3A

TO PILGRIM VILLAGE
AND WAMPANOAG
SUMMER CAMPSITE

TO MYLES STANDISH
STATE FOREST

Plymouth Beach

PLYMOUTH HARBOR

Plimoth Plantation

WARREN AVE.

SANDWICH RD.

RTE. 3A

LONG POND RD.

RTE. 3

COURT ST.

SUMMER ST.

SAMOSET ST.

RTE. 44

Plymouth

group — fishing, hunting, tending crops, and preserving foods.

For a change of pace, **Plymouth Beach** is just across the street from the village. The beach, home to a tern colony, has a long man-made breakwater that's great for walking, and a sandy area at low tide. Parking's free here in spring and fall.

> The **trolley ride** is a fun bargain, only $.25 for a 3-mile ride on a nineteenth-century replica complete with white oak woodwork and etched glass. You can get off along the way, but reentry is another quarter or a merchant's token (usually free with purchases). The trolley runs daily, late May through late November, from 9 a.m. to 8 p.m.

No charge and good

Cranberry World Water Street (in town along the waterfront)

PHONE: 508–747–1000, 508–727–2350.
PARKING AND ADMISSION: Free.
OPEN: April–November, 9:30–5 daily. Busiest on weekends in spring and fall, midweek in summer.
AVERAGE STAY: 30–45 minutes.
SPECIAL PROGRAMMING: Concerts on the boardwalk summer Sunday afternoons.
STROLLERS: Allowed.
HANDICAPPED: Accessible.

Cross over the bogs along wooden bridges to the museum. (It's air-conditioned.) Wonderful displays explain the history, lore, and commercial development of cranberries. The whole place — from both architectural and informational points of view — is well done. Visits end with samples of cranberry cooking and juice.

If you walk from Cranberry World to *Mayflower II*, you'll pass Town Wharf, near the Mayflower Restaurant, where fishing boats unload, weigh, and ice their catch. This is also where Captain John's fishing parties leave from.

Mayflower II State Pier

PHONE: 508–746–1622.
OPEN: April–November, 9–5 daily; July–August, until 6:30.
ADMISSION: $2 adults, $1.25 ages 5–13, free under 5. Combination tickets available for village and ship.
SPECIAL PROGRAMMING: In summer, dockside demonstrations by the crew at work and an orientation that focuses on the religion, politics, and economics of the Pilgrims.

You're on and off in 20 minutes — through the cramped

quarters the Pilgrims had during their 1620 voyage. The role-playing captain will remind you that he hasn't yet returned to England.

> Two miles north of Plymouth Rock, in Cordage Park on Route 3A, is **Commonwealth Winery,** in a turn-of-the-century building once the library of the world's largest hemp rope manufacturer. Free tours Monday through Saturday 10 to 5, Sundays noon to 5. It's busiest here from late August to mid-September, when the grapes are crushed (some by hand-operated equipment), and in March, April, May, and August, at bottling time. Tasting is for adults only. Phone: 508–746–3148.

Waterfront Houses

PHONE: 508–746–1622.
OPEN: April–November, 9–5 daily.
ADMISSION: $.25 to each.

If you haven't been to the village, you may want to see First House, an example of the earliest permanent house built by the Pilgrims, and 1627 House, which shows later refinements.

Portsmouth, New Hampshire

LOCATION: 56 miles north of Boston.
DIRECTIONS: Tobin-Mystic Bridge to Route 1 north, to I-95 north, to New Hampshire exit 7.
PARKING: Park once, and walk to just about everything.
BUS: Greyhound (423–5810) and Trailways (482–6620), 1½-hour ride.
INFORMATION: The booths in Market Square and opposite the Viking Cruise dock are open weekdays during the summer from 10 to 2. They'll fill you in on walking tours, harbor cruises, historic sites, and chamber concerts.
RESTAURANTS: There are nearly seventy in town, many of them outstanding. Most places are busy at lunch, when locals join tourists for reasonably priced specials. Lucia's has Greek food. The Library has unbelievable cheesecake. Metro is famous for its chowder. Warren's Lobster House, just over the bridge in Kittery, has a good salad bar. Hector's Country Kitchen, on Route 1 in Rye between Portsmouth and Hampton, is a big, family place that offers seconds on house specials.

Good eating, browsing (antiques and crafts), and entertainment (Theatre by the Sea) are some of the many reasons visitors come to this revitalized port town. In summer, the Prescott Park Arts Festival adds to a varied and inexpensive day trip.

Strawbery Banke   Hancock Street

PHONE: 603–436–8010.

DIRECTIONS: Follow the signs to the parking area on Hancock Street.

OPEN: April 15–November 15, 9:30–5 daily.

ADMISSION: $4.50 adults, $3.50 senior citizens, $2.50 students 16–22, $1.50 ages 6–15, free under 6.

GROUPS: Special tours by appointment.

Built in 1630, along a riverbank lined with wild strawberries, this urban community became important during the clipper ship era. Thirty-five buildings now stand within the 10-acre area, all but five on their original foundations. Of the twenty-three that are open, five are furnished with period furniture and have guides. Others have exhibit rooms or serve as shops for working craftspeople. There's work in progress too in the boat shop and archaeological excavations. It's easy to spend a couple of hours (more if construction and architecture are your thing) exploring three centuries of change in New Hampshire's first permanent settlement.

NEARBY: Across the street are the colorful **experimental gardens** of the University of New Hampshire. . . . Here, too, on the banks of the Piscataqua River is **Prescott Park,** a busy place during much of the summer. Plan to stay for a free Friday or Saturday night outdoor concert. The sight lines are good, the audience is attentive, and it's fun. . . . It's about a 5-minute walk to the **old harbor area,** where glassblowing is done at Salamandra Glass from March through December.

Rockport

CROWDS WILL GREET THE
DAY-TRIPPER

MAP: Page 60.

LOCATION: 44 miles north of Boston.

DIRECTIONS: Tobin-Mystic Bridge to Route 1 north, to Route 128 north, to exit 10 (Route 127 north).

PARKING: The town is coping with traffic and parking by providing a bus from a parking lot a mile out of town, at 182 Main Street (Route 127). Service is available from 10 to 7 weekends in May, June, September, and October, and daily during the summer. Parking is $3; there's no charge for the bus, which leaves every 12 minutes or so.

TRAIN: 1¼-hour ride from North Station (227–5070).

INFORMATION: The booth on Upper Main Street (Route 127) is open year-round from 8 to 6.

RESTAURANTS: Oleana at 29 Main Street has a dining room and coffee shop. The decor is Norwegian; the menu, American. Delightful atmosphere, fantastic fish or clam chowder on Fridays, wonderful homemade baked goods, and moderate prices and a children's menu. Open April through December and some winter months, closed Mondays. Some consider Peg Leg at 18 Beach Street the best value in town. Plan on a long wait.

PICNICKING: No areas right in town. You can park on the jetty at Granite Pier Wharf (in summer, $1). Take Granite Street to Wharf Road on the right. Or go to Halibut Point Reservation (page 186).

BIKE RENTALS: Full size only at L. E. Smith, 17 Railroad Avenue, 546-6518. Open until 8 Thursday and Friday evenings, 5 other days; closed Sundays. (Rockport does have hills.)

COMBINATION IDEA: Hammond Castle Museum (page 61) in Gloucester.

The shoreline here gives the feeling of Maine. In the center of town are open spaces, galleries, artists at work along the harbor, the much-photographed and -painted, and reconstructed, Motif #1, inviting lanes, and history. Main Street is full of contrasts: the tombstones in the Old Parish Burying Ground, saltwater taffy made in the window of Tuck's at Number 15, the handcrafted candles shaped at Number 5. Most Bearskin Neck shops don't open until 1 on Sundays, making Sunday mornings, before the crowds arrive, a good time to walk the Neck. Be sure to go the full length for a good view of the harbor.

Many people bypass the town and head straight for **Halibut Point,** the outermost tip of Cape Ann.

PIGEON COVE

A DIFFERENT PERSPECTIVE

This area is a 10-minute drive along Route 127 or a healthy bike ride from the center of Rockport. Turn at the Tool Company to see lobsters unloaded and weighed (no set schedule).

Not far from the post office is the **Paper House.** It took twenty years to build this house in which everything — lamps, chairs, grandfather's clock, even the walls (215 thicknesses) — is made of paper. The fireplace mantel is rotogravure sections; the writing desk, newspaper reports of Lindbergh's flights. Mrs. Curtis, your guide for the 15-minute tour, will happily point out any unusual birds bathing in the shallow spot near the ledges. Open June through October 12, 9 to 5 daily. Admission is $.50 for adults, $.25 ages 6 to 15, free under 6.

Salem

LOCATION: 20 miles northeast of Boston.

DIRECTIONS: Callahan Tunnel to Route 1A north right into town.

PARKING: One time in a garage or metered lot may be all that's necessary. This is a compact, well-signed town.

TRAIN: B&M from North Station (227-5070), 29-minute ride; then 6 blocks to the center of town.

T: Haymarket on the Orange or Green Line; then a 50-minute bus ride (722–3200).

INFORMATION: The Chamber of Commerce at 32 Derby Square, between Pickering Wharf and Essex Street Mall, is open weekdays. Four information centers, including one at Pickering Wharf, at 221 Derby Street, are open daily during the summer.

RESTAURANTS: Plenty, including Romagnoli's Table in the Essex Street Mall for homemade pasta; Soup du Jour at 7 Central Street, near Derby Square, for soups, salads, quiches, and pizza; the Lyceum at 43 Church Street, with brick walls and hanging plants, for crepes and veal; and Folsom's Chowder House at 7 Dodge Street, for seafood in a real family-type place.

PICNICKING: Eat on the common or go to Salem Willows Park (page 213), a mile from town.

> Enjoy the **Voyage** or the **witch museum,** or explore on your own. . . . Spend part of the day here, and then see **"Le Grand David"** (page 43) in Beverly. . . . Ride the waves with a **harbor cruise** from Pickering Wharf or Salem Willows. . . . Go **fishing** or **whale watching** from Pickering Wharf. . . . Walk along quiet, elegant **Chestnut Street,** past the magnificent houses once owned by sea captains.

Restored homes are part of the neighborhood

Pickering Wharf

OPEN: Daily. Summer, Wednesday–Saturday evenings until 8:30, Sundays 10:30–5:30; winter, Friday and Saturday evenings until 8:30, Sundays noon–5.

The spot for Faneuil Hall Marketplace lovers, people who enjoy shops and browsing, restaurants, and street entertainment. Go into the Voyage lobby (no charge) to see dioramas that show the changes here from 1805 to 1981.

Voyage of the India Star Pickering Wharf (next door to Putnam Pantry and its ice cream smorgasbord)

PHONE: 508–741–0426.

OPEN: Summer, Mondays and Tuesdays 10–5:30, Wednesday–Saturday 10–8:30, Sundays 10:30–5:30; winter, Monday–Thursday 10:30–5:30, Fridays and Saturdays 10:30–8:30, Sundays noon–5.

ADMISSION: $2 adults, $1.50 ages 13–18, $1 senior citizens and ages 6–12, free under 6. Family (2 adults and 4 children) and group rates available.

The 25-minute show gives a sense of the life of those who

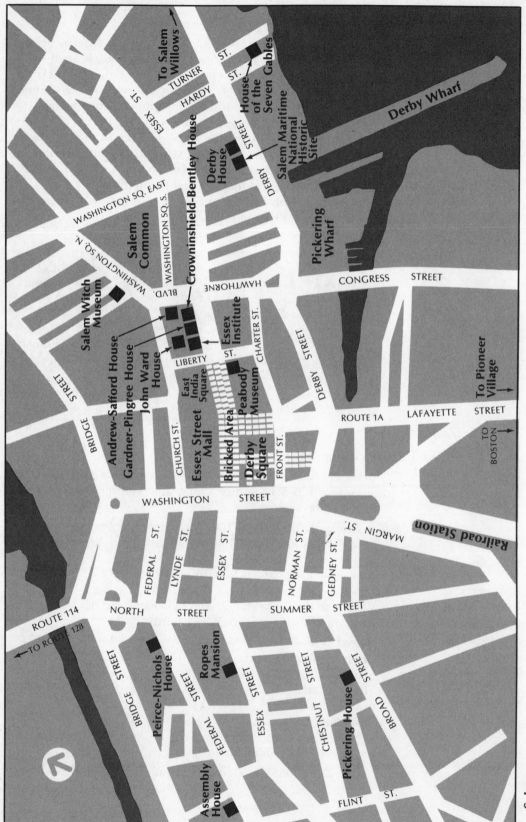

Salem

took risks and reaped rewards through long voyages at sea. In this multimedia presentation of an 1804 clipper ship's trip around the world, souvenirs and tea are bought in Calcutta. The stop in Sumatra is complete with a pirate attack off the coast. There's even a thunderstorm at sea, and a Fourth of July celebration in Salem. Times change. After twenty-two years of voyages, the ship is sold for scrap.

Near the wharf

Salem Maritime National Historic Site Derby Street

PHONE: 508–744–4323.
OPEN: Year-round, 8:30–5 daily, in summer until 6.
ADMISSION: Free.
SPECIAL PROGRAMMING: Activities, and demonstrations during school vacations. Reservations required for school groups.
REST ROOMS: Open 9 to 4:30 in the gray building at the end of the cobblestone driveway.

The site includes the **Custom House,** with an office once used by Nathaniel Hawthorne. You can sign up for a free 45-minute tour that takes you into **Bonded Warehouse,** with its sample cargo; **Scale House,** with its weighing and measuring demonstrations; and **Derby House,** a merchant's home.

Andersen and Vining Sailmakers 155 Derby Street (just beyond Derby Wharf)

OPEN: Monday–Saturday.

Watch sailmakers sewing (on their knees) through the window, or go in and talk with them while they work.

Harbor Sweets 85 Leavitt Street

PHONE: 508–745–7648.
DIRECTIONS: A 10-minute walk from Pickering Wharf to the end of Congress Street, then left onto Leavitt.
OPEN: September–May, weekdays (mornings are best). Call a day in advance.

Up to eight people at a time are welcome to watch the cooking, dipping, foil wrapping, and packing of this "best and most expensive" small candymaker. Free samples are part of the fun.

Off Derby Street, overlooking the water

House of the Seven Gables (1663) Turner Street

PHONE: 508–744–0991.
PARKING: Free and plentiful.
OPEN: July 4–Labor Day, 9:30–6:30; the rest of the year, 10–4:30. Closed Thanksgiving, Christmas, and New Year's.
ADMISSION: Combination ticket (three houses): Available mid-June–Labor Day and fall weekends, $3 adults, $1 ages 13–17, $.50 ages 5–12, free under 5. Single tickets: Available the rest of the year, $2. Proceeds support Settlement House.

EATING: The garden coffee shop is open mid-May through mid-October.

Those who've read Nathaniel Hawthorne's novel will enjoy the 20-minute tour through the six rooms he made famous. Most memorable is the winding climb to Clifford's room, up the narrow secret staircase. Summer tours include Hawthorne's Birthplace (1682), moved to its present site in 1958, and a seventeenth-century counting house.

About 5 minutes from Pickering Wharf

The Salem Witch Museum 19½ Washington Square North

PHONE: 508–744–1692.

OPEN: Year-round, 10–5 daily; in summer until 7.

ADMISSION: $2.50 adults, $1.75 senior citizens, $1.25 ages 6–18, free under 6.

What caused the witchcraft hysteria in late-seventeenth-century Salem Village? An effective half-hour multimedia show explains some of the whys and wherefores of the witch trials.

Many return again and again

Peabody Museum of Salem East India Square

PHONE: 508–745–1876, 508–745–9500 (recorded information).

PARKING: Across Essex Street on Liberty Street, $.30 an hour.

OPEN: Year-round, Monday–Saturday 10–5, Sundays and holidays 1–5. Closed Thanksgiving, Christmas, and New Year's. Busiest on rainy days in summer, from 10 to 3.

ADMISSION: $2 adults, $1.50 senior citizens and students with IDs, $1 ages 6–16, free under 6. Group rates available.

PROGRAMMING: Lectures, courses, performances, films, bus tours, field trips, and children's programs.

STROLLERS: Allowed.

HANDICAPPED: Accessible.

If your children are museum-goers, this is worth a special trip. The collections of maritime history, ethnology, and natural history have been growing ever since the East India Marine Society was organized by a group of Salem captains and merchants in 1799. Step inside the reproduction saloon, and see the full-size cabin from Cleopatra's barge (built in Salem in 1876) and the enormous tusks said to come from 150-year-old elephants. Here are ship models — in and out of bottles — nautical instruments, paintings, and bird and plant exhibits. The Chinese, Japanese, and Pacific Islands ethnological collections have everything from flower holders and costumes, to armor and ornate saddles.

A museum too

The Essex Institute 132 Essex Street

PHONE: 508–744–3390.

OPEN: June–July 3, Monday–Saturday 9–4:30, Sundays 1–5; July 4–Labor Day, Monday–Saturday 9–6, Sundays and holidays 1–6;

September–May, Tuesday–Saturday 9–4:30, Sundays and holidays 1–5. Closed Thanksgiving, Christmas, and New Year's.
ADMISSION: $1.50 adults, $1 senior citizens, $.75 ages 6–16, free under 6 with a parent. Some buildings in the rear (see below) are free during the summer.
EDUCATIONAL PROGRAMS: Grades K–12 use the museum as a living classroom. Themes include privateering, Hawthorne, the witch trials, and family life.

Visitors of all ages from all over the world enjoy the old dolls and dollhouses, toys, early costumes and uniforms, portraits, furniture, silver, and pottery. You're allowed to use the heavy rubber mallet (one time only) to strike the tall bell, which was cast at the Paul Revere Company.

In the rear gardens are the **Doll House,** probably the original seventeenth-century Salem Quaker meetinghouse, and since 1947 the home of a unique collection of dolls, doll furniture, and toys; the 12-foot-by-14-foot **Lye-Tapley Shoe Shop,** which represents the shoe industry during its handcraft period, from 1750 to 1850; and the **Lucius Beebe Summer House,** recently restored and moved from its lakeside location in Wakefield. Also behind the museum is the **John Ward House,** one of the institute's six historic houses (see box). It's a small seventeenth-century house with old parlor, kitchen, apothecary shop, and "cent shop" (nothing for sale) — ideal for a family visit. The house is open June through October 15, Tuesday through Saturday from 10 to 5, Sundays from 1 to 4:30.

The Essex Institute maintains six **historic houses,** dating from the seventeenth to the nineteenth century. Volunteer guides, schooled in the period of "their home," give a very informative tour that's geared to your interests. Admission to each house is $1 for adults, $.75 for senior citizens, $.50 for ages 6 to 16, and free under 6. Combination tickets are available. Each house has its own hours. Call 508–744–3390 for a current schedule.

A 10-minute drive from Salem Center

Pioneer Village Clifton Avenue
OPEN: June–Labor Day, 9:30–6:30 daily; Labor Day–mid-October, 10–5 daily.
AVERAGE STAY: 30 minutes.
ADMISSION: $1.50 adults, $.50 ages 5–11, free under 5.

As you walk past the reproduction thatched-roof houses, bark-covered wigwams, dugouts, pillory and stocks, and brick kiln and bellows in the blacksmith shop, you can almost feel the Salem of 1630. The printed signs are helpful, but young children may get impatient while you're reading.

Sandwich and the Canal Area

FOR A TASTE OF THE CAPE IN A DAY

LOCATION: 65 miles south of Boston.

DIRECTIONS: I-93 south to Route 3 south, to the canal. Cross the Sagamore Bridge and take Route 6A east.

RESTAURANTS: Simple Fare on Route 6A is just that — simple and reasonable. Sandy's on Route 6A, next to the motor lodge (also on Route 28 at the Bourne Bridge approach on the mainland), is known for its fried clams. Children's plates and take-out too. There's usually a line, but it moves quickly. Townspeople like to take out fried seafood from Captain Scott's on Tupper Road next to the Sandwich boat basin, and eat by the canal right around the corner. Horizons at Town Neck Beach serves sandwiches in a new building overlooking all of Cape Cod Bay, from Plymouth to Provincetown.

Sandwich, settled in 1637, is the oldest town on Cape Cod. Along Route 6A are several interesting stops. See the troughs filled with all-different-size fish at the **state fish hatchery.** No charge. . . . Near the cranberry bogs there's **Green Briar Nature Center and Jam Kitchen,** open June to mid-December. In the 1903 kitchen, stoves are lined up two by two, and fruits are being cooked by the sun in the greenhouses. . . . **Titcomb's Bookshop** is good for browsing among books, magazines, and old maps. . . . The **Wing Fort House** (1641) on Spring Hill Road (opposite Quaker Meetinghouse Road) was recently restored. Its two floors are furnished with Wing family antiques from different periods of its three-hundred-year history. Open weekdays from 10 to 4. Admission is $.75 for adults, $.25 under 12.

The **Cape Cod Canal** area spans a 4-mile stretch between the Sagamore and Bourne bridges. For a close look, take Route 6 at the Sagamore Bridge and stop at the herring run (page 280). Or use the level service roads (no cars allowed) that run on each side of the canal for walking, cycling, pushing a stroller, picnicking, and watching passing freighters and tankers. Crossing one of the bridges is an experience in itself — more frightening to many adults than to children.

June through August, the U.S. Army Corps of Engineers runs free day and evening **walks and campfires** for families. For a schedule of programs, call 508–759–5991. Come with sturdy shoes and insect repellent.

Summer parking in the center of Sandwich is difficult. Find one place and choose from several attractions.

- **Sandwich Glass Museum:** Lovely shapes and colors, and rare pieces handsomely displayed in well-lit cases and windows. The beautiful collections are arranged in sequence of production, from 1825 to 1888. A scaled diorama of the Boston and Sandwich Glass Works depicts the stages of glassmaking. Not a child's paradise. Open daily, 9:30 to 4:30, April through October. Plan to stay about 45 minutes. Admission is $1.50 for adults, $.25 for children under 12.
- **Underground spring:** Next to Town Hall. It's been flowing for hundreds of years. Bring a jug and fill up. It's delicious and free.
- **Dexter's Grist Mill:** Open daily mid-June to late September, Monday through Saturday 10 to 4:45, Sundays from 1. It's only a 5-minute visit to see the old machinery (modern gears) in full operation, grinding corn. Admission is $.75 for adults, $.50 for children.
- **The Thornton W. Burgess Museum:** At 4 Water Street, on Shawme Lake, a picture-book setting with swans and aggressive ducks that like to be fed. Inside the restored 1756 home children can listen to taped Burgess stories, and look at his original manuscripts and Harrison Cady's original illustrations. Free admission. Open April until late December, Monday through Saturday 10 to 4, Sundays from 1. Call 508–888–3083 for information.
- **Hoxie House:** A restored saltbox, said to be the oldest (1637) on Cape Cod. Most visitors spend no more than 15 minutes looking at utensils by the fireplace, an early convertible bed, the Indian board lock, and the place where children slept. Open daily mid-June to late September, Monday through Saturday 10 to 5, Sundays from 1. Admission is $.50 for adults, $.35 for children.
- **Yesterday's Museum:** Two floors filled with hundreds of beautifully costumed dolls in labeled glass cases, furnished Nuremberg kitchens, tiny shops, and miniature rooms. (That's a lot of looking! Plan to stay at least an hour.) Open daily May through October, Monday through Saturday 10 to 5, Sundays 1 to 5. Admission is $2 for adults, $1.50 for senior citizens, $1 under 16; $5 maximum for families.

A mile down Pine Street from the glass museum

Heritage Plantation Pine and Grove streets

PHONE: 508–888–3300.
OPEN: May–mid-October, 10–5 daily.
ADMISSION: $4 adults, $1.50 ages 6–11, free under 6.
PICNICKING: In the pine grove. No fires allowed.

PROGRAMMING: Cultural events throughout the summer, and an extensive educational outreach program.

Allow a couple of hours to ride the open-air shuttle or walk through the meticulously maintained 76 acres of views, running space, and rhododendrons (from three continents), azaleas, and laurels. This is an indoor-outdoor museum with several air-conditioned buildings. The Round Barn houses an antique car collection in mint condition. Other beautifully displayed collections include Currier and Ives lithographs, early American tools, carved birds, and antique firearms. The miller grinds corn and explains the workings of the windmill all season long. A highlight for children: a ride (one each) on the restored carousel in its glass-walled rotunda.

A special train ride

Cape Cod & Hyannis Railroad Box 57, Hyannis 02601
PHONE: 508–771–1145.
ROUND-TRIP FARE: $5 adults, $3 under 13.

The train runs between Sandwich and Hyannis (corner of Main and Center). The conductor calls, "All aboard," the whistle toots, and you're off for an hour's ride (each way) along cranberry bogs, salt marshes, and the dunes at Sandy Neck.

For the "real" Cape, **walk a boardwalk** across marsh and creek to beach and dunes. It's a special place that some natives call Plank Walk Beach. To get here from Route 6A heading toward Barnstable, turn left on Tupper Road, left on Town Neck Road to the end, then right on Freeman Avenue. Out of season, nonresidents can park in the town beach lot.

A highlight

Pairpoint Glass Works 851 Sandwich Road, Sagamore
PHONE: 508–888–2344.
DIRECTIONS: Under the Sagamore Bridge, on the Cape side of the canal.
OPEN: Weekdays 10–4:30.
ADMISSION: Free.

Stand on the balcony overlooking the blowing room, and watch skilled craftsmen as they put a rod into the furnace, gather molten glass, and then shape it into a vase, bowl, candlestick, or paperweight. Whether it's the formation of a handle, spout, or foot, the reheating of molten glass for more shaping, or the removal of the finished work, this is an art that fascinates all ages.

Wayside Inn Area

A SMALL OPEN AREA,
A MIXTURE OF HISTORY,
ARCHITECTURE, AND
RECREATION

LOCATION: Sudbury, 20 miles west of Boston.

DIRECTIONS: Follow Route 20 west, and you're there. Or take the Mass. Pike to Route 128 (I-95) north, to exit 49 (Route 20 west), for 11 miles.

Even if the **Gristmill,** on Boston Post Road (Route 20) just beyond the Wayside Inn, is closed, you'll have lots of company in the grass and fields during the first-sign-of-spring weekend or in the fall. The miller (508–443–6451) is on duty April to November, from 8:30 to noon and 1 to 5; grinding hours vary. The 5-minute explanation of the eighteenth-century reproduction mill, complete with huge water wheel and millstones, is free (but donations are accepted). In late spring, beside the path that leads from the mill along Hop Brook, there's often snow in the woods.

On the other side of the road are several buildings built or restored by the Ford Foundation. The **Martha-Mary Chapel,** open by appointment, was built from timber felled on the hill in the hurricane of 1928. The **Red Schoolhouse,** attended by Mary and her little lamb, was built in Sterling, Massachusetts, in 1798, and was in actual use until 1952. It's usually open from noon to 5 during the summer.

If you're in the area at dusk, you may see the oil lamps being lit outside the **Wayside Inn** (508–443–8846). The country's oldest operating inn, having known time and fire, is part original (1686) and part restored. It's open year-round except Christmas. Dinner guests are welcome to look through, but after 6 the light isn't good. Guided tours by appointment only.

A 5-minute drive west brings you to the **Country Store** in Marlborough at the Sudbury line. This complex, open seven days a week, has been very popular since the store, originally built in 1799 in Sudbury Center, was moved and restored by Ford in 1930. The parking area has lots of ice cream lickers, but not too much atmosphere. Inside, the aroma of fresh baking greets visitors, who find interesting old and new items in chock-full displays. And the candy shop has a wide selection of what used to be penny candy.

Organizations

Detours Page 122.

Special for teenagers.

Let's Take the Babies Cambridge YMCA, Youth Program Office, 820 Massachusetts Avenue, Cambridge 02139

PHONE: 876–3860.

A model program designed for support and for travel, an opportunity to see the worlds of Boston with infants and toddlers

(3 months to 3 years). Sessions include information (nutrition, child rearing, travel, and safety) and trips.

Mystic Valley Railway Society Box 32, Mattapan 02126
PHONE: 361-4445.

The thrust of this organization is to teach people about the field of transportation through trips. All fifteen annual day trips, and the longer trips (as far as the West Coast), are open to nonmembers. The average number of riders per trip is 50. Children are usually in the minority, and get plenty of attention.

Several other organizations have day trips open to individuals and families:

- **American Youth Hostels** (page 220)
- **Appalachian Mountain Club** (page 251)
- **Sierra Club** (page 201)

Opportunities vary, but usually include some active participation: hiking, cycling, climbing, touring, or cross-country skiing.

Historic Sites

In Boston

THE FREEDOM TRAIL

Several historic sites in Boston that are not part of designated trails are in the Back Bay (page 125) and Beacon Hill (page 128).

INFORMATION: The National Park Service has visitors' centers at 15 State Street (page 97) and the Charlestown Navy Yard (page 105).

PARKING: The best place is in Charlestown at the navy yard, where there's free space and a good information center. Elsewhere, particularly in downtown Boston, parking demands time, luck, and often the expense of a garage. The best bet: the Boston Common Underground Garage (page 10) and its shuttle bus.

Ⓣ: Most downtown sites are within short walking distance of one another, and near a Ⓣ stop. The Charlestown sites, also close to one another, are harder to get to by Ⓣ.

HOURS: Most are open daily during the summer, but hours vary. During the winter it's a good idea to call ahead to see whether a particular site is open.

AVERAGE STAY: 10–15 minutes at most sites.

ADMISSION: Most sites are free. The Old South Meeting House, the Old State House, and the Paul Revere House charge a minimal fee. There's also a charge for the museum and the multimedia show at the navy yard.

FREE GUIDED WALKS: 1–1½ hours, all outside. History from the time of the Revolution through 1812. Offered four times daily in summer, weekends in spring and fall. Reservations (suggested) at the visitors' center, 15 State Street. For a schedule call 242-5642. The navy yard tours (page 97) are free too.

"The Freedom Trail wasn't so great because of all the walking, but the places we went to were interesting. . . . It was a kind of hike. . . . I would like a dirt path."

— BOY SCOUTS

Freedom Trail sites are neither numbered nor sequential, so the trail can be picked up at any point. . . . It's possible to go in and out of the buildings and completely cover the trail in one exhausting day. But the city invites diversion, and it's okay to take detours! . . . Determined tourists find the most direct route for a complete tour begins at the State House or the Charlestown Navy Yard. Most visitors (with or without children) choose the navy yard, the sure way to see the USS *Constitution*. . . . Those with limited energy — or young children — may find the North End most fascinating.

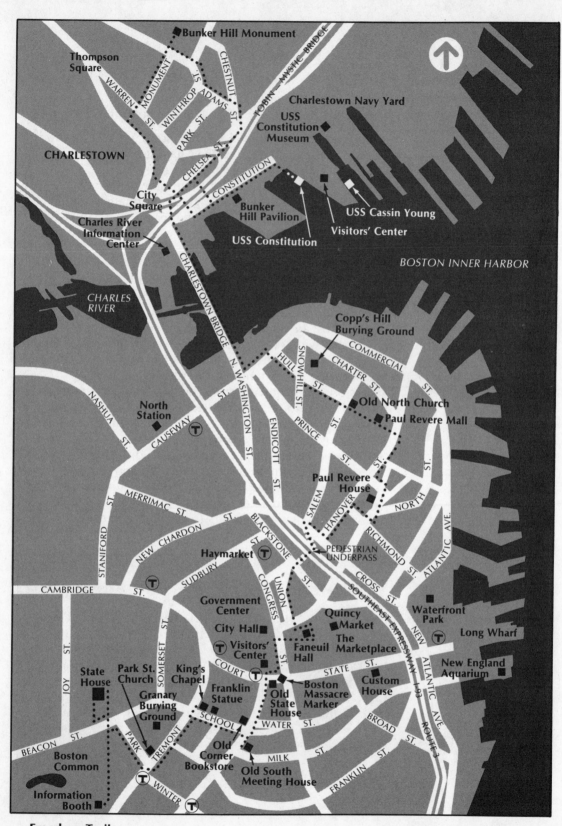

Bunker Hill Monument

Thompson
Square

CHARLESTOWN

Charlestown Navy Yard

USS
Constitution
Museum

WARREN ST.

MONUMENT

ST. ADAMS ST.

WINTHROP

PARK ST.

CHESTNUT ST.

TOBIN — MYSTIC BRIDGE

CHELSEA ST.

City
Square

CONSTITUTION

Charles River
Information
Center

Bunker
Hill Pavilion

USS Cassin Young

Visitors' Center

USS Constitution

BOSTON INNER HARBOR

CHARLESTOWN BRIDGE

CHARLES
RIVER

Copp's Hill
Burying Ground

COMMERCIAL

CHARTER ST.

HULL ST.

SNOWHILL ST.

Old North Church

Paul Revere Mall

N. WASHINGTON ST.

ST.

NASHUA ST.

North
Station

CAUSEWAY

ENDICOTT ST.

PRINCE ST.

ST.

ST.

NORTH ST.

ATLANTIC AVE.

Paul Revere
House

MERRIMAC ST.

STANIFORD ST.

NEW CHARDON ST.

SUDBURY ST.

BLACKSTONE ST.

SALEM ST.

HANOVER ST.

RICHMOND ST.

PEDESTRIAN
UNDERPASS

Haymarket

CAMBRIDGE ST.

CONGRESS ST.

UNION ST.

CROSS ST.

SOUTHEAST EXPRESSWAY — I-93

NEW ATLANTIC AVE.

Waterfront
Park

Government
Center

Quincy
Market

Long Wharf

City Hall

Visitors'
Center

Faneuil
Hall

The
Marketplace

SOMERSET ST.

JOY ST.

State
House

Park St.
Church

King's
Chapel

COURT ST.

STATE ST.

Custom
House

New England
Aquarium

Granary
Burying
Ground

Franklin
Statue

Old
State
House

Boston
Massacre
Marker

BROAD ST.

ROUTE 3

SCHOOL ST.

WATER ST.

BEACON ST.

TREMONT ST.

PARK ST.

Boston
Common

Old
Corner
Bookstore

MILK ST.

FRANKLIN ST.

Old South
Meeting House

Information
Booth

WINTER ST.

Freedom Trail

The trail covers a 3-mile stretch — sixteen historic sites — in downtown Boston and Charlestown. Tourists, with eyes on maps and feet on red-brick or painted sidewalk lines, sometimes miss the basement book shop, the blend of rooflines, the ghosts of painted signs on old buildings, and the posts with original street names — like Crooked Lane and Shrimpton's Lane — above today's street signs.

The trail combines the resources of federal, state, city, and private organizations.

In the city, the recommended first stop

Boston National Historical Park Visitor Center 15 State Street
PHONE: 223-0058.
DIRECTIONS: Across from the Old State House, 1 block from Faneuil Hall (away from the waterfront).
Ⓣ: State on the Orange or Blue Line.
OPEN: Year-round, 9-5 daily except Thanksgiving, Christmas, and New Year's.
EDUCATIONAL PROGRAMS: Always something — special tours, orientation and follow-up, games, activities, or print materials. Current programming is for Grades 4 to 8.

Helpful staff, free maps and plenty of printed information (some in French, Spanish, Italian, German, and Japanese), and welcome rest rooms. Check downstairs (in person only) for brochures on other sites in New England and on national parks all over the country. From here decide whether you'll go south (not through any neighborhood really) to the State House (and maybe on to the swan boats) or north by the Marketplace, through the North End, and on to the navy yard.

On historic Beacon Hill

State House Beacon Street at Park
PHONE: 727-3676, 727-2816 (Archives Museum).
Ⓣ: Park Street; then walk 1 block up Park Street.
OPEN: Weekdays, except legal holidays, 9-5.
AVERAGE STAY: Depending on interests, this could be a major stop — 1½ to 2 hours.
ADMISSION: Free.
TOURS: Free guided tours (¾ to 1 hour) are available year-round, weekdays (except holidays) from 10 to 4. Groups should make advance arrangements; individuals are welcome to join a group. The information desk in Doric Hall has the day's schedule (and printed information for self-guided tours). Also available are tours in Spanish, French, German, and Italian. For appointments and information, call 727-3676 or write to the State House, Room 272A, Boston 02133.
OPEN SESSIONS: Meetings of the legislature and committee hearings are open to the public. Call 727-2860 for a schedule.
MOCK SESSIONS: By arrangement (with the help of a legislator), groups can conduct their own sessions.

HANDICAPPED: Many stairs, but arrangements can be made with advance notice.

What was once John Hancock's pasture is now the site of a gold-domed building with impressive marble staircases and Bulfinch architectural details everywhere. The *Sacred Cod* still hangs in the senate chamber, a reminder of one of the first major industries in the state. The Hall of Flags displays battle flags from Civil and Spanish-American wars, from World Wars I and II, and from the Vietnam conflict. Look up to see a stained-glass skylight with the state seal.

You could spend some time in the house and senate; even when they're not in session, you can look at the roll board and think about procedures. In the Legislative Document Room, Room 428, are copies of all of the bills under consideration. In the library, Room 442, are microfilms of newspapers dating back to the 1800s. It's $.25 for a single-page copy.

The **Archives Museum** has its own entrance from outside — just to the left of the main stairway — or can be reached from inside the State House. This is an exciting place for people who enjoy original documents. (For some that excitement is diminished when the visit comes at the end of the State House tour.) You might help children read from Governor Bradford's diary, a Revolutionary War muster roll, or the Charter of the Massachusetts Bay Colony. Exhibits do change, but usually include maps, photographs, and the copperplates for Paul Revere's famous engravings of the Boston Massacre and Boston Harbor.

NEARBY: The restored Robert Gould Shaw and 54th Regiment Memorial (page 108) is right across Beacon Street.

Across from Boston Common

Park Street Church Tremont and Park streets

PHONE: 523-3383.

Ⓣ: Park Street.

OPEN: Mid-June–August, Tuesday–Saturday 9:30–noon and 12:30–4. Closed July 4. Young people with parents or group leaders are welcome.

AVERAGE STAY: 10–15 minutes.

ADMISSION: Free.

It's a two-flight climb to the sanctuary, whose spire and clock have been landmarks since 1810. When the town granary occupied the site, the sails for the USS *Constitution* were made here. Parishioners of 1829 heard William Lloyd Garrison give his first antislavery address. And two years later they heard the first public performance of "America."

When the church bells announce noon, there's a villagelike feeling in the area.

Right next to the church

Granary Burying Ground Tremont Street

Ⓣ: Park Street.

OPEN: 8–5 daily.

Originally the site of the town granary. Here are the graves of John Hancock, Robert Treat Paine, Samuel Adams, "Mother Goose," and the victims of the Boston Massacre. Finding specific gravestones is a treasure hunt; there are no maps anywhere. Sorry, no gravestone rubbing allowed.

Across from the Parker House

King's Chapel 58 Tremont Street (corner of School)

PHONE: 523-1749.

Ⓣ: Park Street.

OPEN: Year-round, Tuesday–Friday 10–4. Sunday services at 11.

ADMISSION: Free.

HANDICAPPED: Accessible; the threshold is low.

As you walk up the central aisle, there's a feeling of beauty and history in this living church. You're in a place with a history of "firsts" — the first church of England in the Massachusetts Bay Colony, the first Unitarian church in America, the first church to use organ music. Its bell was made by Paul Revere; the governor's pew was used by George Washington. It is the oldest stone (Quincy granite) church in Boston. The 4-foot-thick walls were built in the 1750s around the original wooden structure, while the church was still in use. The steeple isn't pointed because the congregation ran out of money.

In the **Burying Ground,** the first cemetery in town, are the graves of Governor Winthrop and Reverend John Cotten. Many of the markers aren't legible today. Sorry, no rubbing allowed here.

In back of King's Chapel, on the Old City Hall grounds

Benjamin Franklin Statue School Street

The statue dates back to 1856. The four bronze panels at its base show Franklin in several of his many areas of involvement — as a Founding Father, signing the Declaration of Independence; as a diplomat, signing a treaty with France; as a printer; and as an inventor, experimenting with lightning and electricity.

The original site of Boston Public Latin School, the first public school in the country, was on this block.

Old Corner Bookstore Washington (formerly Cornhill) and School streets

PHONE: 929-2602.

OPEN: Monday–Thursday 9–4:45, Fridays 9–3.

AVERAGE STAY: 10 minutes.

ADMISSION: Free.

The building has a varied history. It was a private home, an apothecary shop and home, and a printing shop before it became a book shop and gathering place of literary figures like

Holmes, Longfellow, Lowell, Whittier, and Hawthorne. And changes continued. Before it was restored, it was a pizza parlor. On the ground floor, now the *Boston Globe's* in-town office, are first editions behind glass, a Franklin stove, and period furniture, including Oliver Wendell Holmes's desk. The newest addition is the Globe Corner Bookstore with thousands of New England titles for sale.

Across Washington Street is **Spring Lane,** site of the spring that attracted John Winthrop's colony from Charlestown to Boston. It gave water to the people of Boston for over two centuries. Slagle's Restaurant at Number 9 is a simple place with a strong soup following.

Old South Meeting House   310 Washington Street

PHONE: 482–6439.

DIRECTIONS: 2 blocks north (toward Government Center) of Filene's and its famous basement, on the corner of Milk.

Ⓣ: State on the Orange or Blue Line.

OPEN: Year-round, daily except Thanksgiving, December 24 and 25, and New Year's. Spring and fall, 10–5; summer, 10–6; winter, 10–4.

AVERAGE STAY: 30 minutes.

ADMISSION: $.50 adults, $.25 ages 6–16, free under 6. Fees for school groups (reservations preferred) depend on programs (may be combined with the Tea Party ship or Faneuil Hall).

SPECIAL PROGRAMMING: In summer, an old-fashioned town meeting in the park across the street on Saturdays at 2. It's free, and everyone's invited to take part.

Sit in the pews at this historic site, now filled with prints, documents, and artifacts that explain the building's 250-year history. Many important town meetings were held here, including the one that fathered the Boston Tea Party. During the siege of Boston its pews were used for firewood; the building, as a riding academy for British soldiers. The "new" Old South Church was built in Copley Square in 1872. During busy times — and by request — talks are given by knowledgeable guides.

Across from the National Park Service visitors' center

Old State House   206 Washington Street (actually in the middle of State Street)

PHONE: 242–5655.

Ⓣ: State on the Orange or Blue Line; and you're right underneath the building.

OPEN: Year-round, daily, except Thanksgiving, Christmas, and New Year's. April–October, 9:30–5; November–March, weekdays 10–4, Saturdays 9:30–5, Sundays 11–5.

ADMISSION: $.75 adults, $.50 senior citizens, $.25 ages 6 up, free under 6.

GROUPS: No charge for Massachusetts school groups; $.10 (if

teacher collects) for out-of-state school groups. All groups should make advance arrangements for guides.

HANDICAPPED: Steps make it difficult.

After climbing the circular staircase to the second floor, visitors can stand near the balcony where laws were proclaimed. It's a good vantage point for the site of the Boston Massacre. Built in 1713, the building, once the seat of colonial government, is now a museum. There are shop signs, a doctor's kit, pictures of early Boston, and revolutionary relics. John Hancock's embroidered velvet waistcoat, in the room next to the one where he was inaugurated the first governor of the commonwealth, shows the difference in height between early settlers and twentieth-century Americans. Outside are the gables, among the most photographed architectural details in Boston, that still bear the lion and unicorn emblems of England.

A detour: Browse through **Goodspeed's Basement Store** at 2 Milk Street, a side entrance to the Old South Meeting House. The used books at this very organized shop start at $.25 (Few books for children, though.) Open weekdays 9 to 5 and Saturdays, fall through spring, 10 to 1:30. (Closed Saturdays during the summer.) Goodspeed's rare books, autographs, and old prints are at the 7 Beacon Street store.

Several of Boston's used-book shops have a long history. The oldest antiquarian bookstore in America is the **Brattle Book Shop** at 25 West Street, on the block that runs from the Boston Common Information Booth to new Lafayette Place on Washington Street. (It's 4 short blocks from the Old State House.) In addition to books you'll find pamphlets, newspapers, magazines, and a children's section for fun browsing. Introduce yourself to proprietor George Gloss. He'll give you the royal treatment, which includes an introduction to his son and partner, Kenneth. They can lead you to almost anything in the accumulation that's regrown quickly since a fire destroyed the five-floor site a few doors down the street.

With grasshopper weathervane

Faneuil Hall Dock Square

PHONE: 223-6098.

Ⓣ: State on the Orange or Blue Line; Government Center on the Green or Blue Line.

OPEN: Year-round, 9–5 daily except Thanksgiving, Christmas, and New Year's.

ADMISSION: Free.

ARMORY: On the third floor (a good climb). Open weekdays 10 to 4. Call 227-1638 for information.

This is the real Faneuil Hall, the "Cradle of Liberty" that lends its name to the entire Marketplace. It was built in 1742, burned in 1763, and enlarged in 1806. Atop it sits the grasshopper, forged in 1742 by Shem Drowne, maker of colonial weathervanes. To comply with the wishes of donor Peter Faneuil, the ground floor still has markets. But if you climb the steep steps to the second floor, you'll see the hall where eighteenth-century town meetings were held, and where open meetings still take place today. A National Park Service interpreter gives talks on request.

"Did they make it bigger for all the tourists?"

— LARRY, AGE 8

If you climb to the third floor, you'll find the place where the Ancient and Honorable Artillery Company, chartered "as a nursery for soldiers and a school for officers" in 1638, has had its home for over two hundred years. The armory's displays of colonial uniforms, arms, and artifacts are fairly child-proof. Count the stripes on the early flags. Some have fifteen narrow stripes. After Vermont and Kentucky were admitted to the Union, the design was changed, and then changed back again to the original thirteen "broad stripes."

Facing Faneuil Hall

Quincy Market Dock Square

Ⓣ: State on the Orange or Blue Line; Government Center on the Green or Blue Line.

OPEN: Year-round, daily.

This long low granite building and the neighboring north and south markets were completed on filled-in land in 1826. America's first real estate development of its kind has updated stalls that still sell produce, cheese, poultry, and meat, and much more (see page 131).

In the North End

Paul Revere House 19 North Square (between Richmond and Prince)

PHONE: 523-1676.

Ⓣ: Haymarket on the Orange or Green Line; then a 10-minute walk.

OPEN: Year-round, daily except Thanksgiving, Christmas, and New Year's. April 15–October 9:30–5:30; November–April 15, 10–4. Summer afternoons are usually very busy.

AVERAGE STAY: 15–30 minutes. Manageable for children.

ADMISSION: $1.50 adults, $.75 senior citizens and students, $.25 ages 6–17, free under 6. Group rates ($.75 adults, $.50 senior citizens and students, $.10 children) available by reservation only.

EDUCATIONAL PROGRAMS: From November 1 to April 15, there are games, activities, role playing, and debates in the tour and programs for Grades 1 through 12. Reservations required. Borrowing materials include a videotape about Revere's life in a growing Boston.

FOREIGN LANGUAGE BROCHURES: Available in Japanese, French, Spanish, Italian, and German.

HANDICAPPED: The first floor is accessible by wheelchair; alternative interpretations of inaccessible areas are available. Tactile tours for the blind; large-print brochures for the sight impaired. Print materials for the hearing impaired.

It was from here that Paul Revere rode to Lexington in April 1775. Built around 1680, it is the oldest building in Boston, and was already ninety years old when Revere bought it. Most of his sixteen children (with two different wives) lived here. It's the only place in Boston that gives a sense of seventeenth- and eighteenth-century home life. As you walk through — reading a time-line, a detailed chronology of Revere's productive eighty-three years — you'll see cooking implements, cradles, a child's armchair, Revere's silver-working tools, and some of the things he made (a small cannon, copper spikes, a bell).

Next door, at 29 North Square, is the **Moses Pierce–Nathaniel Hichborn House** (1711). Tours (daily June through August at 11 and 3) are geared to adults and teenagers interested in the architecture and social history of the eighteenth century. The house is open at other times by arrangement. Call the Paul Revere House for information.

Following the trail from here to the Old North Church, you come to **Paul Revere Mall** on Hanover Street. It's a few steps down to the small park, where thirteen bronze tablets set in the walls tell the part played by the people of the North End in Boston's history from 1630 to 1918. Visiting children — and everyone carrying a camera — usually focus on Cyrus Dallin's equestrian Paul Revere.

Steps at the far end of the mall lead to

Old North Church 193 Salem Street

PHONE: 523–6676.

DIRECTIONS: Parking is difficult. But if you're driving, take Causeway Street to Hull Street; go up over the hill and down to the church.

Walking from Hanover Street, find St. Stephen's Church (look for its white spire), cross the street, and walk through the mall to Old North.

Ⓣ: Haymarket on the Orange or Green Line; then a 10-minute walk.

OPEN: Year-round, 9–4:40 daily. Sunday services at 9:30 (½ hour), 11 (1 hour), and 4 (½ hour).

ADMISSION: Free.

TOURS: 10–20 minutes for groups, by reservation.

HANDICAPPED: Accessible through the main entrance.

Individual guides may point out the 1724 brass chandelier or the 1726 clock (the oldest working one in a public building in the country), or on rare occasions play the 1759 Johnston organ; but all talk about the role of the church in the Revolution — familiar details and new ones.

This gracious, well-maintained structure, Boston's oldest church, was built in 1723. Visitors can sit in the box pews marked with names of revolutionary parishioners, but the path to the narrow steeple isn't open to the public. The old bells, still rung every Sunday at 10:45, were rung by Paul Revere when he was a fifteen-year-old member of the Bell Ringers' Guild, and later they signaled Cornwallis's surrender at Yorktown.

Replicas of the two lanterns that hung in the steeple to signal the redcoats' leaving for Lexington and Concord are in the small museum next to the church.

"Lots of tourists stop along the bridge to watch the water activity. Sometimes jellyfish are the big attraction."
— BOSTON POLICEMAN

Walking the Freedom Trail across Charlestown Bridge? The **Charles River Information Center** is on the way. Near the Charlestown end of the bridge go through the gate on your left, down the stairs to the park, and into the building with two flags. The center is the place for learning about the river and watching the activity on it. Push a button and activate a 12-minute audiovisual show that dramatically explains flood control and the water level in the Charles River Basin. The observation window overlooks three locks: two for pleasure boats and one for oil barges and other commercial vessels. The center is open year-round, weekdays from 10 to 4 and some weekends, but call 727-0488 for the current schedule. Reservations (recommended) may be necessary. Admission is free.

You can get here by car too. The center is on the river about 10 minutes from the navy yard, between North Station and the Charlestown YMCA. Coming from City Square, park in the small lot after the YMCA; then follow the signs to the new Charles River Dam.

A block away

Copp's Hill Burying Ground Snowhill and Charter streets

DIRECTIONS: From the front door of the Old North Church it's a 3-minute walk up Hull Street. (Directly across from the Hull Street gate is the narrowest house in Boston — only 9 feet 6 inches wide.)

OPEN: July–August, 8–4 daily; September–June, weekdays 8–4.

Thousands of early Bostonians are buried here. Some gravestones show bullet marks from the muskets of the British, who used them as practice targets during the siege of Boston; and weather and time have worn away many of the names. Efforts are under way to improve maintenance at the site, which offers a good view of the harbor and "Old Ironsides." Sorry, no gravestone rubbing allowed.

The **Charlestown Navy Yard** (formerly the Boston Naval Shipyard too) is a complex with many attractions.

ADDRESS: Constitution Road, Charlestown 02129.

PHONE: 242–5601.

DIRECTIONS: From I-93 follow the signs to City Square and Constitution Road in Charlestown. By foot, it's about a half-hour from the waterfront. In summer, Bay State operates the Constitution Cruise (page 226) from Long Wharf, near the Aquarium.

PARKING: Free.

Ⓣ: From Haymarket (on the Orange or Green Line) take Bus 92, 93, or 111 (infrequent runs on weekends), and ask for the stop nearest the yard. Or, even easier, take the Orange or Green Line to North Station, then walk about 20 minutes along the trail, across Charlestown Bridge. Or in summer and early fall, use the Shuttle (page 120).

HOURS: Year-round, 9–sunset daily (until exhibits close in winter).

VISITORS' CENTER: Open year-round, 9 to 5 daily except Thanksgiving, Christmas, and New Year's. Plenty of information about this and other Freedom Trail sites, and a good model ship exhibit showing boat building from the time it began in Massachusetts. The building is accessible to the handicapped.

TOURS: Emphasize the role of the worker in the yard. See the dry dock and floating dock, and shops that made and repaired essentials for shipbuilding. All outside, daily June through Labor Day. Check the schedule at the visitors' center.

EDUCATIONAL PROGRAMS: Many. For current arrangements call 242–5697.

ORAL HISTORY: Write the yard superintendent for access to tapes of yard workers.

SHADE: Under the big old trees near the commandant's house.

A great vantage point for the Boston skyline, the new set against the old. It's a big place where warships were built between 1800 and 1974. At its peak, fifty thousand people worked here. Although part of the yard is being recycled into housing, shops, and recreation areas, a full sweep of exhibits makes it a day trip in itself.

USS Constitution Charlestown Navy Yard

PHONE: 242–5670.
DIRECTIONS, PARKING, AND (T): Page 105.
OPEN: Year-round, 9:30–3:45 daily except one day in July (for the turnaround cruise) and during blizzards. There's often a half-hour wait in summer, less than 10 minutes on spring and fall weekends.
AVERAGE STAY: 45 minutes.
ADMISSION: Free.

"Old Ironsides," the 44-gun frigate launched in 1797 and undefeated in twenty-four battles, is still a commissioned ship of the navy. The fifth restoration in 177 years was completed in 1976; little more than a tenth of the original craft remains. The towering masts, cannons, hammock beds, dentist and surgeon chairs, and galley, where soups and stews were cooked for over four hundred men — all give a feeling of navy life in another century. Crew members in 1812 uniforms will help with young children on the steep stairways that connect the three decks.

*For an understanding of
life on board*

USS Constitution Museum Charlestown Navy Yard

PHONE: 426–1812.
DIRECTIONS, PARKING, AND (T): Page 105.
OPEN: Year-round, daily except Thanksgiving, Christmas, and New Year's. Spring and fall, 9–5; summer, 9–6; winter, 10–4. Air-conditioned.
AVERAGE STAY: Almost an hour.
ADMISSION: $2 adults, $1 senior citizens, $.50 ages 6–16, free under 6. Group rates available by arrangement.
HANDICAPPED: Accessible.

Maybe you expect to see the muskets, vintage navy uniforms, navigational equipment, and the tools used to build the USS *Constitution*, but when you "meet" five members of the 1812 crew (all at different levels), you get a strong sense of daily life at sea. Learn what it took to feed 475 men; read their letters home; climb into a sleeping hammock; steer the wheel and hoist the sail on a moving "deck" with sounds of shipboard life around you; or try your hand at tying knots. Other things to see in this marvelous 1832 granite building: an exhibit of the ship's history with a walk-through model of keel and ribbing, and "Honor of War," a continuous audiovisual program that depicts a bloody battle of 1812.

*Check at the visitors'
center for tours*

USS Cassin Young Charlestown Navy Yard

PHONE: 242–5604.
DIRECTIONS, PARKING, AND (T): Page 105.
OPEN: Year-round, 9–4 daily, weather permitting. Closed Thanksgiving, Christmas, and New Year's.

ADMISSION: Free.

The recently restored ship represents the many ships built here during World War II. The 25-minute tour points out the dangers of serving on a destroyer, and takes you below, through narrow passageways, into cramped crews' quarters, the eating area, and the pilot house.

Next to "Old Ironsides," in the Bunker Hill Pavilion at 55 Constitution Road, is the **Whites of Their Eyes** — a bloody, 25-minute multimedia show that re-creates the Battle of Bunker Hill and the events leading up to it. Lighted areas show authentically dressed mannequins; voices tell of their official roles and personal concerns. Sounds come from seven channels, and pictures flash. Open year-round, daily, June through August, 9:30 to 6; September through May, 9:30 to 4. Closed Thanksgiving, Christmas, and New Year's. It's $1.50 for adults, $1 for senior citizens and students with IDs, $.75 for ages 5 to 16, free (and maybe inappropriate) for children under 5. Family rate: $4. Phone: 241-7575.

From the navy yard it's a 10-minute walk to

Bunker Hill Monument and Museum Breed's Hill, Charlestown

PHONE: 242-5641.

DIRECTIONS: Driving, the natural way to approach the monument is by Park, Commons, and Adams streets. More dramatic, and worth going a minute out of your way, is to go around Winthrop Square (past the memorials to Charlestown men who fought at Bunker Hill), down Winthrop Street, right onto Warren Street, and then right onto Monument Avenue, a hill lined with gas lamps and historic brick residences.

PARKING: Allowed on neighboring streets.

Ⓣ: Haymarket on the Orange or Green Line; then bus to Sullivan Square via Bunker Hill.

OPEN: Year-round, 9–5 daily except Thanksgiving, Christmas, and New Year's. (The monument closes at 4:45.)

ADMISSION: Free.

SPECIAL PROGRAMMING: In summer, interpreters in period costumes describe the battle. They take the roles of two eighteenth-century civilians and two soldiers — one American and one British — each with his own version of the day.

The granite for the monument came from Quincy, first by horse-drawn railroad cars from the quarries to the Neponset River, and then by barge to Charlestown, Boston's oldest neighborhood (settled in 1625). The railroad — America's first commercial railway — was built for this contract. Of course the site is more remembered for the command "Don't fire until you see the whites of their eyes." A highlight: the 294-step climb up the inside of the monument for a view of the harbor and city. Younger visitors may appreciate adult accompaniment up the narrow passageway; some older ones will feel that once was fine, thank you. In the museum are a diorama and a continuous 15-minute slide show of the battle.

BLACK HERITAGE TRAIL

INFORMATION: Printed guides are available at the Boston National Historical Park Visitor Center (page 97). An interpretation center will be located (after restoration is complete) at the African Meeting House (below).

TOURS: By appointment through the Museum of Afro American History (page 156), 445–7400.

Plaques tell the stories of fourteen Beacon Hill churches, schools, and homes that belonged, from revolutionary times to the early twentieth century, to the community of free blacks. The trail, a recent addition to the National Park System, is run cooperatively by public and private organizations.

The **African Meeting House** on Smith Court (off Joy Street, just up from Cambridge Street) is the oldest black church in New England. This is where William Lloyd Garrison founded the New England Anti-Slavery Society in 1832 and began the American abolitionist movement. Near the meetinghouse, also on Smith Court, are the **Abiel Smith School,** a landmark in the struggle for quality education for black children, and the **Smith Court Residences,** five houses typical of the homes occupied by black Bostonians throughout the nineteenth century.

There are three sites on Pinckney Street. The **George Middleton House** at Numbers 5 and 7 is one of the oldest wooden structures on Beacon Hill. The **Phillips School** at the corner of Anderson was integrated in 1855. And the **John J. Smith House** at Number 86, near West Cedar Street, was the home of a Massachusetts legislator.

The **Charles Street Meeting House** at Mt. Vernon and Charles streets, now being recycled into a multiuse building, was originally built for a white congregation. Bought by a black congregation after the Civil War, it was the last black institution to leave the hill. The **Lewis Hayden House** at 66 Phillips Street (near Charles Street Circle) was the home of a leader of the abolitionist movement. At the other end of Phillips, toward Government Center, is **Coburn's Gaming House** at Number 2.

On the Common, just across from the State House, is the **Robert Gould Shaw and 54th Regiment Memorial.** The recently restored bas-relief, by Augustus Saint-Gaudens, depicts the first black division from the North in the Civil War. Shaw, the leader, was white.

In Nearby Communities

Very few historic homes report that they have as many visitors "as the original carpet can take." Actually they're trying to achieve a delicate balance between preservation and education. At other than national historic sites, you're likely to be the only ones in attendance.... Guides may change. Much depends on the mesh of personalities, a difficult aspect to guarantee in a book.... There are dozens of historic homes in Greater Boston. Check with town halls or newspapers (page 6). The extent of restoration, furnishings, and research varies according to interest and funding. Many have participatory programs for schoolchildren.... Unless it's a designated children's day, historic houses request (or require) that youngsters come with adults.... A small early house is a good introduction. If children enjoy it, take on an estate.... Parking at all of these sites is available in the neighborhood.... Many more historic sites are listed in Day Trips (pages 51–92).

ARLINGTON

Jason Russell House & Smith Museum 7 Jason Street

PHONE: 648–4300.

DIRECTIONS: 1 block from Pleasant Street along Massachusetts Avenue.

OPEN: April–October, Tuesday–Saturday 2–5.

ADMISSION: $.50 adults, $.10 under 12. The museum is free.

PICNICKING: It's about a mile up Jason Street to Menotomy Rocks Park (page 197).

A 30-minute tour past revolutionary guns, dolls, cradles — and holes made by the British on April 19, 1775.

The Old Schwamb Mill 17 Mill Lane, Arlington Heights

PHONE: 643–0554, 643–0640.

DIRECTIONS: Massachusetts Avenue to Lowell Street. Second right is Mill Lane.

Ⓣ: Harvard on the Red Line; then Arlington Heights bus (77) to Lowell Street.

OPEN: Drop-ins (no charge) are welcome to see, smell, and hear just about any weekday from 9 to 4.

AVERAGE STAY: 30 minutes.

GROUPS: 1¼-hour tours, by appointment. Fee charged.

"It's like going through a time tunnel to go down Mill Lane and into the mill."

Adjust to the abrupt change from Massachusetts Avenue traffic to this charming landmark. In 1650, the site of a gristmill and sawmill; during the Revolution, the site of the Battle of the Foot of the Rocks on Mill Brook. All over the building are messages, and news and weather reports. (The windows were washed on December 31, 1901, the first major snowstorm of the season took place on ... and more.)

The mill now houses twentieth-century craftsmen using nineteenth-century machinery. (It's hard to predict activity —

craftsmen at work or classes in fine arts and crafts — but there's always someone to turn on an elliptical lathe.) This, the only mill in the country still making museum-quality, hand-turned, oval wood frames, is part of a movement to preserve industrial archaeology. Other sites are in Lowell (page 67), Saugus (page 113), Pawtucket (page 168), and Waltham (page 169).

BROOKLINE

Frederick Law Olmsted National Historic Site 99 Warren Street (corner of Dudley)

PHONE: 566-1689.
DIRECTIONS: Route 9 west. Left onto Warren at the reservoir.
Ⓣ: Brookline Hills on the Riverside–Green Line; then a 15-minute walk.
OPEN: Year-round, at least Friday–Sunday noon–4:30. Closed Thanksgiving, Christmas, and New Year's.
AVERAGE STAY: 1½ hours.
ADMISSION: Free.
PROGRAMMING: May change and grow. Currently, sessions in urban park preservation for schoolchildren.

At this new national site, the home of America's first landscape artist while he was designing Boston's park system, visitors see a slide show, lithographs, maps, photographs, a huge collection of plans, windowed office, and grounds. The house and grounds are being restored, so there are plenty of opportunities to watch work in progress.

JFK's birthplace

John Fitzgerald Kennedy National Historic Site 83 Beals Street

PHONE: 566-7937.
PARKING: Municipal lots (the nearest is 3 blocks away on Fuller Street).
Ⓣ: Coolidge Corner on the Cleveland Circle–Green Line; then a 15-minute walk.
OPEN: Year-round, 10:30–4:30 daily except Thanksgiving, Christmas, and New Year's.
ADMISSION: $.50 adults; senior citizens, under 16, and school groups are free.
EDUCATIONAL PROGRAMS: Call to check arrangements.

The thirty-fifth president of the United States lived here from his birth, May 29, 1917, until 1920. The house has been restored to that period with many original furnishings. It's a 20-minute walk through the hall of the house for a look at three rooms on the first floor and four on the second. Printed material directs

A little lost? Check the map on page 2.

you on a 45-minute walk to nearby places that played a part in the president's early days.

CAMBRIDGE

Also see page 135.

Hooper-Lee-Nichols House 150 Brattle Street
PHONE: 547–4252.
OPEN: Mondays and Thursdays 3–5.
ADMISSION: $.50 adults, $.25 under 12.

Recently restored. It's a 1-hour tour through this 1685 saltbox farmhouse, which was converted in 1760 to a gracious Georgian mansion. You'll also see old decor and construction exposed in an early restoration.

Longfellow National Historic Site (1750) 105 Brattle Street
PHONE: 876–4491.
DIRECTIONS: .6 mile from Harvard Square.
OPEN: Year-round, 10–4:30 daily except Thanksgiving, Christmas, and New Year's.
ADMISSION: $.50 adults; senior citizens and children under 16 are free.
GARDEN CONCERTS: Free. Held every other Sunday afternoon throughout the summer.

"Even Melinda and Mort were interested — and they're both five."
— ANDREW, AGE 10

Longfellow lived and wrote here for forty-five years. The half-hour tour appeals to visitors of all ages who are familiar with his writings. There are many reminders of "The Children's Hour" and "The Village Blacksmith." Visitors also learn about the role of the house in early American history. Check for information about the National Historic Park Tory Row walking tours (page 138).

CONCORD

See page 54.

DEDHAM

Fairbanks House (1636) 511 East Street (corner Eastern Avenue)
PHONE: 326–1170.
OPEN: May–October, Tuesday–Sunday 9–5.
ADMISSION: $2 adults, $1 under 12. (Minimum suggested age: 7.)

The 45-minute tour takes visitors through eleven rooms filled with treasures that belonged to eight generations (eighty-four members) of the family that lived here from 1636 to 1903. In the country's oldest frame dwelling, you'll see how each addition was made (with its own stairway to the second floor), the change in ceiling height from one period to another, a three-cornered hearth, the careful penmanship of an eleven-year-old, and a cradle that rocked forty-seven babies.

LEXINGTON

See page 63.

MEDFORD

Royall House 15 George Street (at Main)

PHONE: 396-9032.
OPEN: May–September, 2–5 daily except Mondays and Fridays.
ADMISSION: $1.50 adults, $.50 under 12 (with adult).

Originally a seventeenth-century farmhouse owned by Governor Winthrop, it was rebuilt and enlarged by a wealthy merchant in 1732. Now restored with formal gardens and four furnished rooms on each of the three floors. Guided tours (not really youth oriented) last 30 to 60 minutes.

NEWTON

The Jackson Homestead 527 Washington Street (2 minutes from Newton Corner)

PHONE: 552-7238.
OPEN: Year-round. July–August, Tuesday–Friday 10–4; September–June, weekdays 10–4, Sundays 2–5.
ADMISSION: $1 adults, $.50 senior citizens, $.25 ages 6–17, free under 6.
PROGRAMMING: Lectures from fall through spring; outdoor folk concerts (admission about $1) in summer.

All of the furnished period rooms, with their frequently changed mannequins in authentic nineteenth-century dress, are open. Children can card wool in the spinning-weaving room with its beautiful collection of samplers and quilts; or handle some of the old toys. In a bedroom closet is a collection of children's clothing often used to dress the mannequins. Tours last about a half hour, and take visitors down to the basement, where abolitionist Jacksons once hid fugitive slaves.

NEARBY: Cabot's Ice Cream is a 5-minute walk. Hemlock Gorge–Echo Bridge (page 197) is about 2 miles away.

QUINCY

Adams National Historic Site 135 Adams Street

PHONE: 773-1177.
DIRECTIONS: I-93 south to exit 24 (Furnace Brook Parkway). At the third set of lights, turn right on Adams Street for 1.5 miles.
ⓣ: Quincy Center on the Red Line (air-conditioned); then a 10-minute walk.
OPEN: April 19–November 10, 9–5 daily. Summer and Sundays are busiest. Reservations requested for large groups.

ADMISSION: $.50 adults; senior citizens and under 16 are free.

Built in 1731 and enlarged several times, this was the home from 1787 to 1927 of four generations of the Adams family. The changing style and taste of its occupants is explained during the 45-minute tour, a tour adapted to the level of visitors. In a corner of the lovely nineteenth-century garden is the surprise of the visit — a stone library filled from floor to ceiling, and balcony too, with books.

Colonel Josiah Quincy House (1770) 20 Muirhead Street, Wollaston

PHONE: 471-4508.
OPEN: June 1–October 15, Tuesdays, Thursdays, and weekends noon–5.
ADMISSION: $1.50 adults, $.75 under 12.

The tour is geared to the visitor, who learns about the economic success of the Quincy family — witness Quincy Market and Quincy Co-Operative Bank. There are no ropes across doorways, and children can try on old-fashioned hats.

NEARBY: Wollaston Beach (page 215) is 4 blocks away.

Dorothy Quincy Homestead 1010 Hancock Street

PHONE: 472-5117.
OPEN: April 19–October, Tuesday–Saturday 10–5, Sundays noon–5.
ADMISSION: $1.50 adults, $.50 under 13 ("welcome anytime").

The guided tour of the eighteenth-century mansion-farm-house explains the architecture, decorative arts, furniture making, religion, and customs of the period. In the carriage house is an eighteenth-century carriage once owned by John Hancock, Dorothy Quincy's husband.

SAUGUS

Saugus Ironworks National Historic Site Central Street

PHONE: 233-0050.
DIRECTIONS: Tobin–Mystic Bridge to Route 1 north, to Main Street (Saugus). Left on Central, and follow signs to the site.
OPEN: Year-round, daily. April–October, 9–5 with guided tours every half hour; November–March, 9–4 with less dramatic self-guided arrangements. Suggested for Grades 5 up.
AVERAGE STAY: 1 hour.
ADMISSION: Free.

It's best to visit the museum first for an orientation before seeing the demonstrations at the rolling and slitting mills where the working power waterwheels, the huge wooden gears, and the bellows and giant forge hammer make an impressive sight. Stones from the original structure were used to rebuild the blast furnace, a replica of the three-hundred-year-old forge where cast iron "sow" bars from the furnace were reheated and beaten into usable wrought iron. The original plant, built by John Winthrop in 1646, started America's iron industry, and was in operation on the banks of the Saugus River for twenty years.

WALTHAM

Gore Place 52 Gore Street (Route 20)

PHONE: 894-2798.

OPEN: April 15–November 15, Tuesday–Saturday 10–5, Sundays 2–5. Closed holidays.

ADMISSION: $2 adults, $.50 under 13. (Minimum age: 8.)

All twenty-two rooms of this outstanding house of the federal period are covered during the 1-hour tour. Young people enjoy the flying staircase, which spirals up for three full flights, the delightful nursery, and Governor Gore's shower room. Located on acres of ground with a restored herb garden, apple trees, and a stable.

And not far away

Lyman House Lyman and Beaver streets

PHONE: 893-7232.

OPEN: Year-round, Thursday–Sunday, 10–4.

ADMISSION: $1.50 adults, free under 12.

"The Vale," one of Samuel McIntire's most ambitious houses, has tours for groups of ten or more. In the greenhouses, built in 1800, are grapevines and camellias over a hundred years old, and several examples of early solar heating.

NEARBY: DeVincent's at 378 Beaver Street (894-7342) has wonderful plants — most from its own greenhouses — flowers and vegetables too. (Ever had purple cauliflower?) Open year-round, daily except Tuesdays in winter.

Looking Around

> Look up! Tops of buildings often have original architecture. . . . Play the identification game before or after a trip. From pictures (there are several collections on Boston) see who can identify this doorway or that weathervane.

Viewpoints

IN BOSTON

Charles River Information Center Page 104.

Custom House Observation Tower 1–8 McKinley Square (State Street entrance near India Street, 5 minutes from the Aquarium)

PHONE: 223–2633.

Ⓣ: Aquarium on the Blue Line (those steep, single-width escalators are an adventure in themselves); then a 5-minute walk.

OPEN: Mid-April–October, weekdays 9–noon and 1–3. Closed holidays and in bad weather.

ADMISSION: Free.

GROUPS: Plan to separate, and allow extra time.

Outdoors and free. Bostonians read the tower clock from the Southeast Expressway or Haymarket; but the real treat is from topside down, on the open-air balcony (there's protective caging) that encircles the tower (built in 1915 atop the 1847 building). Take two elevators to see (without telescopes) rooflines, construction, Government Center, the Tobin-Mystic Bridge, excursion boats, freighters, and tugboats, and as far as Blue Hills in clear weather.

The best introduction to Boston

John Hancock Observatory John Hancock Tower, Copley Square (enter across from Trinity Church on St. James Avenue, right next to the Copley Plaza Hotel)

PHONE: 247–1976.

DIRECTIONS: Mass. Pike to exit 22 (Copley Square).

PARKING: Several garages nearby.

Ⓣ: Copley on the Green Line.

OPEN: Year-round, daily except Thanksgiving and Christmas.

Where to from the Observatory or Skywalk?

From the reflecting pool at the **Christian Science Center,** walk through the passageway between the church's Colonnade Building and the church, to the publishing society's bronze doors on Massachusetts Avenue. (Ⓣ: Symphony, Auditorium, or Prudential on the Green Line.) Inside and free is the **Mapparium.**

As you cross the glass bridge through the glass globe (30 feet in diameter), pretend you're at the center of the earth. Notice the time zones, the blue-shaded ocean depths, and the relationships of land and water surfaces. The globe, in 608 individual sections each a quarter inch thick, shows the world's political divisions in 1932. Its brilliant colors are heightened by several hundred electric lights. Speak, and everyone shall hear; the glass doesn't absorb sound. Open year-round, weekdays 8 to 4, Saturdays 9 to 4, and Sundays noon to 4:45. Phone: 262-2300.

What else is here? Tours of the center (page 258), a reading room that offers free copies of the *Christian Science Monitor,* and rest rooms.

Outside again, walk through the archway of the Colonnade Building, past the pool and fountain (beautiful and functional — part of the church's air-conditioning system), to the end of the building that faces the Sheraton-Boston, on Belvidere Street. Here is the **Bible Exhibit** — a history of the Bible compressed into 18 minutes with the visual help of a wall-sized, sculptured-glass map of the Holy Land. A push of a button brings a recorded narration of the journeys of biblical figures. Rare archival Bibles are on display. The triangular theater on the second floor is the setting for a film of the Holy Land and a multiprojector show that uses contemporary pictures — hundreds of Boston scenes — along with Bible verses, music, and narration. Open year-round, Tuesday through Saturday from 10:30 to 5, Fridays until 8, Sundays from noon to 4. Admission is free.

May–October, Monday–Saturday 9 a.m.–11 p.m., Sundays 10 a.m.–11 p.m.; November–April, Monday–Saturday 9 a.m.–11 p.m., Sundays noon–11. Last tickets sold at 10:15 p.m.
AVERAGE STAY: 1 hour.
ADMISSION: $2.25 adults, $1.75 students with IDs, $1.50 senior citizens and ages 5–15, free under 5.
FOREIGN LANGUAGE BROCHURES: In Spanish, French, German, Italian, and Japanese.
HANDICAPPED: Accessible.

Visitors expect a spectacular view from the tallest tower in New England, but the exhibits, each using a different technique, are what give a sense of time and place. The 15-minute light and sound show describes land changes here from the time of the Revolution until the tower was built. That description is heightened when you look at the city from a grandstand seat. A 7-minute film for all ages has you high above today's Boston in a helicopter. And fixed telescopes (no extra charge) bring details of specific landmarks closer.

Next to Hynes Auditorium and the Sheraton-Boston

The Skywalk Prudential Tower

PHONE: 236-3318.
DIRECTIONS: Mass. Pike to exit 22 (Copley Square).
PARKING: Prudential Center Garage (page 10), underground and relatively expensive.
Ⓣ: Copley or Auditorium on the Green Line.
OPEN: Monday–Thursday 9 a.m.–11 p.m., Friday–Saturday 9 a.m.–midnight, Sundays 10 a.m.–11 p.m.
ADMISSION: $2 adults, $1 senior citizens, $.75 ages 5–15, free under 5. Group rates (15 or more) available.
HANDICAPPED: Accessible.

At any hour, the 32-second elevator ride to the fiftieth floor may be the most memorable part of the visit for youngsters. To fully appreciate the panorama at this observation point — and at its Copley Square competitor (above) — try to go when it's clear. Sunsets are particularly beautiful. Adults often have to remind themselves (while reassuring children) that those moving vehicles below are real.

NEARBY: Take the escalators from the Prudential Shopping Plaza to Boylston Street for the Back Bay (page 125).

WEST OF BOSTON

Babson World Globe Babson College, Babson Park, Forest Street, Wellesley

PHONE: 235-1200.
DIRECTIONS: Route 16 (Washington Street) west to Wellesley Hills Square. Turn left just beyond the theater onto Forest Street, to the main gate of the campus.
PARKING AND ADMISSION: Free.
OPEN: Year-round, 10–5 daily except holidays.
AVERAGE STAY: 30 minutes.

The change from day to night and the progression of the four seasons are simulated as the 25-ton globe, mounted out-of-doors, revolves on its 6-ton shaft. You're seeing countries and their capitals, mountain ranges, rivers, islands, and oceans from 5,000 miles above the earth. For a topside view of the globe look out through the windows of the balcony of the nearby Coleman Map Building, where the largest relief model of the

United States (recently renovated to show late summer vegetation colors) is on display.

NEARBY: A **duck pond** in a pretty setting at Wellesley Town Hall. From Babson drive to Washington Street and turn left. Watch on the right for the building that looks like a medieval castle. Bring bread to feed the ducks and geese. Also nearby, and worth a special trip, are the **Margaret C. Ferguson Greenhouses** (page 199), on the Wellesley College campus.

Observatories

Boston University Observatory 705 Commonwealth Avenue, Boston

PHONE: 353–2625.
OPEN: Year-round, Wednesday nights. School year, 8–9; summer, 9–10.
ADMISSION: Free.

Three (two 7-inch and one 12-inch) telescopes are available to the public on the fifth floor.

Special programs

Harvard College Observatory 60 Garden Street, Cambridge
PHONE: 495–7463.
ADMISSION: Free, but tickets are essential. Call for arrangements.

Children's open nights are scheduled once in the fall and once in the spring for two age groups: 6 to 12 and 12 to 16. It's a very special evening, but with arriving early, a possible tour of the observatory, and, weather permitting, a turn at the telescope, it's a long one for young children.

Getting Around

BUS TOURS

See page 9 for general travel information.

Gray Line Sheraton-Boston Hotel, Prudential Center, Boston
PHONE: 426–8805.
SEASON: Year-round.
GROUPS: For reservations, write to 420 Maple Street, Marlborough 01742, or phone 237–7720 (Wellesley) or 1-800-762-9718 (toll-free in Massachusetts).

Sightseeing tours to Concord and Lexington, Plymouth, and other day trip areas. Two local tours:

- **The Shuttle:** Runs from June through mid-October, to museums (discount admissions at some), specific restaurants, and Freedom Trail sites. The first tour starts at 9; the last, at 3. It's a worthwhile trip if you get an early start and make "Old Ironsides" your first stop. If you're only going to Faneuil Hall, it's not a bargain. The full narrated run takes almost 1½ hours; longer if you get off along the way. The fare is $3.50 for adults, $2 for children 12 and under. Tickets are good only on the date of purchase. (Two-day tickets are also sold.)

- **Boston and Cambridge:** The narrated tour, offered year-round, takes about 3 hours. For those with limited time it's the most efficient way to make a grand sweep. You'll just make two stops: at the Tea Party ship (admission is extra) and at the USS *Constitution.* The fare is $10 for adults, $5 for children 5 to 11, free under 5 (on your lap). Phone reservations accepted.

Trolley Tours of Boston 329 West Second Street, South Boston

PHONE: 269–7010.

LEAVE FROM: Quincy Market (on the harbor side) and Congress Street (between Faneuil Hall and City Hall).

SEASON: Spring and fall, weekends noon–6; summer, 11–7 daily.

FARE: $4 adults, $3 senior citizens, $2 under 12.

The open-air trolley, mounted on a Chevy chassis, has windows and a heater for cooler weather. During the 1-hour narrated tour you get a good overview of Boston's past, present, and coming developments. The 6-mile ride covers the major areas of downtown, from the waterfront to the State House, through Back Bay, to the theater district and Chinatown.

HORSE-DRAWN RIDES

Horse and Carriage Tours 82 Commercial Street, Boston

PHONE: 321–4490, 247–9310.

SEASON: Year-round except when it's very hot or wet. Blankets provided in cold weather.

LEAVE FROM: Faneuil Hall Marketplace (on the harbor side).

Sit in a refurbished, century-old surrey or wagonette for a narrated tour of the waterfront and North End ($5 for 30 minutes), or much of the Freedom Trail ($8 for 45 minutes). Some seasons there's a half-hour tour of Back Bay for $5. Children are half price on all rides.

THE SUBWAY

Park Street Mural

If you start at or pass through Park Street Station, allow some time for the 110-foot, 12-ton mosaic by Lilli Ann Killen Rosenberg. There's no sign, but it's very definitely on the north wall of the tracks near the fare booth. The artist used old trolley parts, railroad spikes, seashells, stones, pieces of slate, marbles, and chips of colored and gold-leaf glass embedded in cast and carved concrete to depict Boston's growth from seaport to commercial complex. You'll notice tunnels and trolley tracks connecting different neighborhoods, and the dominating layers-of-earth theme that represents what was under the

For Teenagers

Members of **Detours** receive information, encouragement, and a constant stream of suggestions for exploring the city on their own by public transportation. Organized trips often go behind the scenes, where the public usually isn't allowed. The Detours Bus, a mobile information center (where-what-when by Ⓣ), visits Greater Boston neighborhoods, schools, and community centers throughout the year. Detours is based at the Children's Museum, on Museum Wharf. Membership, open to ages 11 to 16, is $5 a year ($4 for groups of ten or more). Benefits include Ⓣ tokens, discounts at theaters and museums, and publications (theme brochures and a newspaper). Call 426–6500 for more information.

Two other programs give area teenagers opportunities to explore their interests. The **MIT High School Studies Program** is conducted by college students for young people in Grades 7 through 12. A wide range of offerings — math, science, computers, performing arts, liberal arts, social sciences, and hobbits (a catch-all) — is available year-round for a nominal fee. The noncredit program also schedules SAT preparatory sessions. For information, phone 253–4882 or write W20-467, MIT, Cambridge 02139.

Explorer Posts programs are open to everyone ages 14 to 21. (Scouting membership isn't necessary.) Offerings include mechanics, skin diving, architecture, medicine, marine biology, insurance, hotel management, or even kayaking. Check the phone book under "Boy Scouts of America" for information about current groups.

Common at the turn of the century. And the longer you look at the incredible detail, the more you see.

Where To?

Out-of-towners (particularly children) who've never been on a subway — or even a trolley — often feel that their first ride (not at rush hour, please) is an excursion in itself. Foreign visitors are surprised that most trains stop at every station.

A half-hour ride on the air-conditioned Red Line could start at Harvard Square (page 135). The train surfaces at Longfellow Bridge for a picture postcard scene of sailboats on the Charles, then goes back underground through Park Street Station and on to Quincy. Here, within walking distance, is the Adams National Historic Site (page 112). And right across from the station is the Bargain Center, a store with everything from clothes and toys to fabrics and appliances.

The Riverside–Green Line (35 minutes from start to finish when all goes well) surfaces at Fenway, a familiar stop for Red Sox fans. Then the trolley travels by blossoms, foliage, or snow-laden bushes; a lake used for swimming and skating; and maybe deer (between Chestnut Hill and Newton Center).

WALKING TOURS

Walking tours seem to be everywhere, in every revitalized community up and down the New England coast. Most are led by local historical societies. The guides, young and old, have usually had rigorous training. And their own interests often color the tour, which may focus on a certain period or neighborhood with a strong emphasis on architecture and history.

Boston by Foot 77 North Washington Street, Boston
PHONE: 367–2345.
FEE: $3–$4.

Guides are knowledgeable volunteers, eager to share their enthusiasm for the city's history and architecture. The 1½-hour personalized tours are held in all weather from May through October, on Sundays at 2, and on Tuesdays, Thursdays, and Saturdays at 10. Every Wednesday there's a tour of Copley Square; Saturdays at 3 there's one of the North End; and once a week there's a 5:30 tour of Beacon Hill. Special monthly Sunday tours start at 2.

Special for children: **Boston by Little Feet** — a 1½-hour tour on Sundays at 2 from May through October. Youngsters may stop to pace a plaza, examine a statue, or measure a doorway on the route past the Old State House, Old South Meeting House, old and new city halls, and Faneuil Hall. Suggested for ages 8 to 12, with an accompanying adult. The fee is $1.

Cambridge Page 135.

Freedom Trail For free guided walks see page 95.

Historic Neighborhoods Foundation 90 South Street, Boston
PHONE: 426–1898.

Walking tours, lectures, and teaching projects that focus on urban architecture and social and landscape history are year-round activities for this nonprofit educational group. Bilingual tours can be arranged. Walks through Back Bay ($5) and Beacon Hill ($4.50) are 2 hours each. Children's tours (an adult must come along) run 1½ to 2 hours, and usually begin mornings at 10.

Make Way for Ducklings (through Beacon Hill and on Mrs.

Mallard's route) is designed for ages 5 to 12. The fee is $3.75 for adults, $3.25 for children. **A Kid's View of the North End** inside and out ($4) is for ages 8 up, as are the **waterfront tours** ($3.75), which include a visit to the Custom House tower, part of the look at Boston's origins as a port city.

The Victorian Society 137 Beacon Street, Boston
PHONE: 267–6338.

Walks in October and May. Call for a schedule of walks and year-round lectures and activities.

Exploring on Your Own

BACK BAY

LOCATION: See map (page 127).
PARKING: Boston Common Underground Garage (page 10).
Ⓣ: Green Lines. Arlington and Copley are near the Public Garden; Auditorium and Prudential are closer to Massachusetts Avenue.
VIEWPOINTS: Page 117.
RESTAURANTS: Page 14.
MUSEUMS: The Institute of Contemporary Art (page 154). The Gardner Museum (page 153) and the Museum of Fine Arts (page 156) are nearby, in the Fenway area.

You don't have to be an architecturel afficionado to appreciate the hundreds of details — chimneys, gables, balconies, bay windows — in this area. The elegant town houses are built on tidal flats, filled through forty years' time. The area is laid out in a grid, with perpendicular cross-streets progressing alphabetically from Arlington, at the Public Garden, to Hereford, just before Massachusetts Avenue. Number 32 Hereford has an iron balcony that was salvaged from the Tuileries during the Paris riots of 1871. Number 12 Fairfield, built in the late 1870s, has twenty different shapes of molded brick.

Wide, tree-lined **Commonwealth Avenue** is complete with benches and dog walkers along the promenade. The white limestone at Number 287, built in 1899, contrasts sharply with earlier homes nearby. To see the magnificent ballroom with parquet floor, chandeliers, and mirrors in the Boston Center for Adult Education at Number 5, make advance arrangements with Donnie Curtis.

Marlborough Street feels residential. The French Library at Number 53 has a charming children's area on the second floor. On **Newbury Street** you need rooftops and stoops to give a sense of scale. Many of the homes have become art galleries (contemporary and traditional) and one- to three-level shops (featuring clothes, antiques, crafts, and china from around the world). Outdoor cafes abound spring through fall. F. A. O. Schwarz, with its wide selection of children's toys and games, is

The **Boston Public Library** is the oldest free municipal library in the world, and its collections are extraordinary.... The bas-relief doors on Dartmouth Street, the work of Daniel Chester French, lead to a large hall where the names of famous Bostonians are set in the mosaic ceiling, and where marble lions guard an impressive staircase. Here too are dioramas of Alice in Wonderland and of Dickens's London.... The Wiggin Gallery on the third floor has wonderful changing exhibits.... The Newspaper Room has papers from all of New England and from every major city in the United States and the world.... Small screens in the microtext department make it possible to see back editions of local, regional, national, and even some international newspapers. (What was happening the day you were born? Children — with an adult along — can ask to see particular editions.) ... A bubbling fountain and shade trees make the courtyard a pleasant, cool place to relax in summer.... In 1969 an addition was made to the library — an addition widely acclaimed for its architectural blend with the old.... There are regularly scheduled programs (page 38) both in the auditorium and in the inviting children's room, near the Boylston Street entrance. (The children's room has its own rest rooms.) ... Listening tables are available in the audiovisual department, the place also for organizational film loans (page 40).... Borrowing privileges are free to all state residents who present an ID with a picture and address. Phone: 536–5400.

at Number 40 just around the corner from **Berkeley Street,** where Bonwit Teller occupies a building that was the first home of MIT and later of the Museum of Science (then known as the Museum of Natural History). Also at Berkeley and Newbury is the First and Second Church in Boston. Very little of the old building is left from a devastating fire in 1968, but from Berkeley you can see the remaining wall with rose window frame, the porch, and the steeple and bell tower of the oldest church in the city.

Copley Square is surrounded by buildings that could fill a day of looking. Trinity Church (page 263) and the new Old South Church are National Historic Landmarks. The observatory in the mirror-covered John Hancock Tower (page 117) gives a good orientation to the Back Bay and all of Boston. The magnificently appointed Copley Plaza Tea Court serves high tea ($1.50, more for victuals) among the palms from 2 to 5. (Denim accepted, but not preferred.) Copley Place, a complex with two hotels, offices, and shops — including Neiman-

Marcus — is under construction. At Dartmouth Street a central escalator will take visitors to the Westin Hotel and to eleven parts of the complex.

Along **Boylston Street,** toward Trinity Church, a canopy of locust trees leads to the New England Mutual Life Insurance Company Building at Number 501, on the left between Berkeley and Clarendon. The lobby is open weekdays from 8:45 to 4:45. Go in to see the dioramas, among them "The Filling In of Back Bay 1858" and "The Boylston Street Fishweir" (exposed during the 1913 excavation for the subway). Beautiful postcards of the Hoffbauer murals of colonial New England are given free to visitors on request.

It's another block to the **Boston Public Garden.** Bounded by Arlington, Boylston, Beacon, and Charles streets, the park offers colorful formal flower beds, rare old trees, statues, an oft-photographed bridge, and winding paths for strolling. But you'll have no peace with the children if you don't head for the swan boats (page 228) first.

Inside Views

The **Gibson House** at 137 Beacon Street (between Arlington and Berkeley) isn't far from the Public Garden. The house is filled with Victoriana — from the kitchen in the basement to the cat's bed in the upstairs music room. In less than half an hour you'll see four floors of the home, built in 1860 and always lived in by the Gibson family. It's just as bachelor son Charles Hammond Gibson left it when he died in 1956. Open May through October, Tuesday through Sunday from 2 to 5; No-

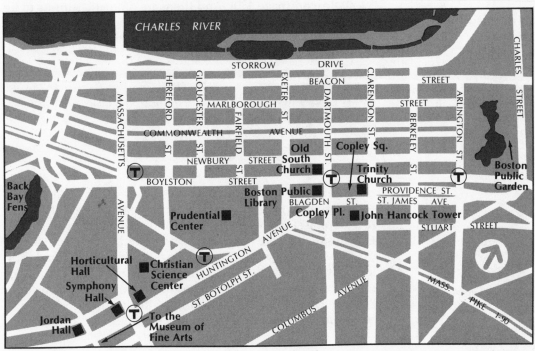

Back Bay

vember through April, some afternoons (call 236–6338 for hours). Closed legal holidays. Admission is $2.

At **Fisher Junior College,** 118 Beacon Street, is a very different interior. The hanging marble stairway has a metal balustrade that's covered with 24-karat gold. Rugs are woven with the Greek design of the balustrade and walls. And the carved rosewood doors in the library have handwrought silver knobs. The school is open weekdays from 9 to 4:30. And there's no charge for the tour through the 1803 home.

BEACON HILL

LOCATION: See map (facing).
PARKING: Boston Common Underground Garage (page 10).
Ⓣ: Park Street on the Red or Green Line.
RESTAURANTS: Page 15.
NEARBY: Boston Public Garden (page 127) and the swan boats (page 228).

A good starting point is the State House (page 97). Then wind your way to the river (Storrow Drive pedestrian overpasses are at Beacon and Arlington, and at Charles Street Circle). During the summer, the entire scene is splashed with the color of flower boxes. As you wander up, down, and across the hill (which was at least 60 feet higher before its dirt became part of Back Bay fill), you'll find antique gaslights, foot-scrapers at doorsteps, stables now converted to homes, interesting doorways, patterned brick sidewalks, underpasses and tunnels, and cobblestone driveways. Purple windowpanes — the original glass affected by the sun — can be seen from inside out at 39–40 Beacon (page 130). And there are dramatic sunsets to be seen looking toward MIT from Pinckney and Joy streets, where the river is framed by buildings on each side of the hill.

> How did Beacon Hill get its name? Some say from the beacon once erected at the top to warn of oncoming danger. (It was never used.)

Use the map to find **Acorn Street,** bordered by Willow and West Cedar (which runs off Chestnut near Charles). This narrow sloping street is one-car wide and paved with river stones. Early residents were coachmen who served nearby families.

Follow Willow with its iron railings (used for support during icy weather and in the past as hitching posts) to Mt. Vernon for one of the entrances (Pinckney is the other) to **Louisburg Square** (pronounced *loo-is-burg*), with its simple doorways, bowfront three- and four-story brick homes, and central park

Beacon Hill

Charles River

Hatch Shell

LONGFELLOW BRIDGE

CHARLES RIVER

Charles Street Circle

TO MASSACHUSETTS GENERAL HOSPITAL AND HARRISON GRAY OTIS HOUSE →

STORROW DRIVE

EMBANKMENT RD.

EMBANKMENT RD.

ARTHUR FIEDLER FOOTBRIDGE

CHESTNUT STREET

MT. OTIS STREET

BRIMMER STREET

CHARLES RIVER STREET

CEDAR STREET

WEST

PRIMUS

PHILLIPS ST.

GROVE

ANDERSON

BEACON STREET

MT. VERNON STREET

REVERE ST.

Boston Public Garden

CHARLES STREET

STREET

REVERE

MYRTLE ST.

ROLLINS ST.

GARDEN ST.

IRVING ST.

Louisburg Square

CHESTNUT STREET

BRANCH ST.

ACORN ST.

WILLOW STREET

SPRUCE ST.

PINCKNEY STREET

MYRTLE STREET

Nichols House Museum

African Meeting House

SMITH

Boston Common

FROG POND

BEACON STREET

WALNUT ST.

MT. VERNON STREET

JOY STREET

HANCOCK STREET

DERNE ST.

State House

Shaw Memorial

PARK ST.

BOWDOIN STREET

ASHBURTON PL.

TREMONT STREET

SOMERSET ST.

open only to proprietors of the square. While you're looking for Number 4, where William Dean Howells, an editor of the *Atlantic Monthly* lived, or Number 10, once the home of Louisa May Alcott, the children may still be looking for a way into the iron-fenced, oval-shaped park, with its statues of Aristides the Just (on the Mt. Vernon side) and Christopher Columbus (on the north side). Both were gifts of Joseph Iasigi, a Boston merchant; and both came as ballast in ships from Italy.

Mt. Vernon Street has several sizable old homes with elaborate iron fences. Number 55 (below) is open to the public. Number 50, only 13 feet high, was once a stable for three horses. Some say it was planned so that the gentleman across the street could see his cattle grazing on the Common.

Joy Street brings you to the Museum of Afro American History (page 156), one of fourteen Black Heritage Trail sites on the hill (page 108). At the end of **Rollins Place,** facing 24 Revere Street, is a housefront without a house. Those closed green shutters hide a brick wall. Walkers with the energy to cross the hill for one more block will find **Primus Avenue,** off Phillips near Charles. It has an iron grillwork entrance and an ascending path with a series of steps, and interesting doors at each level.

Charles Street, another filled-in area of Boston, is lined with antique shops, and others with elegant wares of the "don't touch" variety. Businesses and interiors change, but the architecture will remain as is. In 1963 the National Park Service designated Beacon Hill a National Historic Landmark.

Inside Views

WITH LITTLE APPEAL FOR CHILDREN

The **Beacon Hill Mansions** at 39–40 Beacon Street, across from the Common, are lovely furnished federal homes (1818) maintained by the Women's City Club of Boston. Open for tours (fee charged) by appointment only. Phone: 245-2423.

The **Nichols House Museum** at 55 Mt. Vernon Street (between Joy and Walnut) was designed in the nineteenth century by Charles Bulfinch. It now houses the Boston Council for International Visitors. Guides share anecdotes about the family and the house, which has been carefully and lovingly preserved as it was lived in for eighty years. Open Mondays, Wednesdays, and Saturdays from 1 to 5. Admission is $1. Phone: 227-6993.

On the north side of the hill, at 141 Cambridge Street (midway between the Massachusetts General Hospital and Government Center), is the **Harrison Gray Otis House,** the oldest (1796) freestanding town house in Boston. Originally designed by Charles Bulfinch for Otis, a lawyer, congressman, and mayor of Boston, the federal-style mansion is now a museum and headquarters of the Society for the Preservation of New England Antiquities. Tours, weekdays (except holidays) at 10, 11, 1, 2, and 3, go through the first two floors — a magnificent sampling of town house living from 1790 to 1802. Admission is $2 for adults, $1 for children under 12. Phone: 227-3956.

CHINATOWN

LOCATION: See map (page 7).
DIRECTIONS: Driving, take the Chinatown exit off the expressway (look for the pagoda). Walking from Downtown Crossing, follow Chauncy Street (in back of Jordan Marsh) to Harrison.
PARKING: Meters on clogged streets. Some nearby garages.
Ⓣ: South Station on the Red Line.
RESTAURANTS (THE BIGGEST DRAW FOR MOST VISITORS): Page 15.

The pagoda atop the Chinese Merchants Building is a landmark of Boston's small Chinatown. (And the area, centered on Beach, Hudson, and Tyler streets, is growing even smaller, as businesses and roadways eat into its boundaries.) The official entrance — a recently installed gateway with green roof tiles and traditional lions, a gift from the government of Taiwan — is at Beach and Edinboro. Just down the street is a pagoda-shaped phone booth, one of several in the neighborhood.

There's a sense of community in the markets, where Chinese is spoken by both shopkeepers and customers. The C. W. H. Company at 55 Beach Street has a meat lady who knows how to cut small pieces with a huge cleaver. In back there's a big display of whole fresh fish, and one of the aisles is filled with a selection of noodles. In the smaller groceries, where many shopkeepers still total purchases on an abacus, you'll see fresh chestnuts (in winter), Chinese vegetables, suspended dried meats, dried fish, dried shrimp in apothecary jars, litchi nuts, dried lotus roots, and bamboo leaves. Wing Fung Lin, 79 Harrison, stocks individual iced soybean drinks. Gift shops, on almost every street, feature clothing, dolls, scrolls, tea sets, and chopsticks from China and Japan.

Ho Yuen Bakery at 54 Beach, open 9 to 9 daily, sells delicious mixed-nut pastries, macaroons, black bean cakes, moon cakes, huge walnut cookies, and more. (The pastries filled with meats aren't really desserts.) A full assortment — still warm from the oven — is available in late morning. Through the open doors of Hing Shing on Beach, at the corner of Hudson, you can see bakers at work. Their golden fish and Happy Buddha cookies are decorative and reasonably priced. Bo-Shek Coffee House at 63 Beach has a smaller selection of pastries, but they're all marvelous. Across the way on Oxford Street, Wai Wai Ice Cream sells take-away ginger, coconut, and pineapple cups.

FANEUIL HALL MARKETPLACE

OFTEN CALLED QUINCY MARKET

PHONE: 523–2980.
DIRECTIONS: From the expressway south, take the Dock Square exit; going north, take the Atlantic Avenue exit.
PARKING: Limited meter parking under the expressway. Quincy Marketplace Garage.
Ⓣ: State on the Orange or Blue Line; Government Center on the Green or Blue Line.

OPEN: Shops are open Monday through Saturday 10 to 9, Sundays noon to 6. Restaurants stay open later in the evenings. The flower market never closes.

STREET ENTERTAINMENT: Free and popular. April–October, 11–11, between Faneuil Hall and Quincy Market.

REST ROOMS: In obscure locations near the middle of the central building, downstairs, and on street and second levels in the north and south markets. Look for signs or ask the guards.

BOSTIX (TICKETS AND PERFORMING ARTS INFORMATION): Page 34.

Step onto traffic-free cobblestones, one of the million visitors each month. The Marketplace, an ongoing urban pageant, is a dependable spot for people watching and listening.

Clipper ships and fishing boats no longer dock at the back doors of the copper-domed, granite center building conceived by Boston's early-nineteenth-century mayor, Josiah Quincy. But today, one hundred and fifty years later, that building is still a market. Walk through crowded aisles past dozens of stalls with freshly baked bread, and arrays of chicken, meats, and seafood. Lots of little tables inside (often filled in winter) and benches outside for eating Greek salads, cookies, bagels, pizza, or yogurt cones. The two flanking brick buildings are filled with jewelry, gifts, clothing, and home furnishings for sale. If you're looking for the personal touch, talk to the craftspeople in the Bull Market. You'll find an informed staff and an incredible selection of quality children's books at the White Rabbit & Company in the North Market.

There are plenty of restaurants with good (moderate to expensive) food, hanging plants, and piano players. And lines still form at Durgin Park (page 17). The whole place takes on a different feeling at night, with the sounds of music from open-air cafes. Early morning and some early evening hours are about the only times the area isn't mobbed.

Beyond the Marketplace

Haymarket, just across from the North Market on Blackstone Street, behind the new Bostonian Hotel, is open year-round Fridays and Saturdays, until about 8 in summer, 7 in winter. Vendors sell fruits and vegetables (at low prices) from inherited pushcart positions once occupied by horse-drawn wagons. The tradition includes displays and sales pitches. Go quickly! It's changing and shrinking with every new development.

Step into one of the wholesale meat markets for a look at hamburg in the making. At Prosperity, 78½ Blackstone, three generations still service our family. . . . The aroma alone makes Al Capone's Cheese Shop at Numbers 72–76 worth a visit. In addition to a wall stacked with dozens of cheeses, the shop sells its own ricotta and yogurt, and four kinds of spreads. (The walnut and fig creme de creme is out of this world.) Samples cheerfully given. You'll hear many languages spoken in the line at the meat counter, where customers are waiting for Al's personal service complete with cooking instructions. Open Monday through Saturday, until 7 on Friday and Saturday nights.

The **waterfront** (page 140) is just minutes away.

Faneuil Hall (page 101) is the real place. Minutes and a long stairway away from the crowds, in the auditorium on the second floor, there's a National Park ranger who'll tell you about the building and its grasshopper weathervane, both dating back to 1742.

Where's Boston 60 State Street (near Faneuil Hall), Boston

PHONE: 367–6090.

Ⓣ: State on the Orange or Blue Line; Government Center on the Green or Blue Line.

OPEN: 10–5 daily (sometimes later).

ADMISSION: $3.50 adults, $3 students with IDs, $2 under 14, $1.75 senior citizens.

HANDICAPPED: 18 steps from the Marketplace; none from the State Street entrance.

A show with pizzazz. Music, voices, and sounds, and thousands of slides flashing on eight screens. Most Bostonians identify with parts of the 50-minute portrait; out-of-towners get a whirlwind, breathless tour of contemporary Boston.

In **Dock Square,** north of the flower market toward City Hall, is a small park with Lloyd Lillie's statues of mayor-governor-congressman James Michael Curley — a Boston legend. Most people sit down on the bench to chat with the figure; others sit right on its knee (the shiny bronze attests to it).

This is very close to a precious pocket of the Freedom Trail (page 95). Along **Union Street,** as you pass the eighteenth-century Union Oyster House, you'll probably see Tommy Butt shucking oysters at the U-shaped mahogany bar, where he's worked for almost sixty years. Look up to see old rooflines, windows, and doors still traceable on blank brick walls.

Don't miss **Marshall Street,** a taste of old Boston just steps away from all the latest changes. Here is the Boston Stone, used by an early-eighteenth-century painter to grind pigments. Legend says that all distances from Boston were measured from the stone. You're in the **Blackstone Block,** where Marsh Lane, Salt Lane, and Creek Square are part of the seventeenth-century street pattern, the most extensive in the city.

From this area, it's a short (rather grubby) tunnel walk to the

bustling **North End** (page 138), or a swing right, through Haymarket, back to the Marketplace.

Government Center is also just a couple of blocks from the Marketplace. In City Hall Plaza, an area paved with two and a half million bricks, there's often free live entertainment during the summer at lunchtime and in the evening.

Across from the Government Center Ⓣ station, at the end of Sears Crescent (once lined with bookstores and busy with literary activity), is the Steaming Kettle Coffee Shop, a Boston landmark high above its Court Street door. The 200-pound, gold-leaf-covered copper kettle, which simmered over a century ago in front of the Oriental Tea Company in Scollay Square, still spouts steam constantly.

On the other side of the plaza is the John F. Kennedy Federal Building. Of interest may be the government information desk, passport office, and bookstore (open weekdays 8 to 4) with over a thousand government publications for sale.

From here it's a 5-minute walk to the Harrison Gray Otis House (page 130), and then another 10 minutes to the Massachusetts General Hospital (page 261).

HARVARD SQUARE

JUST ACROSS THE RIVER IN CAMBRIDGE

DIRECTIONS: Follow the signs on Memorial or Storrow Drive.

PARKING: Difficult. Try the Eliot Street lot near Brattle Square.

Ⓣ **(THE BEST WAY):** Harvard on the Red Line, 11 minutes from downtown Boston.

INFORMATION: Harvard Information Center (page 137).

RESTAURANTS: Page 17.

TOURS: Harvard University tours (about an hour long) leave mid-June through mid-September, weather permitting, from the information center (page 137) Monday through Saturday at 10, 11:15, 2, and 3:15, and Sundays at 1:30 and 3. The rest of the year they leave weekdays from the university's admissions office (call 495–1573 for a schedule) and on Saturdays from the information center at 10:30. For walking tours of nearby residential areas see page 138.

OUTDOOR ENTERTAINMENT: Evenings from late spring through summer find musicians, jugglers, thespians, and mimes performing in doorways and between the flower stands in Brattle Square. Uneven talent. Good fun. And free (donations always welcome).

INDOOR ENTERTAINMENT FOR CHILDREN: Alternative Family Cinema (page 35) in Central Square and the Children's Workshop (page 41) in North Cambridge.

REST ROOMS: On the third floor of the Coop's bookstore and on the second floor of the main store.

MEETING PLACE: Under the Coop clock.

Harvard Square isn't a square at all. It's a wide area of historic and cultural resources interspersed with shops that reflect the

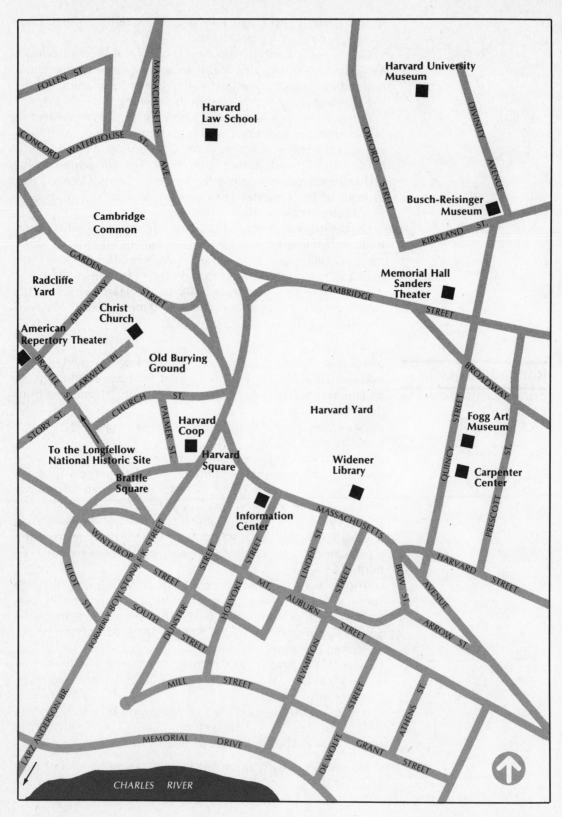

Harvard Square

international flavor of the community. Browsers find minimalls everywhere, traffic aplenty, and bookstores every few feet.

Right in the square, on the plaza at **Holyoke Center,** are benches, crafts vendors (when allowed), and musicians. It's a good place for people watching and ice cream licking. . . . The **Out of Town Newspapers Stand** has hundreds of American and foreign newspapers and magazines. . . . That yellow frame house at the edge of **Harvard Yard** is now used by the alumni association, but it housed Harvard presidents for over a hundred years. Step inside the gate and walk through the yard, a quiet enclave of eighteenth-century red brick buildings. (Harvard is the oldest university in the country.) Go by Widener Library (the largest university library in the world), the statue of John Harvard, and the water pump for the best route to the **glass flowers,** in the Botanical Museum (page 163). That Victorian building just beyond the yard is Memorial Hall, built as a Civil War memorial. Its wooden auditorium makes an interesting setting for lectures and concerts. At this point you're close to the Botanical Museum and the other Harvard museums, and the **Law School yard** — more famous to some as the setting for the film *Love Story* than for its history.

Information? Notices about poetry readings, performances, lectures, and gatherings for the latest cause are posted throughout the square on all sorts of vertical spaces — telephone poles, store windows, and walls. And there's a recorded-information number for campus events (see page 33).

But the best source for personal attention and printed information is the **Harvard Information Center** in Holyoke Center, at 1353 Massachusetts Avenue (next to the Cambridge Trust Company) in the square. Free area maps in English, French, German, Japanese, Portuguese, and Spanish. The center is open year-round, Monday through Saturday from 9:45 to 4:45, and summer Sundays from 1 to 4. Phone: 495-1573.

Brattle Street starts in the square. The first right, Palmer Street, leads to the **Harvard Cooperative Bookstore,** three floors full of books (a huge selection in the children's department on the first floor), posters, and records. Back on Brattle, some people spend hours in **WordsWorth,** a bookstore with a well-informed staff and a discount policy of 15 percent off trade hardcovers and 10 percent off paperbacks (not texts). **Calliope** has a delightful window display of children's items. **Reading International** has bargain books and a selection of new titles. The **Cambridge Center for Adult Education** at Number 42 was a country estate when it was built in 1736. Now it's a bustling center of activity with over two hundred on the faculty.

If you pull yourself away from the shops and continue past the home of the **American Repertory Theater** (page 256), you'll find yourself on **Tory Row,** among lovely old Brattle Street homes. Two — the Hooper-Lee-Nichols House and the Long-fellow National Historic Site (page 111) — are open to the public. Organized **walking tours** (fee charged) along Brattle Street and other Cambridge areas are conducted by the Cambridge Historical Society, based in the Hooper-Lee-Nichols House. Tours run June through mid-September. Call a day in advance for reservations. The Longfellow Historic Site operates free Tory Row tours on Saturdays at 10, weather permitting.

If you're in the square with young children, you're not far from the playground on **Cambridge Common.** Across from the common is the oldest church in the city. **Christ Church** has a bullet hole "made by a stray shot fired by the British soldiers marching to Lexington, April 19, 1775." From here there's a short quaint path to Brattle Street between the church and the Old Burying Ground, where many early settlers are buried.

On Mt. Auburn, near Elsie's (famous for roast beef sandwiches), the triangle-shaped building with brightly painted door is the home of the **Harvard Lampoon.** Attached to it, and filled with used books, is the **Starr Book Company.** A bit on the dark and dusty side, but an old favorite.

By the **Charles River,** two blocks down from the square, are views of domed Harvard dormitories, the Business School, and the boat house, and sculls and small craft. There's grass enough for Frisbee throwing and picnicking. The sidewalk is used for jogging, cycling, roller skating, and walking too. To the west of Boylston Street is a row of enormous old sycamore trees, survivors of a battle to widen the road a few years back.

NORTH END

DIRECTIONS: From the expressway south, take the Dock Square exit; going north, take the Atlantic Avenue exit. From the Marketplace, walk along Haymarket to Blackstone Street, to the cluttered pedestrian underpass.

PARKING: It's just about impossible to park on North End streets. The Government Center Garage (page 10) is nearby.

Ⓣ: Haymarket on the Orange or Green Line; then walk through the underpass.

RESTAURANTS: Page 18.

FESTIVALS: Page 285.

NEARBY: Several Freedom Trail sites (pages 102–105) and the waterfront (page 140).

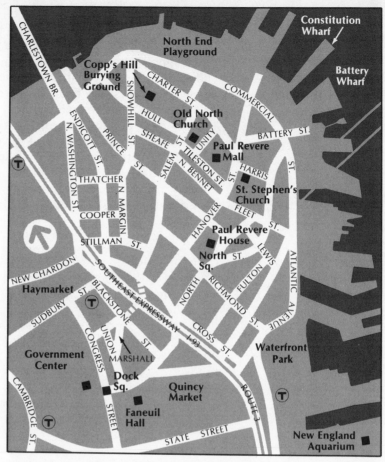

The Italian section of Boston, now separated from the rest of the city by a maze of highways, is a cohesive community with, some say, the feeling of Rome or Milan. The narrow streets — busy with small shops and neighborhood activity — are beginning to show some change, the result of recent condominium and commercial development.

The shops on **Hanover Street** serve all needs, but browsers are often drawn to the elaborate window displays and tempting aromas of the bakeries. The huge wedding cakes at Mike's seem a mile high. At M. M. Rocco's, bakers can be seen working at big tables in the back. Modern Bakery shapes marzipan (almond paste) into fruits and vegetables. Several places serve cappuccino; Pompeii also has pastries and "the best pistachio ice cream in the world."

One block over, on **Salem Street,** vegetables are sold from sidewalk stalls in good weather. There are barrels of live snails and squid, hanging meats in a real butcher shop, olives in bulk, drums of olive oil, and grains in burlap bags. Polcari's on the corner of Richmond Street sells several varieties of coffee beans from old copper bins, hundreds of spices in bulk, and about twenty-five different kinds of dried beans.

More food talk: Salumeria Italiana at 151 Richmond is known for its superb cheeses. The enormous rounds, huge quantities, and wide variety are particularly impressive at Purity Cheese (closed Mondays), 55 Endicott, corner of Cross, near the expressway. Pizza is everywhere, including the bakeries. Cannoli (hollow fried-dough pastries), usually filled to order, are featured in many places, but a favorite — Prince Pastry — is around the corner from the Paul Revere House (page 102) at 2 Prince Street. On North Street at Number 229, Cara Donna Grocery has inexpensive sandwiches and subs to go (to the waterfront perhaps). A pasta machine is at work at Roberto's, 187 North.

The North End branch of the Boston Public Library on Richmond Street, between Salem and Hanover, has ceiling-high plants and a charming children's area. It's one of the most inviting and lively libraries anywhere. Near the section of Italian books is a large diorama of the ducal palace in Venice. In the colorful sixteenth-century setting are figures of the doge in his state gondola, merchants, monks, ladies of the court, peasants, and beggars.

Opposite Paul Revere Mall (page 103) is **St. Stephen's Church,** at 401 Hanover Street. Just inside the door is an exhibit of before-during-after photographs of its restoration. In 1965 the building was lowered (by hydraulic lifts) almost 7 feet, to the original entrance level. The steeple is a reproduction, but the bell is the one made by Paul Revere. If you walk through the mall (which leads to the Old North Church), you're very much part of a neighborhood scene: children playing tag, men playing cards, and others simply watching the tourists.

THE WATERFRONT

DIRECTIONS: Follow signs off the expressway to Atlantic Avenue and the waterfront.
PARKING: Impossible on the street. Garages nearby.
Ⓣ: Aquarium on the Blue Line.
BOAT TRIPS: Page 226.
RESTAURANTS: Page 18.
MUSEUMS: New England Aquarium (page 160). The Children's Museum (page 151) on Museum Wharf and, nearby, the Boston Tea Party Ship and Museum (page 148).

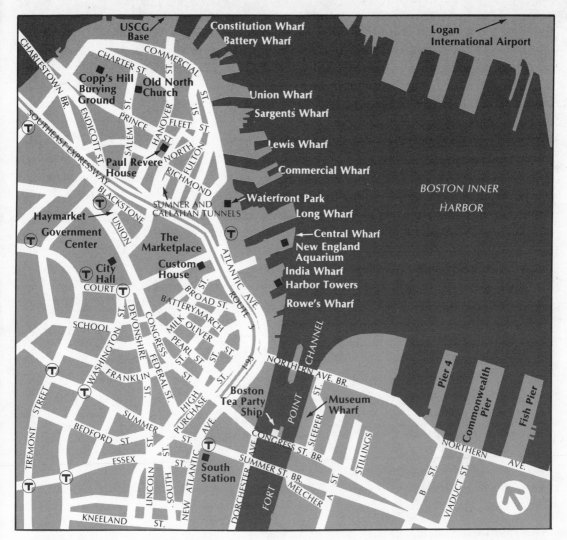

Waterfront

Rehabilitated, renovated, reconstructed. There's a lot of history behind — and under — the many new restaurants, condominiums, and shopping malls. For a free overview, go to the **Custom House tower** (page 117). (It's closed weekends.) . . . The **Fish Pier** continues to be active. Until the major overhaul is finished, though, visitors aren't encouraged to watch unloading. Some wholesalers also sell retail. . . . **Fort Point Channel**'s lobster boats and tugboats can be seen from Museum Wharf and the Northern Avenue Bridge.

Head for the **New England Aquarium** (page 160), where it's possible to spend at least 45 minutes without spending a dime. Attention-getting harbor seals cavort in the outside pool near the front entrance. Visitors of all ages step (carefully) on the planks in the plaza's inviting fountain. Beyond the Aquarium, a

walkway (often missed) juts into the harbor for a ground-level panorama of water and airport activity.

Long Wharf, Boston's oldest (built in 1710), used to reach Dock Square before this area was filled in. Now it's home to the Chart House Restaurant (closed for lunch) in a 1724 pilot house, excursion boat landings, and the Marriott Long Wharf Hotel, complete with pedestrian passageway and dramatic atrium.

Harborwalk

This 2-mile trail — a painted blue line — links sites of Boston's maritime history and has wonderful viewpoints of old and new. The official starting point (the trail can be walked backwards too) is the Old State House (page 100). From there you walk down State Street (filled-in land) to the Custom House tower (page 117) and Waterfront Park, through the Marriott Long Wharf Hotel (exhibits of changes in the area), and around the Aquarium on the sea walk. From here the blue line leads along Atlantic Avenue to the Northern Avenue Bridge (still operating in its turntable style), Museum Wharf, and the Tea Party ship. Tired? Take the free shuttle bus back to the Old State House.

A brochure (free) about the sites and HarborPass ($1), a package of discount coupons for museums, boat rides, and restaurants, are available at BOSTIX (page 34) and the Boston Common Information Booth (page 3).

Waterfront Park, also called Christopher Columbus Park, is a promenade day and night. An unobstructed view of the harbor, and green, open space for picnicking, Frisbees, and festivals. The playground attracts plenty of older admirers, along with kids to the ropes and sand. (More than one adult has rescued an overly courageous young one from the crow's nest.)

Commercial Wharf, where the second sails for the USS *Constitution* were made in the Greek Revival building, is now home to condominium owners who have flower-filled barrels and a marina in their front yard.

Architecture buffs and city planners will continue along Atlantic Avenue, but there's nothing of particular interest until you get to **Battery Wharf,** home of Bay State Lobster. The store has an enormous array of quality seafood, huge pools of lobsters, fair prices, and employees who are happy to show youngsters "the real thing before it's red."

Museums

So many people converge on Boston's museums on Sunday afternoons, fall through spring, that museums in surrounding communities can be a pleasant change. . . . It helps to be aware of a child's attention span. . . . Special programs for children may be scheduled. . . . Museum membership often includes free or reduced admission, a newsletter, special events, preferred enrollment for courses, and savings in the gift shop. . . . Education departments have become very active. Ask about courses, special events, and outreach programming. . . . Outdoor museums — Mystic Seaport, Old Sturbridge Village, Plimoth Plantation, Strawbery Banke — are included in Day Trips (pages 52–92). . . . Leading a group? Have you seen page xi?

Museums in General

RECORDED INFORMATION

EVENTS AND FEES

BUSCH-REISINGER MUSEUM: 495–2338.

CHILDREN'S MUSEUM: 426–8855.

FOGG ART MUSEUM: 495–2387.

GARDNER MUSEUM: 734–1359.

HARVARD UNIVERSITY MUSEUM: 495–1910.

INSTITUTE OF CONTEMPORARY ART: 266–5151.

JOHN F. KENNEDY LIBRARY: 929–4567.

MUSEUM OF FINE ARTS: 267–9377.

MUSEUM OF SCIENCE: 742–6088.

NEW ENGLAND AQUARIUM: 742–8870.

PEABODY MUSEUM OF SALEM: 508–745–9500.

EVENING HOURS

Schedules do change periodically. The following is a good outline, up to date at press time, but check for current arrangements.

BOSTON TEA PARTY SHIP AND MUSEUM: Open summer evenings until 8.

CHILDREN'S MUSEUM: Open Fridays until 9.

GARDNER MUSEUM: Open Tuesdays, September through June, until 9.

INSTITUTE OF CONTEMPORARY ART: Open Tuesdays, Thursdays, and Fridays until 7, Wednesdays until 8.

MUSEUM OF FINE ARTS: The entire museum is open Wednesdays until 10; just the West Wing is open Thursdays and Fridays until 10.

MUSEUM OF SCIENCE: Open Fridays until 10.

MUSEUM OF THE NATIONAL CENTER OF AFRO-AMERICAN ARTISTS: Open summer Sundays until 7.

NEW ENGLAND AQUARIUM: Open Fridays until 9 and summer weekends until 7.

CLOSED DAYS

HOLIDAYS: Some museums are open. Check individual listings, or call the recorded-information numbers (page 147).

MONDAYS: Beware. Several are usually closed. Check!

FREE OR REDUCED ADMISSION

Several museums offer free or reduced admission in their membership benefits. . . . Coupons are sometimes available in discount packets, including those sold at BOSTIX (page 34).

Nonmembers are eligible for free or reduced rates at the following museums:

- **Addison Gallery of American Art:** Always free.
- **Brockton Art Museum–Fuller Memorial:** "Pay what you can."
- **Busch-Reisinger Museum:** Always free.
- **Cardinal Spellman Philatelic Museum:** Always free.
- **Children's Museum:** Reduced rates schoolday afternoons; free Fridays after 6.
- **Danforth Museum:** Always free.
- **Fogg Art Museum:** Always free.
- **Gardner Museum:** Always free ($1 donation suggested).
- **Harvard University Museum:** Free on Mondays except holidays.
- **Institute of Contemporary Art:** Free on Wednesdays.
- **Museum of Fine Arts:** Free on Saturdays from 10 to noon.
- **Museum of Our National Heritage:** Always free.
- **Museum of Science:** Reduced rates Fridays after 5.
- **New England Aquarium:** Reduced rates Fridays after 4:30.
- **Worcester Art Museum:** Free on Wednesdays.

In Boston

Boston Tea Party Ship and Museum Congress Street Bridge (off Atlantic Avenue on the way to Museum Wharf)

PHONE: 338-1773.

DIRECTIONS: Driving from the north, take the High Street–Congress Street exit off the expressway; then the third left on Congress Street. From the south, take the Downtown–Chinatown exit off the expressway; then right on Kneeland, left on Atlantic Avenue, and second right to Congress Street. From the west, take the Mass. Pike to the Downtown–South Station exit; then right on Kneeland, left on Atlantic Avenue, and second right to Congress Street.

Walking from the Freedom Trail, follow the "Tea Party" signs down Congress Street.

PARKING: On weekends, free 2-hour parking on the Congress Street Bridge. Commercial lots on Atlantic Avenue and Congress Street.

Ⓣ: South Station on the Red Line. Go up the old wooden escalator to the street, and follow signs 1 block along Atlantic Avenue.

FREE SHUTTLE BUS: From the Old State House, May–October, 10–4 daily; from the Marketplace (harbor side), June–August, 10–4 daily.

OPEN: Year-round, daily except Thanksgiving, Christmas, and New Year's. April and October, 9–6; May and September, 9–7; June–August, 9–8; November–March, 9–5.

AVERAGE STAY: 30 minutes.

ADMISSION: $2.25 adults, $1.50 ages 5–14, free under 5. Group rates available.

SCHOOL GROUPS: Ask about guided tours.

HANDICAPPED: Steps. Difficult access.

Inspect the rigging, galley, and reconstructed captain's cabin on this small ship, a privately owned replica of a Tea Party ship. Museum exhibits show the economic and political conditions of prerevolutionary Boston. One audiovisual program tells the story of the Tea Party; another, of the 1973 voyage of this brig, *Beaver II.*

Reactions to the ship and museum have been interesting: Danish tourists are intrigued with the fact that the two-masted brig was built in Denmark. Children enjoy throwing tea (bundles attached to a rope for retrieval) into the harbor and seeing costumed staff members climb the rigging. Tired Girl Scouts report they had seen enough ships and audiovisual programs by the time they arrived here. (The audiovisual programs, however effective, seldom have an attentive audience, unless it's a school group that comes with orientation.) But everyone welcomes the tea (hot or iced) served to all guests.

An unexpected attraction: being on deck when wood-planked Northern Avenue Bridge opens. At the moment there's a lot of discussion about the swing bridge, an historic landmark that's almost seventy years old. When it opens for boats, it holds up road traffic — a problem, some say, for businesses on the other side.

Children's Museum Museum Wharf, 300 Congress Street
PHONE: 426-6500 (voice/TTY-TDD), 426-8855 (programs and hours). Before you come, call the recorded-information number to plan your visit around today's events.

DIRECTIONS: Look for "Museum Wharf" signs. From the north, take the High Street–Congress Street exit off the expressway; then the third left on Congress Street. From the south, take the Atlantic Avenue–Northern Avenue exit; then right over the Northern Avenue Bridge and right onto Sleeper Street. From the west, take the Mass. Pike to the expressway north, to the Atlantic Avenue–Northern Avenue exit; then right over the Northern Avenue Bridge and right onto Sleeper Street.

PARKING: On weekdays use the public lot at Northern Avenue and Sleeper Street (fee charged). On weekends spaces are available on the street.

Ⓣ: South Station on the Red Line. Go up the old wooden escalator for a 3-block, 7-minute walk. Head 1 block north on Atlantic Avenue; then turn right across the Congress Street Bridge.

OPEN: July–Labor Day, 10–5 daily, Fridays until 9; rest of year, holiday and school vacation Mondays and Tuesday–Sunday 10–5, Fridays until 9. Closed Thanksgiving, Christmas, and New Year's. Crowded and especially noisy during school vacation weeks and on rainy weekends. Air-conditioned.

ADMISSION: $4 adults, $3 senior citizens and ages 2–15, free under 2. Free Friday nights between 6 and 9. Free admission to the museum shop, resource center, and recycle shop.

GROUPS: *Community group* arrangements (first come, first served) should be made at least 2 weeks in advance, and are not available during school vacation weeks. *School groups* can make arrangements starting the day after Labor Day, at 9. Previsit orientation session at the museum for teachers. Friday morning reservations are set aside for *special needs groups*, so that there's a minimum of noise and competition.

RESTAURANTS: McDonald's has indoor facilities. Victoria Station, moderately priced, is steps away. S.S. John Wanamaker (not the best place for children), an interesting converted tugboat, has a cocktail lounge; and serves on deck in summer, below in winter.

PICNICKING: A few benches on the wharf, facing harbor activity. The milk bottle stand sells snacks in summer.

MUSEUM SHOP: Free admission. Great stock of books, gifts, games, antiques, and reproductions. The kids' shop offers items from $.05 to $5.

RESOURCE CENTER: Develops, publishes, lends, and rents materials. Good browsing in the extensive collection of educational kits, games, books, and audiovisual materials. Activity kits suitable for classrooms and families.

"I still don't think we're too old for this."
— ELDERLY COUPLE

RECYCLE SHOP: Free admission. Industrial by-products sold by volume, weight, and measure.

PROGRAMMING: Plenty. Call 426–8855. Friday Night Performance Series (page 40) too.

WORKSHOPS: Everything from family music making to specific curriculum areas for teachers. Registration required and fee charged.

FOR TEENAGERS: Detours (page 122).

STROLLERS: Allowed. Backpacks loaned free.

HANDICAPPED: Fully accessible. Parking in front. For group programming, see page 151.

WHEN YOU ENTER: If you're with preschoolers, pick up "Exploring the Museum with Children Under Five" — a helpful brochure. Go to the second-floor desk for tokens (no extra charge) for the Japanese House.

> **A Children's Museum landmark:** The genuine giant milk bottle moved here from Taunton. The wooden bottle (children may never have seen the real thing) is now a food stand during summer months.

This is the original touch-look-ask museum. The computer terminals are a magnet for older children. Preschoolers like Playspace, which happens to be a good place for parents to meet and talk. Climb to grandmother's attic (circa 1900) to explore treasures; come down through the furnished house on the way to grandfather's cellar. Check construction through slices that expose wiring, carpentry, and plumbing. Turn an old zoetrope. Join an assembly line and make a top. Discover similarities and differences in exhibits about ethnic diversity.

Visitors with tickets (see above) for the Japanese House take part in a wonderful exchange (not a lecture) about lifestyle. The house was brought over in pieces from Japan and assembled here.

"What you need is an adults-only night."
— MOTHER OF THREE

Every exhibit in the open, free environment is designed for involvement by choice. Kids are everywhere, exploring, discovering, roaming, running — and learning. This is not a quiet place (particularly during school vacation weeks), and occasionally the lack of structure (no lines to take a turn) bothers visitors who prefer a more directed approach. Still the success of the hands-on approach, an informal way to present concepts, has reached another generation. Almost half the visitors are adults, and the college crowd comes too.

NEARBY: It's a 5-minute walk to the Federal Reserve Bank (page 259); 15 minutes to the Marketplace (page 131) or the Aquarium (page 160). Coming: residential use of neighboring industrial property, and possibly more art galleries.

A block from the
Museum of Fine Arts

Gardner Museum 280 The Fenway
PHONE: 566-1401, 734-1359 (concert schedule).
DIRECTIONS: From Copley Square, follow Huntington Avenue past the Museum of Fine Arts, to Museum Road on the right. Left on the Fenway for 1 block to the Gardner (look for the red roof and wrought iron fence) on the left.
PARKING: On neighboring streets.
Ⓣ: Ruggles-Museum on the Arborway–Green Line; then a 3-block walk.
OPEN: July–August, Tuesday–Sunday noon–5; September–June, Tuesdays noon–9, Wednesday–Sunday noon–5. Closed national holidays.
AVERAGE STAY: 1½–2½ hours.
ADMISSION: Free, but $1 contribution suggested.
RESTAURANTS: The Cafe, with indoor and outdoor seating, serves quiches, salads, sandwiches, fruit plates, and desserts.
PICNICKING: Across the street in the Fenway.
TOURS: Taped units are $1 for one person, $1.50 for two. Free guided tours Thursdays at 2:30 focus on Mrs. Jack's life.
CONCERTS: September through June, free 1-hour programs Tuesdays at 6, Thursdays at 12:15, and Sundays at 3. (Busiest on Sundays.) Performers are students or well-known musicians. The room is long and narrow, with no elevation. No seat holding allowed.
STROLLERS: With rubber wheels allowed. Long flights of stairs mean some carrying.
HANDICAPPED: One wheelchair available. Elevators on request.

Reminder: If you're combining a visit to the Gardner Museum with one to the Museum of Fine Arts, it helps to remember that the Gardner doesn't open until noon.

Recommended for children over 8. Thirty unusual display areas show Isabella Stewart Gardner's eclectic, extraordinary collection of paintings (many Dutch Baroque and Italian Renaissance), sculpture, tapestries, stained glass, furniture, tiles, doorways, gargoyles, and more. Every room is decorated in a different style, none true to any one era.

Many visitors return to the Italianate building just to sit in the central court with its magnificent seasonal displays of flowers. (It's particularly peaceful here on weekdays.) The nasturtiums, trailing from third floor to ground, are usually in bloom from late March through April. The outdoor garden, with its beautiful brick wall, is an added joy in warm weather.

Across from the Prudential Center

Institute of Contemporary Art 955 Boylston Street (corner of Hereford)

PHONE: 266-5152, 266-5151 (recorded information).

Ⓣ: Auditorium on the Green Line (except Arborway).

OPEN: Tuesday–Friday 11–7, Wednesdays 11–8, Saturdays 11–6, Sundays noon–6. Closed national holidays.

ADMISSION: $2 adults, $1 senior citizens and students with IDs, $.50 under 12. Free on Wednesdays.

PROGRAMMING: A full and diverse schedule of films, lectures, and performances.

COURSES: Art classes for all ages.

HANDICAPPED: Inaccessible.

Although the exterior is unchanged, the recycled police station now has two and a half floors of gallery space. Rotating exhibits, each lasting about two months, represent the vanguard of national and local art scenes.

Outside, take the time to walk toward Massachusetts Avenue, then turn back toward the institute to see artist Richard Haas's illusory palace. The mural, on a wall of the Boston Architectural Center, challenges your sense of perspective. Children too wonder, question, and smile.

On the campus of the University of Massachusetts

John F. Kennedy Library Columbia Point, Dorchester

PHONE: 929-4584, 929-4567 (recorded information).

DIRECTIONS: From the north, take the expressway to exit 17; from the south, take exit 18. Then follow signs.

PARKING: Free.

Ⓣ: Columbia on the Red Line; then a very long walk. (Call the library for current shuttle bus arrangements.)

OPEN: Year-round, 9–5 daily except Thanksgiving, Christmas, and New Year's. Last showing of film at 3:50. Air-conditioned.

ADMISSION: $1.50 adults, free under 16.

SCHOOL GROUPS: Visits geared to grade level. Admission is free for elementary school through senior high with reservations. Call 929-4555.

RESTAURANTS: Drive 5 minutes south to Linda Mae's. At the light across from the Dorchester gas tanks, take the right fork for 200 yards to 120 Victory Road. It's big, informal, and reasonable (a children's menu), and has everything from hamburgers and lobsters to homemade desserts.

PICNICKING: Right on the library's beautiful grounds at tables set along the walkway and plaza.

TOURS: By appointment.

PROGRAMMING: Archives Film Series (2:30 weekday afternoons), special school vacation programs, and more. During the Kids'

Caucus, held some weekends, youngsters (ages 7 to 11) see the 30-minute introductory film shown to all visitors, tour the museum, and then deal with a particular topic, say taxes. They may see an animated film on the topic, and then hold a mock town meeting. Free, but advance registration is required.

HANDICAPPED: Accessible. Wheelchairs available.

Most visitors never go into the library area, with its 7 million presidential pages, personal papers, congressional papers, oral histories, and audiovisual materials. Unless you're a scholar or researcher, what you've come to see are the public exhibits, which start with a superb introductory film, one that seems shorter than its 30 minutes. Then you line up for nine sequential exhibit areas, starting with JFK's formative years, his heritage in Ireland and Boston. A time line parallels world events with each Kennedy milestone.

"Gosh you get a lot of junk when you're president."

— TEENAGERS

Some visitors are intrigued with every document (and read them all), memento, and experience. Others choose exhibits here and there — major crises during the short administration, campaign material, press conference film segments, a page from young JFK's journal, Robert Kennedy's political career, and the popular display showing the president's desk as it appeared in the Oval Office. Among all the glass cases there's a flood of information that fills you in on the historical and personal aspects of a life in politics.

JFK's birthplace in Brookline (page 110) is open to the public. And the Historic Neighborhoods Foundation (page 123) offers a Kennedy Roots Tour from April through November.

On the library's landscaped grounds are hundreds of pine trees, locust trees for shade, and thousands of rose bushes. The high bank along the water is planted with dune grass. The walkway to the right of the library leads to a good view of freighters in the only deep-water access to Boston Harbor.

NEARBY: The **Boston Globe tour** (page 257), and parkland and swimming at **Castle Island** (page 180). And it's only minutes by car to **Dorchester Heights.** (Ask at the library for a map.) There's nothing to do here yet (the monument will open in a couple of years), but the open park on a hill — with a good breeze — is set so that you're looking beyond (not up at) cupolas to a part of the harbor that can't be seen from downtown vantage points. The historical significance? It was from here that Washington controlled the port of Boston and forced the British to evacuate.

Museum of Afro American History African Meeting House, Smith Court

OFFICE: Box 5, Dudley Station, Roxbury 02119.

PHONE: 445-7400.

DIRECTIONS: 1 block up from Cambridge Street, off Joy Street, on Beacon Hill.

PARKING: Charles River Garage on Cambridge Street (near the Holiday Inn) or the Boston Common Underground Garage (page 10).

Ⓣ: Bowdoin on the Blue Line.

ARCHAEOLOGICAL LABORATORY: At 149 Roxbury Street, Roxbury (445-7400). Open by appointment.

PROGRAMMING: Call for a schedule of Sunday afternoon programs, films, and exhibits. Tours of historic sites on the Roxbury Heritage Trail include Roxbury Burying Ground, First Church, and an optional climb to the top of Cochituate Standpipe, a water tower atop Roxbury's highest hill, which served as a lookout during the Revolution.

The meetinghouse, built by Afro-Americans in 1806, is the oldest extant black church in the country. It has seen several uses, the most recent as a synagogue. It's being restored (with space allocated for a museum gallery). When it opens late this year, its appearance will resemble that of 1850.

A Roxbury branch of the museum is planned for the Dillaway-Thomas House in John Eliot Square.

Museum of Fine Arts 465 Huntington Avenue

PHONE: 267-9300, -9377 (information) 267-9703 TTY/TTD.

DIRECTIONS: 1 mile west of Copley Square on Huntington Avenue. (See map, pages 4–5.)

PARKING: A small lot on Museum Road, next to the West Wing entrance ($.75 for members, $1.25 for nonmembers). On-street parking in the neighborhood.

Ⓣ: Ruggles-Museum on the Arborway–Green Line.

OPEN: Tuesday–Sunday 10–5, Wednesdays until 10. West Wing (only) stays open Thursdays and Fridays until 10. Closed Mondays and most holidays. Air-conditioned.

ADMISSION: Adults: $3 when the entire museum is open, $2 when only the West Wing is open; senior citizens: $2 at all times; under 17: free at all times. Free for everyone Saturdays 10 to noon. No admission charge for those visiting only the Museum Shop, restaurants, library, and auditorium (depending on the program). Umbrellas must be checked (no charge).

SCHOOL GROUPS: Make arrangements through the education department.

RESTAURANTS: Three, with casual to more formal menus.

LIBRARY: Open to the public. Books and slides of museum collections for loan or purchase.

CHILDREN'S ROOM: Free drop-in workshops for ages 6 to 12 include creative dramatics, art projects, poetry, photography, and music. Held weekday afternoons and Saturday mornings for about an hour. Limited to 30, first come, first served. Call for a schedule.

PROGRAMMING: Regularly scheduled gallery walks, guided tours, lectures, films, and performances. Call for details.

COURSES: An extraordinary array for all ages, preschoolers to senior citizens, and families too. Fees charged. Contact the education department.

HANDICAPPED: Fully accessible. Designated parking near the barrier-free West Wing entrance. The West Wing elevator has tactile markings for the blind. Call the education department for a place on the mailing list for special needs programming (workshops and tours).

Allow time. This great cultural resource is much more than a setting for permanent and traveling exhibitions. Special events and educational programs are frequently planned. The Remis Auditorium has a full schedule of performances, films, and lectures. The restaurants provide indoor and outdoor opportunities for people watching and rest.

The celebrated West Wing, designed by I. M. Pei for major international exhibitions, is an exhibition itself with its use of natural light and open space.

Among the 160 galleries: the finest Old Kingdom sculpture outside Cairo, the reward of a forty-year expedition, includes mummies, altars, and hieroglyphics. The Decorative Arts Wing has a 1695 room from England's Hamilton Palace and a 1760 Louis XVI salon complete with rococo work, mirrors, tapestries, and chandeliers. There are also Greek and Roman galleries, an authentic Catalonian chapel, an Asiatic gallery, Early American furnished rooms, twentieth-century sculpture and paintings, and one of the best collections of French Impressionist art in the country. The work of Paul Revere, a master silversmith before he became a legend, is an important part of the American silverware collection.

The fascinating instruments in the Musical Instruments Room (hours may differ from regular museum hours) include a Jingling Johnny (a late-eighteenth-century percussion tree that's shaken), a trombone with a dragon's head, and a 32-glass armonica (the kind invented by Benjamin Franklin). Many of the instruments are in playing condition, and are still used in concerts.

Museum hours and prices change. Call for today's information.

During the next few years, some of the older galleries will be closed for refurbishing. But there's still plenty to see.

NEARBY: The Gardner Museum (page 153) and the rose gardens in the Fenway (page 181).

Expansive, and something for everyone

Museum of Science Science Park

PHONE: 723-2505, 742-6088 (recorded information — a valuable number for planning a visit).

DIRECTIONS: On the river, at the end of Storrow Drive. (See map, pages 4-5.)

PARKING: Attached garage, with reasonable rates.

Ⓣ: Science Park on the Lechmere–Green Line; some steps, then a 5-minute walk.

OPEN: Hours change often; call 742-6088 to check. Memorial Day–Labor Day, Monday–Thursday and Saturdays 9-5, Fridays 9 a.m.-10 p.m., Sundays 10-5; rest of year, holiday Mondays and Saturdays 9-5, Tuesday–Thursday 9-4, Fridays 9 a.m.-10 p.m., Sundays 10-5. Closed Thanksgiving, Christmas, and New Year's. Not too crowded on summer weekends. Air-conditioned.

AVERAGE STAY: 1½-2½ hours.

ADMISSION: $4.50 adults; $2.75 senior citizens, students with IDs, and ages 5-16; free under 5. Reduced rates ($2 adults, $1 everyone else) Friday evenings after 5.

GROUPS: Spring is heavily booked. No guided tours, but ask about scheduled programs.

RESTAURANTS: The Skyline Cafeteria, where everyone wants a window seat, is open daily for lunch and Friday nights for dinner. Friendly's Fast Serve is open daily until a half hour before the museum closes.

MUSEUM STORE: Free (no museum admission) for 30 minutes, if you leave an ID at the front desk.

LYMAN LIBRARY: Film loops, periodicals, books, and a children's corner. Everyone can browse; members and those currently enrolled in courses can borrow.

HAYDEN PLANETARIUM: A 45-minute lecture-demonstration with a realistic depiction of skies — past, present, and future. Scheduled several times daily and at 7:30 Friday nights. Programs change seven times a year. Admission is $.50 extra. Children under 5 aren't admitted except for the special Christmas program (page 291).

COURSES: Offered fall, winter, and spring, for kindergartners through adults. All fill early, especially the classes for younger children.

VOLUNTEER PROGRAM: Ages 14 up.

QUESTIONS: Members of the education department, library staffers, and guides are wonderful — and imaginative; they may have an immediate answer, a bibliography, or at least a lead.

On the Grounds and Free!

Picnic on benches at the pavilion overlooking the river. . . . Sit on the banks of the Charles and watch the boats going to and from the harbor. (Locks are now near the Charlestown Bridge, page 104.). . . Climb into the cab of the steam locomotive, and see what's what. Everything's labeled, and touching's allowed. Hours vary, but it's usually open spring through fall except in bad weather.

STROLLERS: Allowed, and a help. Changing rooms available.
HANDICAPPED: Floors accessible by elevator. Several wheelchairs available. Group visits and programs by arrangement. Braille materials at the admissions desk.

What to do first?

- **CHECK THE POSTINGS FOR DEMONSTRATION TIMES:** Demonstrations are geared for different age levels and cover a wide range of subjects. Young children especially like the animals; they usually don't appreciate the noise and 15-foot-long lightning bolts in the Hall of Electricity's 20-minute demonstrations.
- **CHECK DISCOVERY ROOM HOURS AND TICKET AVAILABILITY:** A space where kids (Grades K through 4) can examine bones, bird beaks, teeth, and stethoscopes, or weigh themselves in kilograms.
- **BUY PLANETARIUM TICKETS:** If you want to go, get your tickets early. They often sell out.
- **DECIDE WHETHER YOU WANT TO STAY TOGETHER:** You could plan to meet at a designated time and place. It's too big (almost four hundred exhibits), though, to let young ones wander alone.
- **PICK UP "WHAT'S WHERE":** A flyer that tells you just that.

"I weigh almost a kilogram less than I did in December, but I'm 2½ centimeters taller."
— JEAN, AGE 11

From the moment you walk into the lobby, with its spectacular view up the Charles to Boston's skyline, you're curious and questioning. Climb into the Apollo capsule, find your weight on the moon scale, listen to the talking transparent woman, make a sand pattern, see a 20-foot-high dinosaur model, watch a working colony of leaf-cutting ants, or make the energy (pedal a bike) to light a light bulb. Many of the exhibits are self-explanatory. Others are more meaningful for youngsters with help from guides or you.

NEARBY: A tour of Massachusetts General Hospital (page 261). And Community Boating (page 224), where youngsters can sail all summer for a dollar.

Museum of the National Center of Afro-American Artists 300 Walnut Avenue (corner of Crawford), Roxbury

PHONE: 442-8614.

DIRECTIONS: Columbus Avenue to Egleston (about a 15-minute drive from downtown). Under the elevated to the first light, then left on Walnut.

PARKING: Free, in the lot behind the museum.

Ⓣ: Egleston on the Orange Line; then a 6-block walk.

OPEN: Tuesday–Sunday 1–5, summer Sundays until 7.

ADMISSION: $1.25 adults, $.50 senior citizens and children.

SLIDE LIBRARY: African, Afro-American, and Caribbean art. Open to the public for research.

PROGRAMMING: Guided tours, lectures, films, gallery talks, concerts, dance recitals, and arts festivals.

EDUCATIONAL PROGRAMS: Docent training and internships.

HANDICAPPED: Five steps to get in; galleries are accessible.

Exhibitions represent both the permanent collection and loans of paintings, textiles, prints, sculpture, and graphics by Afro-American and African artists. Gallery space is being expanded as renovation on the 1856 structure progresses. A permanent African gallery is the newest to open.

Three blocks from the Marketplace

New England Aquarium Central Wharf (off Atlantic Avenue)

PHONE: 742-8830, 742-8870 (recorded information).

DIRECTIONS: From the north, take the Dock Square exit off the expressway to Atlantic Avenue; from the south, take the Atlantic Avenue exit.

PARKING: Difficult on the street. Lots and the Harbor Tower Garage are nearby.

Ⓣ: Aquarium on the Blue Line (that 42-foot escalator is an adventure); then a 2-minute walk.

OPEN: June–Labor Day, Monday–Thursday 9–6, Fridays 9–9, weekends 9–7; rest of year, Monday–Thursday 9–5, Fridays 9–9, weekends and holidays 9–6. Closed Thanksgiving, Christmas, and New Year's. (This can be a noisy place, but generally Sunday mornings are quiet.)

Museum hours and prices change. Call for today's information.

AVERAGE STAY: 2½–3 hours.

ADMISSION: $5 adults, $4 senior citizens and students with IDs, $3 ages 5–15, free under 5. Fee includes the main building, a film, and the *Discovery* show. Reduced rates ($3.50 adults, $2.50 children) Fridays after 4:30.

GROUPS: A wide variety of programs for all ages. Spring school visits should be booked before Thanksgiving.

COURSES: For ages 6 to adult. Some include field trips. Contact the education department for information.

VOLUNTEER PROGRAM: Ages 16 up.

HANDICAPPED: Accessible. Some report that the ramps are steep if you're pushing. A few steps at the very top of the central tank.

Look and wonder. Look and learn. The visual feast, colorful fish of all sizes and shapes, generates excitement. Rising from the floor is the huge central tank (200,000 gallons — the largest in the world) filled with hundreds of fish, even sharks, swimming through the tunnels and caves of the island reef. The walkway that spirals around the glass tank allows a close-up view of all inhabitants (and the scuba divers who enter to feed six times a day).

There's unusual plant life in the more than seventy gallery tanks, which duplicate the natural environments of their occupants. But even the familiar looks new. Have you ever seen a floating lily from underneath?

"Boy, Mom. I bet those clams don't have to take a bath."
— ARTHUR, AGE 4

The saltwater tray on the first floor, complete with jackass penguins, has several hiding places. Look carefully to see what's there. In the children's aquarium, on the third floor, a tide pool simulates the ebb and flow. And you don't have to be a child to hold the starfish, hermit crabs, sea urchins, or clams.

On board the *Discovery* you'll see dolphins and sea lions, real ones and filmed ones, in demonstrations of their learning and physical abilities. There's a lesson, too, in the interaction between trainers and pets.

Harvard Museums

IN CAMBRIDGE

PHONE: 495-1910 (recorded information).
DIRECTIONS: All are within a 10-minute walk of Harvard Square (page 135). Maps are available at the information center in Holyoke Center (page 137) in the square.
Ⓣ: Harvard on the Red Line.

Busch-Reisinger Museum 29 Kirkland Street (at Quincy)

PHONE: 495-2317, 495-2338 (recorded information).
PARKING: Very difficult near the museum.
OPEN: July–August, weekdays 9–4:45; September–June, weekdays 9–4:45, Saturdays 9–4:15. Closed Sundays and holidays.
ADMISSION: Free.
CONCERTS: Saturday afternoons during the academic year, performances on the famous classic organ. Admission charged.
HANDICAPPED: Not really accessible.

This small museum offers important works in a wonderful setting, but it's not really for children. It has one of the most extensive collections of central and northern European art outside Europe. The twentieth-century German works include sculpture, paintings, drawings, and prints. There are two plaster-cast reproductions of fifteenth-century gates and a fine exhibit on the balcony of eighteenth-century porcelain. A sculpture garden is open during warmer months.

Fogg Art Museum 32 Quincy Street (at Broadway)

PHONE: 495-2387 (recorded information).
PARKING: No facilities.
OPEN: Summer, weekdays 10–5; after Labor Day–school year, weekdays 9–5, Saturdays 10–5, Sundays 2–5. Closed holidays.
AVERAGE STAY: 1½ hours.
ADMISSION: Free.
PROGRAMMING: Lectures by visiting art authorities and courses for children and adults. Call for information about the museum's outstanding loan exhibitions.
HANDICAPPED: Accessible.

With orientation and follow-up this could be a fascinating place for youngsters. The galleries on the two lower floors duplicate — in materials and proportion — a sixteenth-century villa. Here is part of the university's extensive, and growing, collection of French paintings, European and American drawings and watercolors, Chinese jades, and Persian miniature bronzes. An addition, due to open in 1984, will provide more exhibition space, particularly for Oriental and Islamic art.
NEARBY: Right next door, the Carpenter Center for Visual Arts

has exhibits of contemporary art, lectures, and films in the only building in North America designed by the late French architect Le Corbusier.

Four museums under one roof

Harvard University Museum 24 Oxford Street (off Kirkland)

PHONE: 495–1910 (recorded information).

PARKING: For metered parking, follow Everett Street to the end and turn left at the lot beyond the white building. Meters are at the far end.

OPEN: Year-round, daily except New Year's, July 4, Thanksgiving, and Christmas. Monday–Saturday 9–4:30, Sundays 1–4:30.

ADMISSION: $1.50 adults, $.50 under 16. Free on Mondays (except national holidays), and for organized groups of Boston and Cambridge schoolchildren. Adult group rates available.

GROUPS: Please make reservations (495–2248), even for unguided visits.

GIFT SHOPS: Considered special. Botanical has slides, postcards, and books; Geology and Zoology have rocks, minerals, books, shells, jewelry, stuffed dinosaurs, and peacock feathers; Peabody has constantly changing ethnographic items.

GUIDED TOURS: By arrangement (495–2341). Fee charged.

CHILDREN'S PROGRAMS: Series Saturday mornings at the Museum of Comparative Zoology.

HANDICAPPED: Elevators are available by arrangement.

The **Botanical Museum** houses the most popular exhibit. A climb to the third floor is rewarded by the famous Ware Collection — over eight hundred species of hand-blown glass flowers that seem real in every detail. (The few cases of flowers outside the main exhibit may be enough for young children.) The creators, Leopold Blaschka and his son, developed the process and shared it with no one. Their sole customers, the Ware family, gave the collection to Harvard, which uses it as an important teaching tool. Phone: 495–2326.

"Grandma probably has one like that in her backyard in Virginia, and doesn't even know it."
— KEVIN, AGE 9

The **Mineralogical Museum** houses a collection — used for teaching and research too — of over fifty thousand specimens from all over the world. The third-floor exhibits include a large sampling of minerals and gemstones (one display shows the stages between rough and polished), and a meteorite exhibit with several sizable examples. Phone: 495–2356.

In the **Museum of Comparative Zoology** (Agassiz Museum), you're constantly looking up, down, and around. There are dinosaurs, rhinoceroses, elephants, and a 42-foot fossil kronosaurus (sea serpent) discovered in Australia in 1932. The largest turtle carapace ever found — 6 feet by 8 feet, weighing 200 pounds — is here too. From a balcony there's a close-up of three whale skeletons. A recently installed exhibit shows human evolution. And under construction is the new Romer Hall of Vertebrate Paleontology. Phone: 495–2463.

The **Peabody Museum** can be reached from the third floor of the Oxford Street entrance or from its own entrance at 11 Divinity Avenue. Totem poles, canoes, ethnological material from the Pacific Islands, and dioramas of Native American life are distributed throughout the four floors of this archaeological and ethnological museum. A thumbnail directory:

- **FIRST FLOOR:** Northwest Coast and North American Indians.
- **SECOND FLOOR:** Primitive arts and industries, textiles, ceramics, musical instruments, and southwestern United States.
- **THIRD FLOOR:** Archaeology — North America west of the plains and east of the Rockies, Mexico, Central and South America, and the West Indies.
- **FOURTH FLOOR:** Pacific Islands.

Although teaching and research are the museum's primary functions, even a casual visitor will find enough to make a return trip worthwhile.

During the next couple of years, the Peabody will be renovating its storage and exhibition facilities, and certain exhibits may be closed. Call ahead if you want to see a specific display. Phone: 495-2248.

North of Boston

SEE "DAY TRIPS" TOO

Addison Gallery of American Art Phillips Academy, Main Street (Route 28), Andover
PHONE: 508–475–7515.
LOCATION: 23 miles from Boston.
DIRECTIONS: I-93 north to exit 15 (Route 125 north), to Route 28 north.
OPEN: September–July, Tuesday–Saturday 10–5, Sundays 2:30–5. Closed New Year's, Memorial Day, Labor Day, Thanksgiving, and Christmas.
ADMISSION: Free.
HANDICAPPED: Elevator available by arrangement.

Special exhibits and a gallery of American art from colonial times to today. The permanent collection includes paintings, sculpture, graphic arts, furniture, glass, textiles, silver, and models — built to uniform scale — of famous American sailing ships.

The **R. S. Peabody Foundation for Archaeology** at the academy, on the corner of Phillips and Main, is open weekdays (except New Year's, Memorial Day, Labor Day, Thanksgiving, and Christmas) from 8:30 to 4:15. The archaeological exhibits focus on New England and nearby Canada; the anthropological exhibits outline the physical and cultural evolution of man over a period of 2 million years. There's also a study on the comparative evolution of three cities — Boston, Mexico City, and Baghdad. Admission is free. Phone: (508) 475-0248

The **Phillips Academy Bird Sanctuary** is in Andover, at the end of Chapel Avenue, off Main Street. A posted map directs you on a 2-mile walk on wide gravel paths that wind by azaleas, rhododendrons, and laurel, and man-made ponds (look for wild ducks and geese). Sorry, no picnicking allowed.

Hammond Castle Museum Page 61.

Merrimack Valley Textile Museum 800 Massachusetts Avenue, North Andover.

PHONE: 508–686–0191.
LOCATION: 29 miles from Boston.
DIRECTIONS: I-93 north to I-495 north, to exit 43 (Massachusetts Avenue, North Andover). East on Massachusetts Avenue for 1.5 miles. The museum is on the left, a half mile beyond the second traffic light.
OPEN: Tuesday–Friday 9–5, weekends 1–5. Closed New Year's, Easter, Thanksgiving, and Christmas.
ADMISSION: $2 adults, $1 senior citizens, $.50 under 16.
GROUPS: Tours by arrangement. Borrowing materials available.
TOURS: With impressive demonstrations of machinery, Tuesday through Friday at 10:30, 1, and 3; Sundays at 1:30 and 3.
HANDICAPPED: Accessible.

Signs, illustrations, and equipment (only one piece is a reproduction) are well arranged in the two galleries. The exhibits depict the history of wool textile manufacturing, and emphasize the transition from hand to machine production during the Industrial Revolution. But the demonstrations are the most exciting part of the visit. In the hand-spinning gallery, you see carding, spinning, and weaving; in the other gallery, you see and hear (the noise is deafening) the equipment in motion.

Peabody Museum of Salem Page 86.

South of Boston

SEE "DAY TRIPS" TOO

Blue Hills Trailside Museum 1904 Canton Avenue (Route 138), Milton

PHONE: 333–0690.
LOCATION: 10 miles from Boston, next to the Blue Hills Ski Area.
DIRECTIONS: I-93 south to Route 128 north, to exit 64 (Route 138 north).
Ⓣ: Mattapan on the Red Line; then the Canton–Blue Hill bus (828-5010) or the Brush Hill bus (436-4100).

OPEN: Tuesday–Sunday 10–5. Closed Mondays except state holidays, and Thanksgiving, Christmas, and New Year's.

AVERAGE STAY: 45 minutes.

ADMISSION: $1 adults, $.50 ages 3–13, free under 3.

SCHOOL GROUPS: Special programs at the museum and Chickatawbut Hill.

PICNICKING: Anywhere in the Blue Hills except on the museum grounds. Houghton's Pond (page 215) with fireplaces and a playground is about a mile away.

TOURS: By arrangement only, for ages 4 up. Include museum exhibits, a live-animal demonstration, and a hike.

PROGRAMMING: Includes hikes into the Blue Hills, animal talks on most weekend afternoons, and speakers and slide presentations for all ages.

COURSES: For all ages.

JUNIOR CURATOR PROGRAM: Ages 14 up.

HIKING TRAILS: Color coded. The quarter-mile Red Trail (15 minutes) does not go to the top of Big Blue. Follow the Green Trail (30 minutes) to the observation tower, a vantage point for many Boston landmarks. The Blue Dot Trail (Skyline Trail), which joins the Green Trail at the tower, covers almost 10 miles of urban wilderness, crossing only three paved roads.

HANDICAPPED: Special programs by arrangement.

This family-sized museum, the visitors' center for Blue Hills Reservation, is an all-weather place that offers indoor and outdoor activities. Inside are displays of plants, trees, minerals, meteorites, birds, mammals, amphibians, reptiles, and fish. On the touch-table are a snapping-turtle shell, a tree limb chewed by a beaver, a snake skin, and several wasp nests. The outdoor exhibits (free) include a river otter in action, red and gray foxes, quail, pheasant, a hawk, and deer. Marked hiking trails start from the exhibit area.

A shift is beginning to show in programming, and will eventually appear in the exhibits. There's more concentration on the reservation's habitats (forests, fields, and wetlands), human history (Native Americans and early settlers), and creation.

Chickatawbut Hill, about 5 miles from the museum, is an environmental center that offers adult workshops, parent-child outdoor experiences, and resident and field trip programs for school and youth groups (by reservation only). It and the museum make up the Blue Hills Interpretive Centers. Both are operated by the Massachusetts Audubon Society for the Metropolitan District Commission.

Not sure where the town is? Check the map on page 2.

Brockton Art Museum–Fuller Memorial Oak Street, Brockton

PHONE: 508–588–6000.

LOCATION: 25 miles from Boston.

DIRECTIONS: I-93 south to Route 128 north, to Route 24, to Route 27 north. First right onto Oak Street; the museum is 1 mile up, on the left.

PARKING: Free and plentiful.

OPEN: Tuesday–Sunday 1–5. Closed New Year's, July 4, Thanksgiving, and Christmas. Air-conditioned.

ADMISSION: "Pay what you can."

PROGRAMMING: Includes lectures and varied children's series.

COURSES: For all ages.

HANDICAPPED: The second floor is not accessible.

Although a special exhibition or performance may bring you here, the setting alone is worth the trip. The attractive, cedar-shingled structure is built around a courtyard with sculpture, fountains, ferns, and a view of a pond complete with ducks. Shows range from collections of nineteenth- and twentieth-century American masters to avant-garde works.

WHAT ELSE IS HERE? A very large, beautiful wooded park. You can walk a half mile around Upper Porter's Pond to the observation tower, and climb for a good southerly view. Or ride a bicycle through 4 miles of trails (shared with motor vehicles) near the museum. Or fish in the ponds. There's something for everyone.

Museum of the American China Trade 215 Adams Street, Milton

PHONE: 696–1815.

LOCATION: 9 miles from Boston.

DIRECTIONS: I-93 south (very busy at rush hour) to exit 22 (East Milton), to the stop sign at Adams Street. Right onto Adams for about a mile to the museum on the left.

OPEN: Tuesday–Sunday 1–4. Closed holidays.

AVERAGE STAY: 45 minutes (includes guided tour), longer for special exhibitions.

ADMISSION: $3 adults, $1.50 senior citizens and students with IDs, free under 12.

PICNICKING: At tables on the grounds.

HANDICAPPED: Inaccessible.

Special exhibitions quarterly and educational programs for all ages have broadened the audience and dramatically increased attendance here. This no-touch, small decorative arts museum is housed in a Greek Revival mansion filled with made-for-export sixteenth- to nineteenth-century Chinese porcelain, paintings, textiles, furniture, lacquer, and silver. Displays in the Trade Room show the early history of trading with China, the routes taken, and some of what was brought back.

Another room is devoted entirely to porcelain, and two rooms are as they would have been in the times of a China trader.

Well done

The Slater Mill Historic Site Roosevelt Avenue, Pawtucket, Rhode Island

PHONE: 401–725–8638.

LOCATION: 45 miles from Boston.

DIRECTIONS: I-93 south to Route 128 north, to I-95 south, to exit 29. Right on Fountain Street, right on Exchange Street, then left on Roosevelt Avenue.

PARKING: Free, at the door.

OPEN: Memorial Day–September, Tuesday–Saturday 10–5, Sundays 1–5; October–December and March–Memorial Day, weekends 1–5. Closed Thanksgiving and Christmas.

AVERAGE STAY: 1½ hours.

ADMISSION: $2 adults, $.75 ages 6–14, free under 6. Group rates available.

GROUPS: By reservation only, weekdays Labor Day through Memorial Day.

PICNICKING: By the waterfall in the park.

HANDICAPPED: Special tours by arrangement.

It's worth the mileage to see the operating equipment in this expanse of real mill. Guides at the **Slater Mill** convey a strong feeling of early activity as they demonstrate spinning and weaving, before they operate the more sophisticated textile machinery of the eighteenth and nineteenth centuries. The site, now in the middle of a business district, is where the first water-powered cotton spinning machinery built in this country was set in motion.

It's a step back to the 1890s in the **Wilkinson Mill** — a machinery repair shop complete with demonstrations of lathes, drill press, jigsaw, and circular saw. The cavernous wheel pit, part of the tour, houses an awesome (2 tons) operating waterwheel, originally built in 1826. **The Sylvanus Brown House** has been restored and furnished according to an 1824 inventory of its artisan-owner's worldly goods.

WHERE TO FROM HERE? It's a 15-minute drive to Providence and its restored Benefit Street area of colonial, federalist, Greek Revival, and Victorian homes. For a walking tour, contact the Providence Preservation Society at 401–831–7440. Another attraction is the Arcade. It was built in 1828, the nation's first indoor shopping mall — now restored to accommodate twentieth-century shops and boutiques. Eating? Amara's, 231

Museum hours and prices change. Call for today's information.

Wickenden Street, serves natural food dinners in a converted 1750 home. Fireplaces glowing in winter and a pianist add to the atmosphere. Or have a good French meal or just coffee and pastry at Rue de L'Espoir, 99 Hope Street.

West of Boston

SEE "DAY TRIPS" TOO

Cardinal Spellman Philatelic Museum 235 Wellesley Street (between Routes 30 and 20), Weston

PHONE: 894-6735.

LOCATION: 18 miles from Boston.

DIRECTIONS: Mass. Pike to exit 13. Follow Route 30 (Commonwealth Avenue) west, then right at the lights on Wellesley Street. The museum is the first driveway on the left, on the grounds of Regis College. Or Route 20 west, left at the lights on School Street, then bear right on Wellesley Street. The museum driveway is on the right after the entrance to Regis.

PARKING: Free.

OPEN: Tuesdays and Thursdays 10–4, Sundays 2–5; other times by appointment. Closed holidays. Sundays are busiest. Air-conditioned.

AVERAGE STAY: 1 hour.

ADMISSION: Free, but donations are welcome.

TOURS: By arrangement.

PROGRAMMING: Stamp show and course on the second Sunday of every month from 11 to 5.

COURSES: For ages 8 up.

HANDICAPPED: Accessible.

This is the only museum in the country designed and built expressly for the display and preservation (an emphasis here) of stamps. The nucleus of the museum's collection is the famous collection started by Cardinal Spellman in his youth. Among the exhibits are the Dwight D. Eisenhower Collection (received by Eisenhower when he was president of the United States), Papal States stamps and covers, Lincoln memorabilia (including a letter pardoning Wilburn Bybee for robbing the mail), tributes to President Kennedy, a collection of British Commonwealth stamps and covers, and an airmail collection.

Charles River Museum of Industry 154 Moody Street, Waltham

PHONE: 893-5410.

LOCATION: 12 miles from Boston.

The museum is still developing, but it has grand plans for exhibits about the people, processes, and products that were part of the Industrial Revolution in New England. Its first exhibits (opening soon) will relate to the Boston Manufacturing Company, the first successful industrial corporation in the country. Future exhibits will look at other industries — watches and clocks, machine tools, municipal engineering, automobile design, electronics, and photography. Call for a schedule of current programs, tours, and lectures.

The museum is housed in the three-story-high former boiler house of the Boston Manufacturing Company. Today the site is in downtown Waltham. Much of the mill complex has been recycled into elderly housing.

Danforth Museum 123 Union Avenue, Framingham

PHONE: 508–620–0050.
LOCATION: 21 miles from Boston.
DIRECTIONS: Mass. Pike to exit 13 (Route 30 west), to Route 126 south. Follow Route 126 for about 2 miles. Turn right at the traffic circle onto Union Avenue, to the museum on your right.
PARKING: Free, in front.
OPEN: Wednesday–Sunday 1–4:30. Closed most holidays.
ADMISSION: Free.
HANDICAPPED: Ramp and elevator available.

Take one part old school building. Add grass roots support, lots of work, and paintings, graphic art, and other media. The result? A good small museum, quite manageable for families. The theme exhibits include works of art on loan from leading institutions and private collections. The Junior Gallery ties hands-on activities and gallery games to special exhibitions. Beyond that, it's an active place with film festivals, lectures, demonstrations, special children's workshops, and courses for all ages.

NEARBY: Macomber Farm (page 25) and Garden in the Woods (page 194).

DeCordova and Dana Museum and Park Sandy Pond Road, Lincoln

PHONE: 259-8355.
LOCATION: 15 miles from Boston.
DIRECTIONS: Route 2 west to Route 128 (I-95) south, to exit 47 west (Trapelo Road). Follow Trapelo Road for about 3 miles, across Lincoln Road, to Sandy Pond Road.
PARKING: Free.
OPEN: Tuesday–Friday 10–5, Saturdays noon–5, Sundays noon–5. Closed New Year's, Easter, July 4, Thanksgiving, and Christmas.
AVERAGE STAY: About an hour (and you can see it all).
ADMISSION: $3.00 adults, $2.00 senior citizens and students with I.D., free under 6.

PICNICKING: Allowed.
PROGRAMMING: Workshops, tours, special events, and outdoor concerts in summer (page 285).

COURSES: For all ages.
HANDICAPPED: Grounds and main floor accessible; many steps to upper galleries. Sign-language interpreter available by arrangement.

The road up to the turreted museum (built in 1880) is lined with lovely old trees. The estate and art collection were given to the town in the 1940s. Since then, the museum has become a cultural center for the performing and visual arts. Rotating exhibits emphasize, but aren't limited to, contemporary art.

The grounds are a perfect setting for sculpture, and offer plenty of roaming and running space. In spring and summer, wild flowers border the paths in the park (open 9 to 5), and fields of daisies lead to the quiet pond below.

COMBINATION IDEAS: Drumlin Farm (page 24), Concord (page 54), and apple country (page 288).

Fruitlands Museums Prospect Hill, Harvard

PHONE: 508–456–3924.
LOCATION: 30 miles from Boston.
DIRECTIONS: Route 2 west to Route 110. Turn right on Old Shirley Road, cross the intersection where Old Shirley Road becomes Prospect Hill Road, and continue less than a mile.
PARKING: Drive down to the middle parking lot at the reception center to buy entrance tickets.
OPEN: May 30–September, Tuesday–Sunday 1–5. Closed Mondays except holidays.
AVERAGE STAY: 1½–2 hours.
ADMISSION: $2 adults, $.50 ages 7–16, free under 7.
GROUPS: Tours and a program by arrangement.
RESTAURANTS: The Tea Room in Prospect House has a lovely terrace overlooking the valley, with mountains in the distance.
PICNICKING: Not allowed.
STROLLERS: Allowed, and a good place for them.

Although some of the exhibits aren't for young children, the setting makes this a popular place with families. Exhibits are set up in several buildings along a rolling hill, with Mount Wachusett and Mount Monadnock in the background. On busy days (Sundays after 2) there may be an outside wait at some of the houses. (And it's hot in the summer sun.)

Because the **Fruitlands Farmhouse** has so much to see, you may want to make it your first stop — while attention span is greatest. Smell the spices in the restored colonial kitchen, find the mouse in the trap, climb the steps to the drying herbs and the toy collection, and read about Joseph Palmer, who was persecuted for wearing a beard. Memorabilia of Emerson, Thoreau, and the Alcotts — even framed locks of Louisa's hair — are on display.

In **Shaker House,** built in 1794, is a good collection of Shaker handcrafts and products. Weaving and shoe repair were among community industries. In the **Indian Museum** are prehistoric implements, a ceremonial buffalo robe, arrowheads, and all sorts of beading and basketry. In the **Picture Gallery** are collections of portraits by itinerant artists of the nineteenth century, American folk art, and landscape paintings from the Hudson River School.

NEARBY: Apple country (page 288).

John Woodman Higgins Armory 100 Barber Avenue, Worcester

PHONE: 508–853–6015.
LOCATION: 45 miles from Boston.
DIRECTIONS: Mass. Pike to I-495 north, to I-290 west, to exit 20. Turn right onto Burncoat Street, then left onto Randolph Road to Barber Avenue.
PARKING: Free.
OPEN: Tuesday–Friday 9–4, Saturdays 11–5, Sundays 1–5. Closed Thanksgiving, Christmas, and New Year's.
ADMISSION: $2 adults, $1 children, free under 5. Group rates available.
PROGRAMMING: A film and demonstrations that emphasize the relationship of the collection to art and history. Shown weekends at 2:30; weekdays by reservation.
HANDICAPPED: Special programs by arrangement.

Knights in armor line the exhibit hall in a Renaissance, castlelike setting. Centuries-old artifacts, arranged chronologically, tell the story of arms and armor from antiquity to modern times. There are helmets with facial features (even mustaches), armor for children and hunting dogs, swords and other weapons, furniture, tools, stained glass, paintings, and tapestries. No touching in the exhibit areas (perspiration and oil from hands can cause rust), but there is a touch-table on the main (third) floor of the museum.

On Route 2A

Museum of Our National Heritage 33 Marrett Road (corner Massachusetts Avenue), Lexington

PHONE: 861–6559.
LOCATION: 12 miles from Boston.
DIRECTIONS: Route 2 west to the Waltham Street exit. Right at the first lights onto Marrett Road (Route 2A), and up the hill.
PARKING AND ADMISSION: Free.
Ⓣ: Harvard on the Red Line; then bus to Arlington Heights, and bus (no service on Sundays) to the museum.
OPEN: Year-round, daily except Thanksgiving, Christmas, and New Year's. April–October, Monday–Saturday 10–5, Sundays noon–5:30; November–March, Monday–Saturday 10–4, Sundays noon–5:30. Air-conditioned.

PROGRAMMING: At least Sundays and school vacation weeks. May be a film, play, concert, or lecture. Tickets are issued on the day of performance, first come, first served. A small fee is charged for some special events. Children's programs often include participatory activities.

STROLLERS: Allowed.

HANDICAPPED: Accessible.

The museum, a contemporary brick and glass building around an open courtyard, was built and is supported by the Scottish Rite Masons. Exquisite displays in the four galleries may include clocks, quilts, folk art, photographs, books, paintings, or prints — all tied to America's growth and development.

NEARBY: Munroe Tavern (page 66).

A treasure, and manageable

Worcester Art Museum 55 Salisbury Street, Worcester

PHONE: 508–799–4406.

LOCATION: 45 miles from Boston.

DIRECTIONS: Mass. Pike to exit 11 (Worcester-Millbury). Left onto Route 122 (Grafton Street) to I-290 east, to exit 17. Left on Route 9 to Lincoln Square. At the rotary follow Route 9 (Salisbury Street) between the auditorium and the Boys' Club, 2 blocks. Or Mass. Pike to I-495 north, to I-290 west, to exit 18 (Lincoln Square), to Route 9 (Salisbury Street).

PARKING: Free, in two lots on Tuckerman Street.

OPEN: Tuesday–Saturday 10–5, Sundays 2–5. Closed New Year's, July 4, Thanksgiving, and Christmas.

ADMISSION: $1.50 adults, $1 senior citizens and ages 10–14, free under 10 and for everyone on Wednesdays.

RESTAURANTS: In summer, light lunches are served in the garden court. In a Victorian house across Salisbury, at 63 Lancaster, the museum runs the delightful Across the Street Restaurant.

PICNICKING: At Institute Park, 1 block away.

PROGRAMMING: Free public concerts, gallery talks, and films for adults and young people. The auditorium is air-conditioned.

EDUCATIONAL PROGRAMS: Classes for preschoolers through adults in spring, summer, and fall. Younger age groups fill quickly.

STROLLERS: Allowed.

HANDICAPPED: Limited access.

Art of fifty centuries, from a Sumerian stone figure to paintings by Gauguin, Matisse, and Picasso. The collection, arranged chronologically, includes noteworthy Egyptian, classical, pre-Columbian, Oriental, and medieval sculpture; mosaics from Antioch in the two-story-high central court; frescoes from Spoleto; a dark, cool Romanesque chapter house, moved stone by stone from France and rebuilt here; Italian and other European paintings of the thirteenth to twentieth centuries; and English and American art from the eighteenth century to today. It's very much a traditional museum setting, but it's lovely.

Open Space

- What's here? Staffed sanctuaries with programs, huge public parks and lands, and small unsupervised (almost hidden) treasures.
- A reminder (at the request of open space staffers): Wear the right shoes for unpaved paths.
- Another reminder (from tired kids and some of their parents): The return part of a hike often seems longer.
- Picnicking may be allowed even where there's no designated area — if you carry your trash away.
- Generally it's a good idea to go in groups.

Boston Harbor Islands State Park

GETTING THERE

Many of the eighteen islands in the park are now open to the public. Comprehensive information is available from the Department of Environmental Management, 100 Cambridge Street, Boston 02202 (727–3180). The MDC (727–5250) sets rules and regulations for Georges, Lovells, and Peddocks.

For travel information call 727–3180 weekdays, 749–7160 weekends.

- **Georges Island:** See page 227. The longest day trip by commercial ferry from Boston's waterfront allows for 6 hours on one or more islands.
- **Bumpkin, Gallops, Grape, Lovells, and Peddocks:** All are reached from Georges Island — there is no direct ferry from Boston — on a free water taxi that runs daily in the summer. It allows for several hours on one island or for island hopping. Some years the boat runs weekends in June and September. Schedules vary. The information desk at Georges is the only source for the day's schedule.
- **Great Brewster Island:** Accessible only by private boat.
- **Thompson's Island:** Call 328–3900 for a boat schedule and departure points. Round-trip fare: $4 adults, $3 under 13.

WHAT'S WHERE

FREE GUIDED WALKS: On Georges, Bumpkin, Gallops, Grape, Lovells, and Peddocks during the summer. Enthusiastic staff members share their knowledge of the island's botany and history.

Boston Harbor Islands

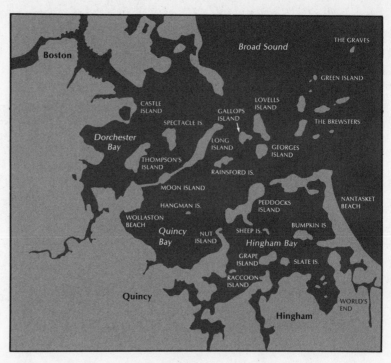

DRINKING WATER: Only on Thompson's.

REFRESHMENT STAND: Only on Georges, during the summer.

PICNICKING: Allowed on all. Only Georges has barbecue pits.

MARKED TRAILS: On all the islands.

FISHING PIER: On Georges, Bumpkin, Gallops, Grape, and Lovells.

CAMPING: On four islands (see page 246). Reservations required.

SUPERVISED SWIMMING: Only on Lovells.

REST ROOMS: Available on all. Most are primitive though.

POISON IVY: Everywhere.

REMINDER: Dress for the occasion. Proper footwear helps.

Georges, open to the public for twenty years, is a popular outing site with a playground for young children, plenty of open space and shade, barbecue pits, a refreshment stand, a baseball field, a volleyball court, and areas for badminton and horseshoes. Explorers like to find their way around old Fort Warren, a defense of Boston Harbor in all U.S. wars and a prison for military and civilian personnel during the Civil War. With tunnels, parapets, and steps to investigate, it can be a long hike. For many years author-historian Edward Rowe Snow led tours here.

Bumpkin is the quietest island. A noticeable solitude. Rocky shoreline for fishing, lots of rabbits, and lovely wild flowers along the trails that lead to stone arches (once part of a children's hospital).

On **Gallops** are many different plants and remains of old

foundations. The high bluffs offer wonderful views of harbor activity.

Grape has variety — including a small forest and tidal salt marshes. Its blackberries, raspberries, and wild rose hips are food for its many birds.

The remains of World War fortifications are an attraction, but most people come to **Lovells** for the beautiful beaches. The harbor side does get crowded.

Peddocks has the longest shoreline of the islands. You're not on your own here: All visits are guided tours that highlight Fort Andrews, built in 1900.

Thompson's is the only private island in the harbor, home of the Boston Farm and Trades School, an alternative school that stresses environmental and natural science programs. The public is welcome spring through fall weekends for day trips, and individual, family, or group overnights (in dormitories). The island, farmland for over two hundred years, is pastoral. The 2-mile northeast trail takes you into a wooded area, along the bluff, beach (no swimming allowed), fields, and coves, and into meadows with abundant bird life and wild flowers. The southwest trail focuses on history, old farm buildings, a weather station, and school sites. About a third of the paths are roadways, accessible to strollers and wheelchairs. Bring a picnic!

In or Very Near Boston

Arnold Arboretum (Harvard University) The Arborway (Routes 1 and 203), Jamaica Plain

PHONE: 524–1718, 524–1717 (recorded information).

DIRECTIONS: Route 1 south to Route 203 east, a little beyond Jamaica Pond.

Ⓣ: Arborway on the Arborway–Green Line; then 4 blocks to the Jamaica Plain gate. Or Forest Hills on the Orange Line; then 2 blocks to the Forest Hills gate.

OPEN: Year-round, dawn to dusk.

ADMISSION: Free.

VISITORS' CENTER: At the Jamaica Plain gate. Open 9 to 4 daily mid-April through early June, weekdays the rest of the year. Maps, rotating exhibits, a gift shop, a meeting room, and rest rooms.

GUIDED TOURS: 1-hour tours in an air-conditioned van. Daily, May–October, $2.50.

PROGRAMMING: Courses for all ages, and walking tours here and at Case Estates.

HANDICAPPED AND ELDERLY: Accessible. Special automobile permits are available at the visitors' center.

A big beautiful place, most colorful in May and June. The 265-acre site was designed by Frederick Law Olmsted to simulate a natural landscape. Paths wind among six thousand different kinds of ornamental trees and shrubs, each labeled with its common and scientific names, age, and origin.

Case Estates, a smaller site on Wellesley Street in Weston, has nurseries and display gardens. Phone: 524–1717.

Beaver Brook Reservation (MDC) Trapelo Road, Belmont

PHONE: 782–9466.
PARKING AND ADMISSION: Free.
Ⓣ: Harvard on the Red Line; then Bus 73 to Waverly Square, and a 5-minute walk.

In the duck pond area, walk across the bridge over the waterfall. Find a rock to fish from, or continue on the short path through the woods around the pond. Shaded picnic tables, swings, and seesaws complete this pleasant spot. (Parking's available at the crest of the hill on Mill Street.)

The larger Trapelo Road area has a wading pool, playground, tennis courts, softball fields, woodland and a brook, and a pretty park with swings down below the hill. Rest rooms are open Memorial Day through Labor Day.

Boston Common Bounded by Beacon, Park, Tremont, Boylston, and Charles streets

Ⓣ: Park Street on the Red or Green Line.

The oldest public park in the country, once the site of public hangings, stocks and pillories, cow pasture, and a British troop station; today, an open area with a bandstand, big old trees, and a playground with good climbing equipment. There's also the underground garage (page 10), the renewed Shaw Memorial (page 108), and festivals. But the Frog Pond is empty some summers, the Old Burying Ground looks forgotten, the grass isn't what it used to be — and people watching has moved to the Marketplace (page 131). Times may change again, but the Common isn't a refreshing place to walk through today.

Across Charles Street

Boston Public Garden Page 127.

Castle Island (MDC) Day Boulevard, South Boston

DIRECTIONS: Southeast Expressway to exit 17. Then follow Day Boulevard to the end.
PARKING AND ADMISSION: Free.
Ⓣ: Andrew on the Red Line; then City Point bus to the island.
GROUPS: For tours of Fort Independence (1801), call 727–5218.

Man-made fill attached the island to South Boston in the 1930s. A great place for all ages with grass, picnic sites, barbecue pits, and a fishing pier that juts out into the ocean. Swimming (page 210) and sailing (page 221) in summer. A good vantage point for watching cranes transfer containers from freighters to waiting trucks.

Charles River Reservation (MDC) Boston and Cambridge, along the Charles

PARKING: The Massachusetts Eye and Ear Infirmary lot on Storrow Drive, near Charles Street Circle, charges $1 an hour ($4 maximum).

Ⓣ: Charles on the Red Line; then cross the footbridge to the Esplanade. Or Arlington on the Green Line; then along the Public Garden to the river.

If you start along the Boston shore at Community Boating, across from the Massachusetts General Hospital, you'll pass Back Bay town houses built long before Storrow Drive, dozens of sailboats, and the Hatch Shell. From here you can walk the Arthur Fiedler Footbridge into Back Bay (page 125). There are several enclosed children's playgrounds, and a lagoon where there may be a model sailboat or two, along the 2.5-mile stretch up to Harvard Bridge (at Massachusetts Avenue).

On the Cambridge side near Harvard is open space, with little to shade the weed-and-grass banks of the Charles. The venerable sycamores at the west end of Larz Anderson Bridge offer shade, and there are benches too, for taking in the river scene.

The Fenway

ORGANIZED WALKS: Contact the Franklin Park Coalition (below).

The Back Bay Fens, established in 1877, is bordered by the Museum of Fine Arts and the Gardner Museum. The area (scheduled for beautification) is full of paths, benches, short rustic bridges, and dog walkers. Just over the footbridge in back of the Museum of Fine Arts is the rose garden, beautiful in season. Neighborhood gardeners grow flowers, beans, corn, tomatoes, pumpkins, even peanuts in 15- by 30-foot plots. The ball park, sometimes flooded in winter for skating, is busy with local competition.

Franklin Park (MDC) Blue Hill Avenue and Columbia Road, Dorchester

The 300 acres of woodland and open space — a surprise to many who think of the park only as the zoo (page 25) — are part of the Emerald Necklace, Frederick Law Olmsted's park design for Boston. Like many open space areas, the park is used mainly by the community. The Franklin Park Coalition, 319 Forest Hills Street, Boston 02130 (522–7431), conducts tours here that highlight native and exotic plants.

Fresh Pond Park Fresh Pond Parkway (at Route 16), Cambridge

Ⓣ: Harvard on the Red Line; then Bus 74.

A popular place for jogging. In summer it offers shaded areas, picnic sites, swings for children, and a large open area for play-

ing ball or just running. In winter the slopes are good for skiing (no tows) and sledding. The only drawback: no rest rooms.

A surprise

Highland Farm Wildlife Sanctuary (Massachusetts Audubon Society) **and Rock Meadow** (Belmont Conservation Commission) Belmont

DIRECTIONS: From Belmont Center, follow Concord Avenue uphill through Pleasant Street. Turn right at the fieldstone gateposts, just before the Belmont Hill Club, and go along the lane to the sanctuary.

PARKING AND ADMISSION: Free.

Ⓣ: Harvard on the Red Line; then a 15-minute ride to Belmont Center on Bus 72. From Belmont Center follow Concord Avenue to the foot of the hill. Enter Rock Meadow through the fields beyond the Mill Street stop sign.

Up to 6 miles of easy hiking in these two adjacent areas of wide open grassland and trees. The sanctuary with marked trails is at the top of the hill; Rock Meadow, at the foot. No rest rooms.

Jamaica Pond Pond Street and the Arborway (Route 1), Jamaica Plain

DIRECTIONS: Route 1 south.

Ⓣ: Pond Street on the Arborway–Green Line; then a 1-block walk west.

The beautiful 65-acre pond, Boston's first reservoir, is circled by a shaded parkway — a fitness course for joggers and cyclists. A good place to picnic or explore water life. Rowboats for rent (page 225). Children can fish the stocked water (no license needed under age 15) from the shore. The refreshment stand is open in summer. Rest rooms in the boat house.

Larz Anderson Park Goddard Avenue and Newton Street (entrances), Brookline

PHONE: 232-9000.

DIRECTIONS: Route 9 west to Lee Street on the left (at the end of the reservoir). Left at the lights, and follow the signs at the fork for parking. The left fork goes to the Goddard Avenue entrance and playground; the right, to the Newton Street entrance, the hill, and skating.

PARKING AND ADMISSION: Free.

Sixty acres of beautiful fields and hillside with a panoramic view of Boston and plenty of running space. Bring bread for the ducks in the picturesque pond. Facilities include a well-equipped tot lot (near the Goddard Avenue entrance), a large picnic area (reservations required for group cookouts), and a baseball diamond. The hill offers good kite flying in warm weather, sledding in winter. Rest rooms at the playground area.

Mount Auburn Cemetery 580 Mt. Auburn Street (Route 16 on the Watertown-Cambridge line), Cambridge

PHONE: 547-7105.

Ⓣ: Harvard on the Red Line; then a 5-minute ride on the Watertown bus.

OPEN: Year-round, daily. April, 8-6, May-October, 8-7, November-March, 8-5. The greenhouses on the Grove Street side are open weekdays and most summer Saturdays.

MAPS: Indicate the graves of famous people and locations of some of the plantings. Available in the office near the main gate, Monday through Saturday, 8:30 to 4.

RULES: No cycling or dogs allowed.

From the first crocus to the last chrysanthemum, the 164 acres blossom with about a thousand varieties of flowers, shrubs, and trees. Many people come just to walk along Tulip, Honeysuckle, Hollyhock, and Camellia paths, past azaleas and dogwood, beech, and Japanese cherry trees; to discover a lake or pond bordered by velvet lawn; or to climb a tower for views of Boston. The cemetery is a marvelous spot, too, for bird watchers (hundreds have their own keys to the Egyptian gates).

The plants and trees — all labeled — date back to 1831, when the Massachusetts Horticultural Society established an experimental garden on what was to become the first garden cemetery in the country.

Stony Brook Reservation (MDC) Turtle Pond Parkway, West Roxbury and Hyde Park

HANDICAPPED: Thompson Center (below).

Three miles of little-used walking paths through woods and grassland, a short bicycle path, a picnic area, barbecues, an ice skating rink, and a pool.

Thompson Center, specifically designed for the handicapped, is open to groups and families by reservation only. (Call 361-6161 or 727-7090.) There's an amphitheater for scheduled performances, a playground, paved trails, trees and grass, a man-made pond stocked with fish and ducks, and, at the top of the hill, a telescope. In the building are accessible rest rooms and a large meeting room with a fireplace.

Waterfront Park Page 143.

North of Boston

Bradley Palmer State Park Route 1, Topsfield

PHONE: 508-887-5931.

LOCATION: 24 miles from Boston.

PARKING: In the picnic area, $3. No charge for cars in the horse van area.

Interesting terrain, beautiful trees and flowering bushes, brooks, open space, hiking trails, and footpaths — all in this large well-kept park. A paved road (cars allowed) takes you through variegated flora, a botanic delight. Watch the Ipswich River flow while you fish or canoe (bring your own). The picnic area is set in a lovely pine grove.

Breakheart Reservation (MDC) Saugus and Wakefield

PHONE: 396–0100.
LOCATION: 10 miles from Boston.
DIRECTIONS: Tobin-Mystic Bridge to Route 1 north, to the Lynn Fells Parkway. The Saugus entrance is on Forest Street, just west of Route 1. Or I-93 north to Route 128 (I-95) north, to Route 129 east, to Farm Road. Left through the Northeast Regional Vocational School parking lot to the Wakefield entrance.
MAPS: Available for $.25 at headquarters, 145 Pond Street, Stoneham (438–5690), weekdays from 9 to 5.

Plenty of trails (some strenuous) for hiking in one of the loveliest wooded spots in the Boston area. Several of the picnic sites have fireplaces, and shelters large enough to drive under.

Halibut Point Reservation (Trustees of Reservations) Rockport

LOCATION: 46 miles from Boston.
DIRECTIONS: Tobin-Mystic Bridge to Route 1 north, to Route 128 north, to Route 127, to Gott Avenue at the Old Farm Inn.
PARKING: Weekdays $1.75, weekends and holidays $2.25. Full by noon on summer Sundays. (The private lot closer to the entrance may be less expensive — and plowed in winter.)
OPEN: Year-round, sunrise to sunset.
PICNICKING: Allowed. Fires allowed on rocks.

Here, at the outermost tip of Cape Ann, is an expansive, open ocean view from huge sheets of granite rock. From the parking area it's a 10-minute walk along a path lined with blueberry bushes (picking in late July) to a summer scene of lobstermen hauling traps and sailboats dotting the coastlines of Plum Island, New Hampshire, and Maine. The tide pools are magnificent. Kids seem to find the ones covered by rocks, big enough to crawl under, where the light patterns are wondrous. (Wear sneakers.) At low tide there's a small natural wading pool, good for children. And many people fish for perch and mackerel from the rocks. Winter visitors see the air filled with white spray. A great place for spring and fall trips when the sun is warm. Always bring jackets. No rest rooms.

AN OTHER-THAN-SUMMER SUGGESTION: To see just how varied the coastline is within a few miles, drive from Rockport along South Street to Penzance Road (on your left), to Pebble Beach — an expanse lined with layers of smooth stones once ballast for Gloucester fishing boats. You can take a long hike on the stones to the footbridge, which brings you to sandy Long Beach. (Driving is a little tricky. Go back to South Street, turn left to Thatcher Road, Route 127A, and double back to the coast on Rockport Road.) Long Beach is actually in Rockport and Gloucester.

Harold Parker State Forest Route 114, North Andover

PHONE: 508–686–3391 (Lawrence).
LOCATION: 29 miles from Boston.
PARKING: $3.

Extensive trails for hiking and cross-country skiing. Popular in the summer for its picnic and beach facilities (page 213), tent and trailer sites (page 247), and large open ball fields.

Ipswich River Wildlife Sanctuary (Massachusetts Audubon Society) Perkins Row, Topsfield

PHONE: 508–887–9264.
LOCATION: 24 miles from Boston.
DIRECTIONS: Tobin-Mystic Bridge to Route 1 north, to Route 97 east (at the lights). Turn left at the first intersection, and follow 1 mile to the sanctuary.
OPEN: Most holiday Mondays and Tuesday–Sunday dawn to dusk. Closed Thanksgiving, December 24 and 25, and New Year's. Office hours are irregular.
ADMISSION: $1.50 adults, $.75 senior citizens, $.50 under 16.
PICNICKING: Allowed, but no designated or equipped areas.
PROGRAMMING: A wide variety, including courses for all ages. Contact Endicott Regional Center, Grapevine Road, Wenham 01984 (508–927–1122).
RULES: No cooking. And sorry, no dogs allowed.

Walk on paths of pine needles, pebbles, moss, and wood chips; cross bridges (are there any two alike?); look at enormous gnarled trees, rhododendrons, yews, greenery, wild flowers, a partially frozen pond in spring, and acres of waterfowl nesting grounds; clamber over and under and in and around the magnificent rockery. A fantastic place with 25 miles of well-marked trails. Somewhat buggy on warm May and June days.

Lynn Woods Lynn

LOCATION: 12 miles from Boston.
DIRECTIONS: Tobin-Mystic Bridge to Route 1 north, to Walnut Street (toward Lynn); then left at the lights onto Penny Brook Road. Or Tobin-Mystic Bridge to Route 1 north, to Lynnfield Street (Route 129), to Great Woods Road.
PARKING AND ADMISSION: Free.

Not many people take advantage of this very pretty area, with its mild hills and unmarked paths. It's about a mile to the observation tower, where all the world looks wooded. The path around the reservoir is almost 5 miles long.

Middlesex Fells Reservation (MDC) Winchester, Stoneham, Medford, Malden, and Melrose

PHONE: 396–0100.
LOCATION: 11 miles from Boston.
PARKING AND ADMISSION: Free.
MAPS: Available for $.25 at headquarters, 145 Pond Street, Stoneham (438–5690), weekdays from 9 to 5.

A big place (3500 acres), with plenty of interesting hiking trails, not all well cleared. The terrain is fairly level.

There are several entrances to the reservation. (Some are unsigned.) **Sheepfold,** the main entrance, is off Route 28, next to I-93, on the Stoneham-Medford line. Here are parking facilities, large open recreation areas, and fireplaces (bring your own barbecue).

Enter from South Border Road in Medford to the **Bellevue Pond** area for parking facilities, picnic tables, and fireplaces. Walk up to Wright Tower, and follow the marked Skyline Trail. The entrance off the **Fellsway East** in Malden also leads to the Skyline Trail, as does the Winchester entrance off South Border Road, opposite Myrtle Terrace.

At **North Border Road** in Stoneham is Hall Pool ($.50 adults, $.25 under 13), a tots' wading pool, and a children's playground. From the area behind the pool you can walk to Bear Hill Observation Tower or around Spot Pond to the zoo (page 28).

Parker River National Wildlife Refuge Plum Island, Newbury-port

PHONE: 508–465–5753.
LOCATION: 32 miles from Boston.
DIRECTIONS: Tobin-Mystic Bridge to Route 1 north, to I-95 north, to Route 113 east, to High Street (Newburyport). Turn left on Winter Street, then right on Water Street to the Plum Island Turnpike.
PARKING AND ADMISSION: Free.
OPEN: Year-round, dawn to dusk.
GREENHEAD FLY SEASON: July and early August. Less troublesome on cool, cloudy, windy, dry days.
RULES: No vegetation picking, pets, or alcohol. And please, no dune climbing.

Hike on nature trails (watch out for poison ivy), walk along the 6-mile beach, sunbathe, swim, picnic, barbecue, go surf fishing. The gravel road, an hour's round trip, is a dusty ride in dry weather. The refuge — a bird watcher's delight year-round — is a resting and feeding area for migrating waterfowl.

(Peak migration periods for ducks and geese are in March and October.) Thousands of acres of dunes, freshwater bogs, and fresh and tidal marshes. Ripe beach plums and cranberries can be picked after Labor Day.

Phillips Academy Bird Sanctuary Page 165.

Ravenswood Park Page 61.

South of Boston

Ashumet Holly Reservation (Massachusetts Audubon Society) Route 151, East Falmouth

PHONE: 508–563–6390.
LOCATION: 77 miles from Boston.
DIRECTIONS: From the intersection of Routes 28 and 51 in North Falmouth, follow Route 151 east for 4 miles. Turn left on Currier Road, 100 yards to the sanctuary.
OPEN: Most holiday Mondays and Tuesday–Sunday dawn to dusk. Closed Thanksgiving, December 24 and 25, and New Year's.
ADMISSION: $1 adults; free for senior citizens and children under 12.
RULES: No dogs allowed.

A quiet place. The paths (you can walk them all in an hour or two) take you completely around the pond, among heather, wild flowers, dogwood, rhododendrons, and sixty-five varieties of hollies (spectacular in early winter). Bamboo grows near the greenhouse. Rest rooms available.

Blue Hills Reservation (MDC) Canton, Quincy, and Milton

PHONE: 698–5840.
LOCATION: 8 miles from Boston.
DIRECTIONS: I-93 south to Route 128 north, to exit 65 (Houghton's Pond–Ponkapoag Trail). Turn right at the top of the ramp.
PARKING: Free, in many areas including the Trailside Museum (page 165) and Houghton's Pond (page 215).

This is a huge (6000 acres) reservation, the highest ground in the metropolitan area. There are woodlands, open spaces, outdoor education centers, well-marked nature and hiking trails from the museum, picnic areas, bridle paths (rentals, page 234), outdoor ice skating areas and an indoor rink, and cross-country trails and ski slopes (page 241). Houghton's Pond offers children's playgrounds, swimming and fishing, tennis courts, two athletic fields, tables and fireplaces, and rest rooms. Miles of little-used trails are indicated on maps available from the Appalachian Mountain Club (page 251) or the MDC Police Station at 685 Hillside Street, Milton.

Cape Cod National Seashore Eastham, North Truro, and Provincetown

PHONE: 508–349–3785 (hdqrs.), 508–235–3421 (visitors' ctr.).
LOCATION: 90 miles from Boston.
PARKING: Charge for beach areas (page 214) in summer only.
ADMISSION: Free.
MAIN VISITORS' CENTER: Salt Pond, Route 6 in Eastham, is open
April through December, 8:30 to 5 (until 6 in July and August).
PROGRAMMING: In summer, wonderful guided walks daily.
Check the schedule for other day and evening interpretive
offerings.

Determined adventurers make the round trip from Boston in
a day. Some exotic highlights: Provincetown has the longest (8
miles) seashore bicycle trail, a paved path by ponds, through
bogs, forests, and dunes. The South Wellfleet parking lot near
the Marconi Station area has an entrance to Cedar Swamp Trail,
a don't-miss short one that leads over a boardwalk. For a more
arduous exploration, the 4-mile Great Island Trail starts in the
woods at the end of Chequesset Neck Road in Wellfleet and
crosses sandbars. (Watch the tides!)

Moose Hill Wildlife Sanctuary (Massachusetts Audubon Society) Sharon

PHONE: 784–5691.
LOCATION: 24 miles from Boston.
DIRECTIONS: Route 1 south to Route 27 east. First right, onto
Moose Hill Street, for 1.5 miles.
OPEN: Most holiday Mondays and Tuesday–Sunday 8–5, until 6
in summer. Closed Thanksgiving, December 24 and 25, and
New Year's.
ADMISSION: $1 adults, $.50 senior citizens and children.
RULES: No picnicking and no dogs allowed.

There are some good introductory courses in natural history
given here, but the oldest (1916) Audubon sanctuary in the
state is basically a hiking place with trails aplenty through fields
and woods, past wild flowers, ferns, brooks, and bogs.

Myles Standish State Forest Page 216.

South Shore Natural Science Center Jacobs Lane, Norwell

PHONE: 659–2559.
LOCATION: 26 miles from Boston.
DIRECTIONS: I-93 south to Route 3 south, to exit 13 (Route 53)
toward Norwell. At the first intersection, right on Route 123 for
.25 mile to Jacobs Lane on the left.
OPEN: Monday–Saturday 9–4, Sundays and holidays 1–4. Closed
New Year's, July 4, Thanksgiving, and Christmas.
ADMISSION: Free.

PICNICKING: Not allowed.

PROGRAMMING: For all ages. Courses, vacation activities, day camp — something every day of the year. A weekend schedule (usually free) might include bird banding or blacksmith demonstrations. Reservations sometimes required.

SENSORY TRAIL: Material available in braille or large print, and on tape.

A great family place. An outdoor smorgasbord. People come to this rural pocket to walk (not really hike) the short trails, and to look and listen near marsh, woodlands, fields, and freshwater pond. A typical visit? A look at the inside exhibits, a walk on one of the short (a half mile or less) trails, a demonstration, and a visit to the nature shop. Rest rooms available.

Stony Brook Nature Center and Wildlife Sanctuary (Massachusetts Audubon Society) North Street, Norfolk

PHONE: 508–528–3140.

LOCATION: 34 miles from Boston.

DIRECTIONS: From Norfolk Center follow Route 115 south 1 mile to North Street. Right on North to the sanctuary.

OPEN: Most holiday Mondays and Tuesday–Sunday dawn to dusk. Closed Thanksgiving, December 24 and 25, and New Year's.

ADMISSION: Donations ($1 adults, $.50 senior citizens and children) requested.

PICNICKING: Not allowed.

Trails and a boardwalk lead visitors over a marsh and along Kingfisher Pond in a 1-hour, 1-mile walk for all ages. Near smaller Stony Brook Pond, part of the Charles River Watershed (and home to a resident family of geese), are ruined foundations of several mills. Always something to see here; it's a good place for young children. Rest rooms open 9 to 5 Tuesday through Friday, 12 to 4 weekends.

Known for its natural spring

Wompatuck State Park Union Street, Hingham

PHONE: 749–7160.

LOCATION: 14 miles from Boston.

DIRECTIONS: I-93 south to Route 3 south, to Route 228 (toward Nantasket). Follow Route 228 for 4.2 miles to Free Street, on the right. Left on Union Street, and first right to the park.

PARKING AND ADMISSION: Free except for camping (page 248).

PICNICKING: Not allowed.

MAPS: Available at the visitors' center, 8 to 4 daily.

PROGRAMMING: In summer, walks, slide presentations, campfire sing-arounds, or telescopes.

Once a military station, now a wooded area open to the public. You'll find good hiking among the geological formations, many dating back to the Glacial period. The 15 miles of paved trails (no cars allowed) make this a popular place for Sunday cyclists. And there are designated areas for minibikes and horses.

If you follow the 2-mile road through the park, you'll come to Mt. Blue Spring (there's a sign), with its delicious water. Rest rooms at the visitors' center.

Boston's skyline from Hingham Bay

World's End Reservation (Trustees of Reservations) Hingham

LOCATION: 14 miles from Boston.

DIRECTIONS: From Route 3A in Hingham, go around the rotary to Summer Street, which branches to the left, toward Nantasket. Follow Summer .25 mile to the lights, and turn left on Martin's Lane (drive slowly, please). If that route didn't please you, coming back cross Route 3A onto Summer Street, right on East Street to Main Street, to Route 228, to Route 128. (Reminder: Nantasket traffic is heavy on weekends.)

PARKING: 10–5 daily, weather permitting.

BUS: The Nantasket bus (472–3450) runs from Quincy Center past Martin's Lane. Or take Bus 220 (Hingham Center) from Quincy to Page's Diner. Walk past the traffic circle (be careful) to Martin's Lane. For a schedule call 722–5657.

OPEN: Year-round, sunrise to sunset.

ADMISSION: $1.25 adults, free under 15.

RULES: Strollers allowed. No picnicking, swimming, fires, firearms, camping, or organized sports and games. Dogs must be under owner's control.

Put on your walking shoes and explore several of the winding 8-foot-wide gravel trails. Over 200 acres of wildlife and magnificent landscaping dating back to 1890. The peninsula is actually two drumlins: the outer elevation, World's End, and the inner elevation, Planter's Hill. Connecting the two is a narrow strip of lowland, about a 40-minute walk from the entrance.

What's "to do" here? Play hide and seek in the tall grass, look for horseshoe crabs in the water, or examine shells on the shore. A good vantage point too for the Boston skyline, harbor islands, sailboats (possibly racing), yachts, unusual birds, and a panorama of the South Shore. No rest rooms.

West of Boston

Ashland State Park Page 216.

A family place, popular for picnics and swimming.

Broadmoor Wildlife Sanctuary (Massachusetts Audubon Society) 280 Eliot Street (Route 16), South Natick

PHONE: 508–655–2296.

LOCATION: 22 miles from Boston.

DIRECTIONS: Route 9 west to Route 16 west. The entrance is 1.8 miles west of South Natick Center.

PARKING: Limited, particularly on Sundays.

OPEN: Most holiday Mondays and Tuesday–Sunday dawn to dusk. Closed Thanksgiving, December 24 and 25, and New Year's.

ADMISSION: $.50 adults, free under 16.

PICNICKING: Not allowed here, but there's a very nice area on the Charles River at South Natick Dam, in South Natick Center on Route 16.

PROGRAMMING: Courses and special events.

RULES: Sorry, no dogs.

Nine miles of partially marked trails (a single one could be covered in an hour) wind along the Charles River — through uplands, wetlands, woods, and fields. Of particular interest are the stone foundations of one of the first gristmills in America, and a sawmill. The solar-heated visitors' center in the renovated barn has natural history exhibits (and public composting toilets).

COMBINATION IDEAS: Cider mills (page 286), a pick-your-own farm (page 283), or a bike ride around Farm Pond and Sherborn.

Cochituate State Park Page 218.

Cutler Park Reservation (MDC) Needham

LOCATION: 17 miles from Boston.

DIRECTIONS: Mass. Pike west to Route 128 (I-95) south, to exit 56 west. First left on Hunting Avenue, for 1 mile to Kendrick Street. Left on Kendrick to the entrance between Polaroid and the Red Cross.

A little gem, good for maybe an hour's leisurely walk (no cars allowed). Paths around the pond go to, but not really along, the banks of the Charles. The pond is used for boating, canoeing, fishing, and ice skating. No facilities. No supervision. Usually underutilized (will it remain so?).

Garden in the Woods (New England Wild Flower Society) Hemenway Street, Framingham

PHONE: 508–877–7630, 237–4924 (Wellesley), 508–877–6574 (recorded information).

LOCATION: 21 miles from Boston.

DIRECTIONS: Route 9 west to Route 30 west (just past the Maridor Restaurant). Right onto Edgell Road for 2.3 miles, right onto

Not sure where the town is? Check the map on page 2.

Water Street at the light, and left onto Hemenway. Or the Mass. Pike to exit 12 (Route 9 east), to Edgell Road. Left onto Edgell Road, right onto Water Street, and left onto Hemenway. Or Route 20 west to Raymond Road (the second left after the lights in Sudbury) for 1.5 miles.

OPEN: April–October, Monday–Saturday 9–4.

ADMISSION: $2 adults, $1.50 senior citizens, $1 ages 3–15, free under 3.

PROGRAMMING: About a hundred programs and courses for adults, year-round. Classes for ages 4 to 8.

RULES: No picnicking, pets, or strollers.

BABYPACKS: Available at no charge.

HANDICAPPED: Please call about access.

More than a thousand (they were counted recently) varieties of wild flowers and native plants grow in this rare and beautiful garden. On the 45 acres are 3 miles of woodland paths, dry wooded slopes, shaded brooks, sunny bogs, open spaces, interesting rocks, even a hemlock dell — a wealth of local natural history. Tall azaleas and lady's slippers bloom during May and June, the most colorful months. To protect fragile plantings, all visitors — including active youngsters — should stay on the paths. Bring insect repellent. Wear walking shoes and long sleeves. Rest rooms are available and accessible.

Great Meadows National Wildlife Refuge Concord and Sudbury

PHONE: 508–443–4661.

LOCATION: 24 miles from Boston.

DIRECTIONS: To the Concord entrance, take Route 2 west to Route 62 east, through Concord Center toward Bedford, for about a mile. Then left on Monsen Road to the parking lot and entrance. To the visitors' center in Sudbury, take Route 2 west to Route 126 south in Concord. Follow Route 126 for 3.5 miles, past Walden Pond and across Route 117. Turn right on Sherman Bridge Road for 1.5 miles to Weir Hill Road. Turn right and follow the signs.

PARKING AND ADMISSION: Free.

OPEN: Year-round, sunrise to sunset.

VISITORS' CENTER: Weir Hill Road, Sudbury.

PICNICKING: Allowed. No sites. Please leave with your trash.

PROGRAMMING: Environmental education leadership training.

The Concord entrance brings you to the 1.5-mile Dike Trail, which divides a submerged meadow from the Concord River. What's to see? There may be turtles and muskrats nesting in the banks of the dike, rabbits, raccoons, ducks, geese — and bird-watchers (there are two photo blinds). From the tower there's a view of all the birds that use the impoundments, among them shorebirds, terns, and gulls.

From the visitors' center in Sudbury there's a signed 20-minute trail. An extension (for a total of almost 3 miles) into adjoining conservation lands will pass Round Hill and its panoramic view. Canoeists along the Sudbury River are welcome to land (no launching) at Weir Hill. Rest rooms are available weekdays 9 to 4 at the visitors' center.

Hammond Pond Woods Chestnut Hill, Newton

PHONE: 552-7135 (Newton City Hall).
LOCATION: 7 miles from Boston.

Enter the MDC land in back of Bloomingdale's II (not the one in the mall) on Route 9, and follow the signs in the adjoining Webster Conservation area. The path leads across a bog bridge, through woods and interesting rock formations. If you go far enough, you may see deer.

A special place

Harvard Forest (Harvard University) Route 32, Petersham

PHONE: 508-724-3285.
LOCATION: 70 miles from Boston.
DIRECTIONS: Route 2 west to Route 32 south, for 3 miles.
PARKING AND ADMISSION: Free.
PICNICKING: Not allowed.

Peace and quiet. Marked trails through pine groves and a birch-bordered meadow — a Harvard University research center for botany, forest economy, and soil science. In the museum, open 10 to 5 workdays (closed Sundays and holidays), are twenty dioramas that show changes over time in land use.

COMBINATION IDEAS: Maple sugaring (page 278) and apple country (page 288).

Hemlock Gorge-Echo Bridge Newton

LOCATION: 8 miles from Boston.
DIRECTIONS: Route 9 west to the Chestnut Street ramp, on the right. Cross Chestnut Street, and turn left onto Ellis Street (Quinnobequin is on your right) to the small parking area.
ADMISSION: Free.
PICNICKING: Allowed.

Stand on the platform below the 130-foot bridge (a nineteenth-century aqueduct), and call out. On a still day, your voice may echo thirteen times. Along the aqueduct, which leads to a small wooded area, are wonderful views of waterfalls.

NEARBY: Within walking distance, at least a dozen shops in the Chestnut Street Antique Market.

Busy some weekends

Menotomy Rocks Park Off Jason Street, Arlington Heights

PHONE: 643-6700 (weekdays).
LOCATION: 10 miles from Boston.

DIRECTIONS: Massachusetts Avenue to Arlington Center, then left on Jason Street. The park is .25 mile beyond Gray Street, on the right.

PARKING AND ADMISSION: Free.

A great view of Boston, trails through woods, rocks to climb on, fireplaces and a picnic area, baseball and soccer fields, a children's playground, and a skating pond.

Prospect Hill Park Totten Pond Road, Waltham

PHONE: 893–4837.

LOCATION: 16 miles from Boston.

DIRECTIONS: Mass. Pike to Route 128 (I-95) north, to exit 48 (Winter Street). Turn right. The entrance is a short way up, on the right.

PARKING AND ADMISSION: Free.

PICNICKING: Some sites have fireplaces, swings, and shelters.

Most people come to picnic at the second highest point in Greater Boston; a few, to walk the steep paved road through the wooded acreage. At the base of the hill is a small farm, a 15- to 30-minute visit depending on the time you spend with horses, goats, sheep, chickens, deer, and donkeys.

Always cool

Purgatory Chasm Sutton

PHONE: 508–234–3733.

LOCATION: 50 miles from Boston.

Where Else?

Reminder: When a specific area is highlighted by the media, crowds come that very weekend.

- **Town forests:** Originally cultivated for wood; now used for hiking, bird watching, and, in some places, swimming. For information about locations and paths, and maps (sometimes distributed for a nominal fee), call town hall.
- **Conservation land:** Many towns and cities are acquiring land before it disappears. The intent is not to develop it, but often paths are cleared for hiking. Whenever space is designated for a specific activity (canoe launching, cross-country skiing), parking lots fill and crowds come. If you want to play discoverer, call local conservation commissions. Several have brochures with maps.
- **Beaches:** Many that are filled in summer offer new perspectives fall through spring. See page 210.

DIRECTIONS: Mass. Pike to exit 11, to Route 122 north, to Route 20 west, to Route 146 south. Then follow the signs.

OPEN: Year-round, dawn to dusk. Very busy spring and fall weekends.

PARKING AND ADMISSION: Free.

EATING: Picnic sites and a refreshment stand (open summer weekends).

The chasm, awesome and beautiful, is a half mile long and at least 60 feet deep in parts. (Climbing and exploring may be difficult for children under 9 or 10.) Some people bring flashlights for finding their way through the caves, but the uninitiated (or timid) can stay above the caves in the chasm. A marked route suggests a path along the jagged rocks, past new trees sprouting through the steep walls and older trees with huge exposed roots. Bring insect repellent!

Outside the chasm, in the park (on both sides of the road): durable playground equipment and picnic sites throughout the large pine-groved area. A 1-mile marked trail through the woods is appealing and little traveled. Also here: a pump for cool, delicious spring water; rest rooms; and Boy Scout campsites.

Well used

Walden Pond State Reservation Route 126, Concord

PHONE: 508–369–3254.

LOCATION: 21 miles from Boston (1.25 miles from the railroad station in Concord).

DIRECTIONS: Route 2 west to Route 126 south.

PARKING: $3 May–October.

PROGRAMMING: Free walks (year-round on weekends) focus on nature and Thoreau. Free guided ski tours in winter. Check the schedule at the reservation, or call 727–3180 (weekdays).

The 1.5-mile, well-worn path around the pond leads, near the north end, to the site of Thoreau's hut. Other paths go through woodlands. Ice fishing in winter; supervised swimming (page 218) and rest rooms in summer.

Wellesley College 106 Central Street (Route 135), Wellesley

PHONE: 235–0320.

LOCATION: 17 miles from Boston.

DIRECTIONS: Route 9 west past Wellesley Hills to Weston Road (toward Wellesley). In Wellesley Square, turn right on Route 135 to the campus, on the left.

On campus is a wonderful combination of outdoor and indoor attractions. There are acres of grass and trees, miles of paths, and the Hunnewell estate's shaped evergreens (topiary) bordering Lake Waban.

An inside highlight: the seventeen **Margaret C. Ferguson Greenhouses.** The first was built in 1887; the rest, in 1926. The collection in the Cryptogram House includes mosses and ferns. You stand on a small rustic bridge and are sure that some youngster (yours?) has touched something when the automatic mist sprays every few minutes. In other houses you'll see cacti, orchids, orange and lemon trees, tea plants, coffee trees, passion flowers, leaves big enough to hide under, magnificent blossoms, even banana trees and pineapple plants. The greenhouses are open just about every day of the year except Christmas. But call to check.

Also on campus are the Jewett Arts Center (closed summers and school vacations), the recycled Victorian Schneider Center, Houghton Memorial Chapel (1899) with the only Renaissance organ in the country, an ultramodern science center, and a small arboretum behind the greenhouses. Lost? The campus police office can orient you.

Organizations

American Youth Hostels Page 220.

Appalachian Mountain Club Page 251.

Massachusetts Audubon Society Great South Road, Lincoln 01773

PHONE: 259-9500, 259-8805 (taped report on bird sightings).

A nonprofit educational organization dedicated to the conservation of the Commonwealth's natural resources. Its sanctuaries offer a tremendous range of experiences (special programs, courses, summer camps) and habitats — from hiking paths in Sherborn, blueberry hills and swamp in Princeton, to rustic bridges and a rockery in Topsfield. All are open most Monday holidays and Tuesday through Sunday, sunrise to sunset. Closed Thanksgiving, Christmas Eve and Day, and New Year's. Directions to each are listed in a descriptive folder available from headquarters.

The society itself is an informational gold mine. It answers questions galore; publishes *Curious Naturalist,* a quarterly magazine for young people; operates a traveling animal program (page 25); and loans films, filmstrips, charts, slides, games, records, and books from its library.

Massachusetts State Parks and Forests Massachusetts Department of Environmental Management, Bureau of Recreation, 100 Cambridge Street, Boston 02202

PHONE: 727-3180.

There are over a hundred state parks and forests in Massachusetts. (Write for a complete list of places and facilities.) Almost all offer picnic areas and trails, and several schedule free interpretive programs. The season varies according to weather and personnel; but generally sites are open April through mid-October, and are busiest during the summer, particularly on weekends.

Metropolitan District Commission (MDC) Page 251.

The MDC develops, constructs, and operates several open space systems in Boston and other communities.

National Park Service See Boston National Historical Park Visitor Center (page 3)

NPS issues a Golden Eagle annual pass ($10) that admits holders to all sites without charge. Senior citizens (ages 62 up), the blind, and the permanently disabled can receive free passes by applying in person. Call 223-0058 for other details.

Outward Bound Page 252.

Sierra Club 3 Joy Street, Boston 02108
PHONE: 227-5339.

The wide variety of day and overnight trips offered year-round includes backpacking, canoeing, cycling, bird watching, beach walks, and issue-oriented city tours. The minimum age depends on the trip; mostly adults attend, but whole families are welcome. The details are announced in a newsletter that also lists information about environmental awareness, conservation, education, and other club concerns.

Trustees of Reservations 224 Adams Street, Milton 02186
PHONE: 698-2066.

Founded in 1891 as the first independent organization in the country for preserving land. Since that time it has acquired sixty-seven places of natural beauty and historic interest throughout the state, from Berkshire County to Nantucket. (Several of the reservations — Halibut Point, World's End, and Crane's Beach are included in this book.) Admission and parking fees, and policies are different at each location.

Recreation

Amusement Parks

Amusement parks — rare, medium, or well done — aren't really an inexpensive adventure. . . . More hoopla, lights, and cotton candy? Try one of the nearby agricultural fairs (page 283).

Canobie Lake Park Salem, New Hampshire

PHONE: 603–893–3506.
LOCATION: 28 miles north of Boston.
DIRECTIONS: I-93 north to New Hampshire exit 2.
OPEN: April–May, weekends only; June–Labor Day, daily. Hours vary. Amusements open at noon, at 1 on Sundays.
ADMISSION: $1. Extra for rides, outdoor pool ($1), and roller skating ($1 an hour). Group rates (25 or more) available.
PICNICKING: Not allowed. Stop at the rest area 2 miles from Canobie just over the New Hampshire line on I-93.

The rides — everything from a roller coaster to a boat trip around the lake — are spread throughout the attractive park. A pleasant setting with lots of shade, a big place that can hold lots of people without feeling crowded. Free circus acts daily in summer and fireworks Wednesday nights.

Lincoln Park State Road (Route 6), North Dartmouth

PHONE: 508–636–2744, 508–999–6984, 289–3300 (Boston, summer weekdays).
LOCATION: 60 miles south of Boston.
DIRECTIONS: I-93 south to Route 128 south, to Route 24 south, to I-195 east, to exit 9 (Sandford Road). Left on Route 6 to the park.
OPEN: Palm Sunday–May, Sundays 1–10 (or 11); Memorial Day–June and Labor Day–Columbus Day, weekends 1–11; July–August, daily from 1.
ADMISSION: Free. Rides are individually priced. An all-day ticket ($3.50) is good on almost all rides.
PICNICKING: Shaded tables and barbecues.

Two roller coasters, two Ferris wheels, dodgems, a tilt-a-whirl, and many more rides for big kids; twenty rides for smaller ones. Also here: flowers and grass, an enclosed pavilion (shows on Sundays), two baseball fields (can be reserved), miniature golf, roller skating (open sessions just about every night; rentals available), and duckpin bowling (mornings and afternoons $.50 a string; nights and holidays $.75).

Paragon Park 175 Nantasket Avenue, Hull

PHONE: 925-0114.

LOCATION: 16 miles southeast of Boston.

DIRECTIONS: I-93 south to Route 3 south, to Route 228.

PARKING: Free.

Ⓣ: Quincy on the Red Line; then the Nantasket bus to the park.

BOAT: In summer, from Long Wharf. See page 228.

OPEN: April, Sundays, beginning on Easter, 1–6; May, weekends 1–6; Memorial Day–mid-June, daily except Tuesdays and Thursdays (hours vary); mid-June–Labor Day, noon–11 daily.

ADMISSION: Free. Rides are individually priced. All-day tickets sold daily except Sundays. Call for time of this season's reduced rate, and check fast-food places and supermarkets for discount tickets.

PICNICKING: Across the street, at Nantasket Beach.

A favorite of many teenagers. At night the whirling lights and crowds make the park exciting. There's everything from a shooting gallery and a merry-go-round to one of the best — and steepest — roller coasters around. One or two new rides are added each year. Four rides for smaller children. (Height, not age, determines admission to some rides.)

Riverside Park Agawam

PHONE: 413-786-9300.

LOCATION: 100 miles west of Boston.

DIRECTIONS: Mass. Pike west to exit 6. Ask at the toll booth for a direction sheet.

OPEN: Memorial Day–Labor Day, 11–11 daily; May and September, weekends 11–11.

ADMISSION: $5.95 (includes $2 in ride tickets); or $8.95 (ages 9 up) and $5.95 (ages 3–8) with unlimited rides. Free under 3.

PICNICKING: Not allowed.

Huge — fifty rides. Many, like the log flume, are spectacular. Another highlight: simulated parachuting in the theater. Lots of live shows — from a strolling musician to Punch and Judy — daily.

Rocky Point Amusement Park Warwick, Rhode Island

PHONE: 401-737-8000.

LOCATION: 62 miles south of Boston.

DIRECTIONS: I-93 south to Route 128 north, to I-95 south, to Rhode Island exit 10 east, past Providence, to Route 117 east. Then follow the signs.

OPEN: Memorial Day–Labor Day. Spring, noon–8; summer, until 11.

ADMISSION: $.75, free under 8. Rides are extra. All-day tickets ($6.05, $4.95 under 4 feet tall) available. Reduced rates

Wednesdays (all tickets are half price) and Friday nights after 6 (admission and rides $5.50). Group rates (25 or more) available. EATING: All-you-can-eat (chowder, clamcakes, watermelon) meals and shore dinners are served in the large dining hall. No picnic facilities.

The park, over a hundred years old, still has the 1898 carousel with wooden horses and fancy carriages, but it's been updated with thirty-three major rides (including a log flume) and an Olympic-sized swimming pool. There are ten rides in Kiddieland. A family place most of the time, except Friday nights.

On Salisbury Beach

Shaheen's Fun Park 26 Ocean Front, Salisbury
PHONE: 508–462–6631.
LOCATION: 40 miles north of Boston.
DIRECTIONS: Tobin-Mystic Bridge to Route 1 north, to I-95 north, to Route 110 east, to Route 1A.
PARKING: Metered municipal facilities.
OPEN: May–mid-June, Fridays from 7 p.m., weekends from 1; mid-June–Labor Day, daily from 1.
ADMISSION: Free. Rides are individually priced. Reduced rates for children on Kiddies Day (Wednesday). Adult specials other days.

A small park with about twenty rides (including a water slide) and several arcades. Fireworks every Friday night at 10 during the summer.

About an hour's drive from Boston

Whalom Park Route 13, Lunenburg
PHONE: 508–342–3707.
LOCATION: 50 miles northwest of Boston.
DIRECTIONS: Route 2 west to Route 13 north.
OPEN: Mid-June–Labor Day, Tuesday–Sunday noon–10.
ADMISSION: Free. Rides are individually priced. All-day tickets ($6, $4 after 6 p.m.) available.
PICNICKING: Groves with tables and barbecue pits.

Thirty-five rides, miniature golf, games, bowling, roller skating, an arcade, and paddle boats, all in "the cleanest park in the East." Puppet shows and live entertainment at least on Sundays. Swimming in Lake Whalom on weekends.

Ballooning

Aeronauts Unlimited 60 North Street, Lexington
PHONE: 861–0101.

Individuals or families can just watch or join in (as ground crew members) the inflation, launching, and chase — all without charge. For a ride, there is a fee — and teenagers are the youngest allowed.

Beaches

Although some of the beaches listed here are miles long, parking areas fill quickly on weekend or holiday afternoons. Try to get an early start. . . . Lifeguards are usually on duty at all these beaches — except Plum Island — during the summer. . . . Bring a kite!

IN BOSTON

Lovells Island Page 179.

MDC Saltwater Beaches

All attract crowds, are accessible by public transportation, and have changing rooms. And all have mudflats at low tide.

- DORCHESTER: **Malibu Beach** (has a tot lot) and **Savin Hill Beach** (not much sand, but grass to lie on) are on Morrissey Boulevard. Ⓣ: Savin Hill on the Red Line. **Tenean Beach** is off Morrissey Boulevard. Ⓣ: Andrew on the Red Line; then bus to Fields Corner and bus to Neponset Circle. Phone for all: 698-3626.
- EAST BOSTON: **Constitution Beach** (near the airport) is noisy, but has a children's playground. Ⓣ: Wood Island on the Blue Line; then bus to Orient Heights. Phone: 567-9272 or 438-5690.
- REVERE: See page 213.
- SOUTH BOSTON: **Castle Island** (no longer an island) is a pleasant spot with an old fort, grass, a picnic area, and a fishing pier; **City Point** (a small park), **Pleasure Bay,** and the **M Street Beach** are all on Day Boulevard. Take exit 17 off the Southeast Expressway, go left on Columbus Road to the rotary and halfway around the rotary onto Day Boulevard. Ⓣ: Bus to City Point from Dudley, South Station, or Copley. **Carson Beach,** on Dorchester Boulevard, has a bathhouse. Ⓣ: Columbia on the Red Line. Phone for all: 727-5118.

NORTH OF BOSTON

North Shore beaches tend to be much cooler — sometimes colder — than South Shore areas. Two outstanding places are Crane's (expensive) in Ipswich and Plum Island (free) in Newburyport.

Gloucester

ALL SALTWATER SWIMMING

LOCATION AND DAY TRIP INFORMATION: Page 59.
NONRESIDENT PARKING: June 15–September 15, $3 weekdays, $4 weekends. All these areas are popular, so lots fill early.

Stage Fort Park

DIRECTIONS: Tobin-Mystic Bridge to Route 1 north, to Route 128 north, to exit 13. Turn right to the beach.

Swings and equipment to play on, an old fort to explore, and rocks to climb — but the beach isn't all that spectacular. Closed fires allowed in the shaded, grassy picnic area. Bathhouse.

Wingaersheek Beach

DIRECTIONS: Tobin-Mystic Bridge to Route 1 north, to Route 128 north, to exit 13, to long, windy (careful, please) Atlantic Street.
PARKING: Fees may be waived for nonprofit organizations. Write to Gloucester City Hall for information.

Small scenic beach, with sand and dunes, at the mouth of the Annisquam River. A good place for young children: smooth rocks to climb on and, at low tide, a sandbar that leads out to a lighthouse. Relatively short beach at high tide. Sorry, no dogs allowed.

Small, sandy, and populated

Good Harbor Beach

DIRECTIONS: Tobin-Mystic Bridge to Route 1 north, to Route 128 north, to the extension. Left on Eastern Avenue, then right just after the IGA.

Ipswich

Crane's Beach Argilla Road

PHONE: 508–356–4354 (summer).
LOCATION: 30 miles from Boston.
DIRECTIONS: Tobin-Mystic Bridge to Route 1 north, to Route 128 north, to Route 1A north, to Argilla Road (on the right).
PARKING (INCLUDES ADMISSION): May, $1 weekdays, $3 weekends; Memorial Day–Labor Day, $4 weekdays, $6 weekends; after Labor Day, $2 weekdays, $2.50 weekends. Buses: $30 May–Labor Day, $16 after Labor Day. Summer weekends the lot fills early.
LIFEGUARDS: May, weekends 9–sunset; Memorial Day–Labor Day, 9–sunset daily. The beach opens at 8.

ADMISSION: Walk-ins $1.

RULES: Barbecues allowed, but no open fires and no camping.

A showplace. Saltwater swimming and over 5 miles of beautiful clean sand. A bathhouse and a refreshment stand. Mid-July through mid-August, insect repellent may help with the greenhead flies (they're very bothersome).

Walking possibilities: It's a good hour round trip to Castle Hill, an estate with rolling lawns and sculpture, and magnificent views of sea, sand, and marsh. Or follow Pine Hollow Interpretive Trail — a 1-mile path over dunes, into pine hollows, and onto a boardwalk in a red maple swamp. (A booklet's available for $.50 at the beach gate or from the patrolling ranger in winter.)

Lynn
SALTWATER, SMALL, AND CROWDED

Lynn Beach (MDC) Lynn Shore Drive

LOCATION: 12 miles from Boston.

DIRECTIONS: Callahan Tunnel to Route 1A north, to Route 129 east, to Lynn Shore Drive.

Manchester
PRETTY, WIDE SANDY COVE

Singing Beach Beach Street

LOCATION: 31 miles from Boston.

DIRECTIONS: Tobin-Mystic Bridge to Route 1 north, to Route 128 north, to exit 15. Turn right (to the center), and left on Central Street to the beach.

PARKING: At the beach for residents only. The free lot behind Town Hall, a mile from the beach, fills early. The lot on Beach Street, near the depot, almost a mile from the beach, charges $3.

TRAIN: It's a 51-minute ride from North Station (227–5070); then a 15-minute walk to the beach (the nearest lovely out-of-town beach accessible by public transportation).

Nahant

Nahant Beach (MDC) Nahant Road

PHONE: 593-2120.

DIRECTIONS: Callahan Tunnel to Route 1A north. Turn right on Route 129.

PARKING: $1.

Ⓣ: Haymarket on the Orange or Green Line; then bus to Central Square and Bus 439 to Nahant.

Saltwater and a children's playground. Band concerts Sunday afternoons.

Newburyport (Plum Island)

Parker River National Wildlife Refuge Page 188.

PARKING AND ADMISSION: Free. Come early (the lot fills by 9) or late (after 3).

Beautiful. Cool-cold open ocean, strong surf (watch the undertow), and dunes along 6 miles of magnificent beach. A good place for walking and picnicking. July through early August is greenhead fly season. No lifeguards.

North Andover

FRESHWATER SWIMMING AND PICNICKING

Harold Parker State Forest Page 187.

DIRECTIONS: Tobin-Mystic Bridge to Route 1 north, to Route 114 north. Left on Harold Parker Road, then left on Middleton Road.

Revere

Revere Beach (MDC) Revere Beach Parkway

PHONE: 284–9534.
DIRECTIONS: Callahan Tunnel to Route 1A north, to the Revere Beach Parkway.
PARKING: $1.
Ⓣ: Revere Beach on the Blue Line.

Some semblance of sand; plenty of water and crowds. Scheduled band concerts.

Salem

LOCATION AND DIRECTIONS: Page 82.

Forest River Park

PARKING: $3.50 weekdays, $4.50 weekends (fills by late morning).

Two beaches and an outdoor pool that's open weekdays until 6.

Salem Willows Park

PARKING AND ADMISSION: Free.

A busy, pleasant place with grass and trees on a stretch overlooking the water, a small amusement area, and a big pier. Picnic tables (jam-packed with cookouts on hot Sundays). Large groups can reserve the sports facilities. Contact the Recreation Department, Broad Street (508–744–0733).

Salisbury

Salisbury State Beach Ocean Front

PHONE: 508–462–4481.
LOCATION: 40 miles from Boston.
DIRECTIONS: Tobin-Mystic Bridge to Route 1 north, to I-95 north, to Route 110 east, to Route 1A.
PARKING: $3.
RULES: No surfing or open fires.

Clean sandbar beach, 4 miles long. Surf swimming (undertow when surf is heavy), fireplaces, barbecue pits, picnic tables, horseshoes, shuffleboard, and a playground. Also here: a boat

A little lost? Check the map on page 2.

ramp, a camping area (page 247), and, across the street, a small amusement park (page 209).

Saugus

Pearce Lake (MDC) Breakheart Reservation (page 186)

PHONE: 438–5690.

Freshwater swimming, a bathhouse, a recreation building, and a picnic area. Crowded.

Swampscott

A GOOD BEACH

King's Beach (MDC) Lynn Shore Drive

PHONE: 593–2120.

DIRECTIONS: Callahan Tunnel to Route 1A north, to Route 129 east.

Ⓣ: Haymarket on the Orange or Green Line; then Humphrey bus to the beach.

Winchester

Sandy Beach (MDC) Mystic Valley Parkway (on Upper Mystic Lake)

PHONE: 438–5690.

LOCATION: 11 miles from Boston.

Freshwater swimming, a bathhouse, picnic areas, and a tot lot. Crowded.

Winthrop

LARGE, SANDY, AND VERY NICE

Winthrop Beach Winthrop Parkway

DIRECTIONS: From Callahan Tunnel take the ramp after the airport exit onto Bennington Street. Right at the fifth light onto Saratoga Street. Right on Pleasant Street to the beach.

PARKING: Limited.

Ⓣ: Orient Heights on the Blue Line — and you're there.

SOUTH OF BOSTON

AND THE TRAFFIC IS STEADY

Cape Cod National Seashore beaches, 100 miles from Boston. (See page 190.) Long, clean, sandy, and beautiful. Eastham has Nauset Light (fills as early as 10) and Coast Guard Beach (parking and a free shuttle bus from the Salt Pond visitors' center or the Doane picnic area). Marconi Beach is in South Wellfleet; Head of the Meadow (usually the last to fill), in Truro. Provincetown has Race Point Beach and Herring Cove Beach (the most accessible for wheelchairs). Summer parking: $1.

Duxbury

Duxbury Beach Route 139

LOCATION: 38 miles from Boston.

DIRECTIONS: I-93 south to Route 3 south, to Route 14 east, to Route 3A, to Route 139. Then follow signs to public parking.

Many outlying communities have lovely beaches that are essentially restricted to residents during the summer months. Off season, for a long walk (up to 9 miles), try Duxbury Beach, which is reached by its Powder Point Bridge — the longest wooden bridge in the country. If you just want some sun in spring or fall, there are smaller beaches in Manchester (north of Boston) and in Scituate and Marshfield (both south of Boston).

PARKING: Fee charged.

The beach is 9 miles of sand, narrow at high tide. A great place for out-of-season walks.

Hull

Nantasket Beach (MDC)

PHONE: 925–0054.
LOCATION: 16 miles from Boston
DIRECTIONS: I-93 south to Route 3 south, to Route 228. It's bumper to bumper on weekends.
PARKING: $1.
Ⓣ: Quincy on the Red Line; then the Nantasket bus.
BOAT: In summer, from Long Wharf. See page 228.
RULES: Surfing in restricted area only.

Large, but still crowded on warm days. A children's playground; band concerts on Wednesdays, weekends, and holidays; and an amusement park (page 208) across the street.

Milton

Houghton's Pond (MDC) Blue Hills Reservation, Hillside Street

PHONE: 696–9875, 698–3626.
LOCATION: 8 miles from Boston.
DIRECTIONS: I-93 south to Route 128 north, to Route 138 north. Right at the first set of traffic lights.

A freshwater pond, tot lot, tennis courts and baseball fields, picnic areas, and a bathhouse. Crowded.

Quincy

Wollaston Beach (MDC) Quincy Shore Drive

PHONE: 773–7954.
Ⓣ: Wollaston on the Red Line; then Bus 217 to the beach.

High tide is great; low tide goes out forever, and is muddy and sometimes smelly. A good family beach during the day. Busy with birders in winter.

Sandwich

Scusset State Beach

PHONE: 508–888–0859.

LOCATION: 59 miles from Boston.

DIRECTIONS: I-93 south to Route 3 south, to South Sagamore Circle (don't go over the bridge).

PARKING: $3.

A popular place for its sandy beach, cool calm water, playground, and fishing pier (jutting out into Cape Cod Canal). Fireplaces and a snack bar.

South Carver

TWO GOOD PONDS WITH SANDY BEACHES

Myles Standish State Forest

PHONE: 508–866–2526.

LOCATION: 41 miles from Boston.

DIRECTIONS: I-93 south to Route 3 south, to Route 44 west. Then follow the signs.

PARKING: $3. Fills to capacity on warm days.

South Dartmouth

Demarest Lloyd State Park Route 6

LOCATION: 60 miles from Boston.

DIRECTIONS: I-93 south to Route 128 north, to Route 24 south, to Route 6 east. Right (south) on Chase Road, right on Russells Mills Road (which turns into Horseneck Road), and left on Barney's Joy Road.

PARKING: $3.

A small saltwater beach, shallow for a distance. Excellent for young children. A shaded picnic area. And not too crowded.

Westport

Horseneck State Beach Route 88

PHONE: 508–636–8816

LOCATION: 55 miles from Boston.

DIRECTIONS: I-93 south to Route 128 north, to Route 24 south, to I-195 east, to single-lane Route 88.

PARKING: $3.

Surf, slight undertow, and warm water. Picnic tables and barbecues (plan to have supper near the protective dunes). A great place for camp groups, families, all ages. Highly recommended. Caution: Watch young children at low tide (there's a sharp drop).

WEST OF BOSTON

Ashland

Ashland State Park Route 135

PHONE: 508–435–4303.

LOCATION: 22 miles from Boston.

DIRECTIONS: Route 9 west to Route 16 (toward Wellesley), to Route 135 west.

PARKING: $3.

Small swimming area in a lovely setting, surrounded by woods and picnic areas (with barbecues). Good family place. Not usually mobbed.

Concord

TENDS TO GET CROWDED

Walden Pond State Reservation Page 199.

PHONE: 508–369–3254.
SEASON: Memorial Day–Labor Day.

Hopkinton

Hopkinton State Park Route 85

PHONE: 508–435–4303.
LOCATION: 26.2 miles from Boston (by Boston Marathon measurements!).
DIRECTIONS: Route 9 west to Route 85 south.
PARKING: $3. The lot fills by 10 on weekends. (Cars are in line by 8.)
GROUPS: Reservations (100 people minimum) for a special area are accepted as of March 1. Fills early.

The long straight beach gets very crowded with teenagers. Picnic tables in a wooded setting. Rest rooms equipped for the handicapped.

NEARBY: Weston Nurseries on Route 135. Vast display of trees and shrubs. Open Monday through Saturday. Phone: 435–3414 or 235–3431 (Wellesley).

Natick

Cochituate State Park Route 30 (near the turnpike interchange)

PHONE: 508–653–9641.
LOCATION: 15 miles from Boston.
DIRECTIONS: Mass. Pike west to exit 13 (Route 30 east.)
PARKING: $3.

A very busy place with a well-used swimming area and boating. Picnic tables in wooded spots.

Bicycling

Although the area has a growing number of cyclists, Boston does not have European-style bikeways. City routes challenge the best of riders. For help in setting a route, check with the Boston Area Bicycle Coalition (page 220).

PATHS

In town, the major path (5- to 25-mile loops depending on the bridge you cross) is along the **Charles.** From Massachusetts General Hospital it's about 2.5 miles to Massachusetts Avenue on the Boston side, another mile to the BU Bridge, another 2.5 miles to the Larz Anderson Bridge. Less traveled is the area beyond here to Watertown, which should all be paved by the time you read this. Around the Esplanade and Back Bay it can be an obstacle course among joggers, skaters, and other cyclists. Pedal with caution.

The signed Watertown to Cambridge side is quiet and pretty, and then it's straightforward all the way to the Charles River Dam.

Other MDC paths: Trails at **Stony Brook Reservation** (page 185) start at West Roxbury Parkway and Washington Street in Roslindale, and lead through 2 to 5 miles of forest. In Somerville, the **Mystic River Reservation** offers a couple of miles.

Near the water, not too far away, is Nahant, a good area for about 5 miles of springtime cycling. Farther out, in Hingham, **Wompatuck State Park** (page 192) has 15 miles of trails without crossroads.

MAPS

American Youth Hostels (page 220) offers routes — all with hostels — north, south, and west from Boston. Among the new maps constantly being added are routes in other parts of the country.

The **Massachusetts Department of Environmental Management** distributes a free atlas of ten rides in eastern Massachusetts. (Write the Division of Forests and Parks, 100 Cambridge Street, Boston 02202, or call 727-3180.) The routes have been designed and tested by local bicycle groups (mostly the Charles River Wheelmen). Families with small children may find the distances a bit difficult to tackle, although several rides can be shortened to 15-mile loops. The route on DEM's free Boston–Cape Cod Bikeway map (from the Charles River to Woods Hole and Provincetown) is not for inexperienced cyclists.

The **Explorer Recreational Map,** $1.95 at most map counters and bike stores, is a great map for "discoveries" — New England barns and rural settings a block in from busy numbered roads. The map indicates carefully selected back roads within a 20-mile radius of Boston. It also shows topographical features of local hiking areas.

REPAIRS

Finding a place that repairs bikes isn't difficult — no satisfaction guaranteed, however. Watch newspaper listings (under "Bicycles") for the repair clinics held by organizations, museums, and bicycle stores.

Of particular interest is the **Bicycle Repair Collective,** 351 Broadway (next to Longfellow School), Cambridge. There are three price levels (all reasonable): for space and tools, for mechanics' help, and for mechanics' work. The staff encourages cyclists to know their own bicycle — and to commute on two wheels. Classes: On bike repair and riding techniques. Open: Monday through Saturday (hours vary). Phone: 868-3392.

RENTALS

Near Boston is **Herson Cycle,** at 1250 Cambridge Street (near Prospect in Inman Square), Cambridge. Other places sometimes rent, but this is the only place close to the city that has for years — and plans to continue. The shop rents 3- and 10-speed bicycles at weekday and weekend rates. Call to check deposit information. Open: Monday through Saturday, and most Sundays. Phone: 876–4000.

To the north, there's **L. E. Smith** (page 82) in Rockport. To the south, **Cohasset Cycle Sports** at 113 Apley Road has maps of scenic routes and 3-speed bikes. Phone: 383–0707. To the west, **Lincoln Guide Service** on Lincoln Road (at the railroad tracks in Lincoln) rents 3-speed and 10-speed bikes. Phone: 259–9204.

ORGANIZATIONS

American Youth Hostels Greater Boston Council, 1020 Commonwealth Avenue (across from Eastern Mountain Sports), Boston 02215

PHONE: 731–6692, 731–5430 (recorded information).

Programs are open to all ages. Call for information (noon to 6 weekdays, until 8 on Thursdays) about day trips, hosteling, and group trips here and abroad. AYH also plans mountain climbing, skiing, sailing, and canoe trips.

Day cycling trips, 15 miles or more round trip, are held in the Boston area almost every Saturday and Sunday year-round. There is no minimum age or membership necessary for these trips. Fees: $.50 up.

Hostels charge between $3.50 and $5.50 a night (depending on place and season). Family rooms (one for the whole family) are available in many locations. Reservations suggested. All have kitchen facilities. Some duties are expected of hostelers. Among the nineteen facilities in Massachusetts are a pullman train in East Bridgewater, a renovated barn in Littleton, and a former life-saving station in Nantucket. New hostels are constantly being added.

Boston Area Bicycle Coalition 3 Joy Street, Boston 02108

PHONE: 491–RIDE.

The BABC is a volunteer organization primarily interested in the bicycle as transportation. Its programs on safe riding encompass weather conditions, heavy traffic, and the "Boston Driver."

Charles River Wheelmen 3 Bow Street, Cambridge 02138

PHONE: 489–3141 (evenings).

Group rides along well-marked routes are open to all — members and nonmembers, individuals and families — without charge. Everything from short 15-mile loops to 100-mile jaunts are scheduled on most Sundays, year-round.

Other Organizations

Day, weekend, and extended trips are offered by many groups. They're usually listed (under "Bicycling") in the *Boston Globe's*

Thursday Calendar. Overnight arrangements include camping, hosteling, and inn hopping.

Bird Watching

A serious activity that's enjoyed by many. (Some get "hooked" at a very young age.) Field trips (no charge), an hour or a day long, start as early as 5 in the morning. Leaders act as narrators, identifying sounds and finding species in marsh, woods, or wherever. They also give directions to beginners. A good clearinghouse for information about how to start, publications, and current trips is the Natural History Services Department of the Massachusetts Audubon Society (page 200).

Boating

LESSONS

Safety courses are offered someplace in the area year-round. Families are welcome; and often there are special sessions for young people. Check with the **Massachusetts Division of Marine and Recreational Vehicles,** 64 Causeway Street, Boston 02114 (727-3900), or with the **U.S. Coast Guard Auxiliary,** 150 Causeway Street, Boston 02114 (223-7073).

Free sailing lessons for all ages at two MDC facilities:

- SOMERVILLE: Shore Drive off Mystic Avenue, near I-93. Phone: 628-9610.
- SOUTH BOSTON: Castle Island (page 180). Phone: 269-9808.

Community Boating (page 224) includes sailing instruction in its reasonable membership rates.

The **Charles River Canoe Service** (page 225) offers canoeing lessons.

LAUNCHING AREAS

There's no charge for most public ramps, including those along the Charles in Brighton on **Nonantum Road** (near the skating rink) and in Cambridge at **Magazine Beach** (off Memorial Drive, near Stop & Shop). For other launching sites under MDC jurisdiction, call 727-5215. For statewide locations contact the Commonwealth of Massachusetts Public Access Board, 100 Cambridge Street, Boston 02202 (727-1614).

There are several canoe-launching areas along the Charles:

- DOVER-NEEDHAM: At the **Charles River Village Falls** canoeists

Before you go out, check marine weather by calling 569-3700.

Sailing

Community Boating 21 Embankment Road (near the Hatch Shell)
PHONE: 523–1028, 523–8571, 523–9763.
Ⓣ: Charles on the Red Line; then across the footbridge over Storrow Drive.
PARKING: Off-hours parking at a discount at the Mass. Eye and Ear visitors' lot.
OPEN: April–October daily.
JUNIOR PROGRAM: For ages 11 to 17 — the biggest bargain in town — $1 for the entire season. Juniors have their own shore school, racing program, social program (outings and canoes), and hours (weekdays 9–3, Saturdays 9–1).

This central, well-equipped facility on the Charles offers everything to everyone at reasonable rates. Open membership — by the month or season — includes the use of sailboats and all instruction. (And members who pass the sailing test have interchangeable benefits with Regatta Point Community Sailing, North Lake Avenue, Worcester, (508) 727–2140.)

travel downstream of the dam. Park at the end of South Street, off Route 135. To paddle upstream of the dam, take a right here onto Fisher Street. Another site in Needham is **Cutler Park Reservation** (page 194).
- NEWTON-WESTON: Off Recreation Road in Weston, at exit 51 off Route 128 (I-95).

RENTALS

CANOES, ROWBOATS, AND SAILBOATS

There are no sailboats for rent in Boston, but free sailboats are available at the MDC sites in Somerville and South Boston (page 221). Although there are no rentals at Community Boating (see box), it may be the best local deal for sailors. Private sailing clubs, listed in the Yellow Pages, do not rent.

Concord

South Bridge Boat House Main Street (just beyond Concord Center, on the Concord River)
PHONE: 508–369–9438.
LOCATION, DIRECTIONS, AND TRAIN: See page 54.
OPEN: April–October, weekdays (except Monday mornings) 10–6, weekends 9:30–dusk. No reservations. Arrive early on week-

ends (plan on up to an hour's wait on sunny weekend after-noons).

CANOES AND ROWBOATS: Weekdays $4 an hour, $16 a day; week-ends $5 an hour, $24 a day. Student rates ($2.50 an hour, $13 a day) available weekdays only.

Bring lunch for a riverbank stop (no fires allowed), perhaps at Old North Bridge (page 54) or Great Meadows National Wild-life Refuge (page 195). You can paddle up to 50 miles here. Re-minder: The return trip is against the current.

Ipswich

Foote Brothers 356 Topsfield Road

PHONE: 508–356–9771.
LOCATION: 32 miles north of Boston.
DIRECTIONS: Tobin-Mystic Bridge to Route 1 north. At the sec-ond light after the Topsfield fairgrounds, take Ipswich Road (which becomes Topsfield Road) to the landing.
OPEN: Whenever weather permits.
CANOES: $5 first hour, $3 after. Day rates: $10 weekdays, $12 weekends. Reservations, accepted up to three weeks in ad-vance, are essential for spring and summer weekends.
CAMPING: Ask about overnight arrangements on an island that's a wildlife sanctuary.

Jamaica Plain

Jamaica Pond Boat House 507 Jamaicaway (Route 1)

PHONE: 522–4944.
DIRECTIONS AND ⓣ: Page 184.
OPEN: Early April–September, dawn to dusk daily. Reservations aren't necessary.
ROWBOATS: $2 an hour; $5 deposit.
FISHING: Bring your rod. The 50-foot-deep pond is stocked.
RULES: Renters must be able to swim.

Marblehead

Marblehead Rental Boat 81 Front Street

PHONE: 631–2259.
LOCATION AND DIRECTIONS: Page 68.
OPEN: May–October daily.
SAILBOATS: $15–$20 first hour, $20–$25 second hour. Morning, afternoon, and all-day rates available. Smallest boat available: 12 feet, for two people.
OUTBOARDS AND ROWBOATS: Call for rates.

Natick

Cochituate State Park Page 218.
Call for this year's arrangements.

Newton

Charles River Canoe Service 2401 Commonwealth Avenue (Route 30)

PHONE: 527–9885.

T: Riverside on the Riverside–Green Line; then a 20-minute walk.

OPEN: April (late March if warm)–October, weekdays noon to dusk, weekends and holidays 9–dusk. On nice afternoons and weekends, there may be a 30-minute wait. No reservations.

CANOES: Weekdays $3.50 an hour, $15 a day; weekends $4.50 first hour, $3.50 each additional hour, $16 a day. Come back with a bounty of trash and your fee is reduced $1. Group rates available.

CAR RACKS: Rentals available.

RULES: Under 18 without an adult must have a signed permission form.

Canoes can take three people; four if two are young children. Most day-trippers paddle 6 miles or so, and bring a picnic to eat along the banks. With portage, it's possible to go farther.

The center offers instruction, and excursions and weekend trips on the Charles and other waterways for novices and experienced paddlers.

Boat Trips

FROM BOSTON HARBOR

BRING A SWEATER!

Several companies sail from the waterfront:

- **AC Cruise Lines:** Pier 1 (Northern Avenue between James Hook Lobsters and Museum Wharf). **T**: South Station on the Red Line; then a 5-minute walk. Phone: 426-8419.
- **Bay State-Spray & Provincetown Steamship Company:** 20 Long Wharf (the red ticket office opposite the Chart House). **T**: Aquarium on the Blue Line, and you're right there. Phone: 723-7800.
- **Boston Harbor Cruises:** 1 Long Wharf. **T**: Aquarium on the Blue Line, and you're right there. Phone: 227-4320 or 227-4321.
- **Massachusetts Bay Line:** Rowe's Wharf, 344 Atlantic Avenue (the south side of Harbor Towers). **T**: Aquarium on the Blue Line; then a 2-block walk. Phone: 542-8000.

Group discounts may be available with advance arrangements.

Harbor Tours

ALL WITH NARRATION ABOUT LANDMARKS

A 90-minute harbor tour can turn into a day trip if you choose to spend time on one (or more) of the islands. All **Bay State** and **Massachusetts Bay Line** trips to Georges Island tour the harbor. **Boston Harbor Cruises** runs tours of the harbor from Long Wharf daily between May 15 and September 15, on the hour between 10 and 4, and at 7. The 10, noon, 2, and 4 departures stop at Georges. For fares and schedules, see Georges Island information (page 227).

Bay State's Constitution Cruise is a 55-minute tour around the inner harbor. It leaves from Long Wharf every hour on the half hour, from 10:30 to 5:30 daily, early June to early October.

Passengers have the option — until 3:30 — of visiting the USS *Constitution*. Round-trip fare: $3 adults, $2.50 senior citizens (weekdays), $2 under 12. One-way fare: $2.

Lunch Cruises

Bay State leaves Long Wharf at noon weekdays from late May to late September. The half-hour trip is $1.

Massachusetts Bay Line offers a 3-hour lunch cruise (from 11 to 2) for senior citizens by group reservation only. The fare ($7) includes food. (Some years sunset and dinner cruises — for everyone — are also scheduled.)

Music Cruises

Water Music summer cruises are very popular. The schedule: Tuesdays, the Dreamboat (music to dance by); Wednesdays, the Jazzboat (traditional and contemporary jazz); Thursdays, the Concert Cruise (chamber music); Fridays, the Cabaret Jazzboat. Most sails run about 2 hours. Tickets: $5–$10. Phone: 876-8742.

To the Harbor Islands

GEORGES ISLAND: A 45-minute ride. Usually spring and fall weekends, daily in summer. **Bay State** leaves Long Wharf weekdays at 10, 1, and 3; weekends at 10, noon, 2, and 4:30. The last boat leaves Georges at 3:45 weekdays, 5:15 weekends. Round-trip fare: $3 (senior citizens $2.50 on weekdays), free under 2.

Massachusetts Bay Line leaves from Rowe's Wharf daily at 10, 1, and 3. Round-trip fare: $3 adults, $2.50 ages 1 to 11, free under 1.

Boston Harbor Cruises leaves from Long Wharf daily at 10, noon, 2, and 4. Round-trip fare: $3 adults, $2 ages 3 to 11, free under 3.

BUMPKIN, GALLOPS, GRAPE, LOVELLS, AND PEDDOCKS: A free water taxi runs to the islands from Georges daily during the summer and weekends in June and September. The schedule varies, but if you want to go to a specific island check with the Massachusetts Department of Environmental Management (727-3180 weekdays, 749-7160 weekends). Once you get to Georges, stop at the information desk for the day's plan.

THOMPSON'S ISLAND: See page 177.

To Nantasket

AN HOUR AND A QUARTER EACH WAY

The best way to get to Paragon Park (page 208) and Nantasket Beach (page 215), but on warm Sunday afternoons it's not a relaxing cruise — it's busy! **Bay State** sails daily late June through Labor Day, weekends in June and September, from Long Wharf. Round-trip fare: $6 adults (senior citizens $4 on weekdays), $3 under 12. Bicycles: $1 extra each way.

Swan Boats Boston Public Garden

PHONE: 522-1966.

WALKING: From Park Street at the State House, walk along Beacon (not through the Common).

Ⓣ: Arlington on the Green Line.

SEASON: First Saturday before April 19–last Saturday in September, daily except when it's rainy or windy. If in doubt, call.

HOURS: Opening day–June 20, 10–4; June 20–Labor Day, 10–6; Tuesday after Labor Day–closing day, noon–4.

FARE: $.75 adults, $.50 under 13. Group rates available.

A young captain sits between the wings of a "swan," in back of benched passengers, and pedals one of the boats that have been a Boston tradition since 1877. Bring feed for the ducks, and try to spot Mrs. Mallard and her ducklings (made famous by Robert McCloskey's *Make Way for Ducklings*) during the 12-minute ride. The setting also has special meaning for *Trumpet of the Swan* readers.

To Gloucester

TWO AND HALF HOURS EACH WAY

The boat docks for 2½ hours at Rocky Neck, the oldest art colony in the country, an area in East Gloucester filled with art galleries and restaurants. **AC Cruise Lines** sails Sundays in June and Tuesday through Friday in July and August. Round-trip fare: $13.50 adults (senior citizens $10 on weekdays), $8 ages 1½ to 12; free under 18 months. Bicycles: $1 extra each way.

To Provincetown

THREE HOURS EACH WAY

Bay State sails from Commonwealth Pier (next to Anthony's Pier 4) weekends in May, June, and September, and daily in July and August. Three decks and two galleys on board. Sing-alongs and a live band for entertainment. The boat leaves Boston at 9:30, docks in Provincetown for 3 hours, and starts back at 3:30. Round-trip fare: $15 adults (senior citizens $12 on weekdays), $10 ages 3 to 12, free under 3. Bicycles: $2 extra each way.

FROM OTHER HARBORS

To Block Island

AN HOUR AND A
QUARTER EACH WAY

The 7- by 3-mile island has fantastic beaches. Cyclists will find the few roads hilly. Boats leave from Port Judith, Rhode Island — a 1-hour drive from Boston — year-round. Fare: $5.75 round trip (same day), $4.50 one way; half fare under 12. Bicycles: $1.15 extra each way.

In summer, boats also leave from Providence (a 3-hour trip) and Newport (a 2-hour trip). Phone **Interstate Navigation** at 401–783–4613 for schedules.

To Cuttyhunk

ONE AND A HALF HOURS
EACH WAY

About 3 hours on this small island, with beautiful beaches (less crowded away from the dock), a general store, gift shops, and two restaurants (in summer). Wildlife (deer maybe), vegetation (huckleberries and bayberries), and great views.

Boat Alert leaves from Pier 3 in New Bedford (page 71) at 10 weekdays, at 9 weekends. Round-trip fare: $9; reduced rates for children. Phone: 508–992–1432.

To Martha's Vineyard

Greyhound (page 10) provides bus connections from Boston to all boats.

FROM FALMOUTH (77 MILES SOUTH OF BOSTON): The **Island Commuter Corporation,** Falmouth Heights Road, operates the *Island Queen* daily from May through October. The ferry docks at Oak Bluffs. It's a 35-minute trip each way. Round-trip fare: $7.50 adults, $4 ages 5 to 12, free under 5. (On some first trips of the day accompanied children go free.) Bicycles: $3.50 extra round trip. Phone: 508–548–4800.

FROM HYANNIS (84 MILES SOUTH OF BOSTON): **Hy-Line** leaves late April through October from Ocean Street Dock, and lands at Oak Bluffs. It's a 1¾-hour trip each way. Round-trip fare: $15 adults, $8 under 16. Bicycles: $8 extra round trip. Phone: 508–775–7185.

FROM NEW BEDFORD (58 MILES SOUTH OF BOSTON): **Cape Island Express Lines** sails from Leonard's Wharf and docks at Vineyard Haven. It's a 1½-hour trip each way. Same-day round-trip fare: $11.50 adults, $5.50 under 12. Bicycles: $3 extra round trip. Phone: 508–997–1688.

FROM WOODS HOLE (74 MILES SOUTH OF BOSTON): The **Steamship Authority** operates ferries to Vineyard Haven year-round, to Oak Bluffs in summer. It's a 45-minute trip each way. Parking: $3.50 a day, in two lots. The one in Woods Hole fills as early as 9 some mornings; the other lot is 4 miles away in Falmouth. (Look carefully; the sign is easy to miss.) Free shuttle bus to the wharf. Same-day round-trip fare: $7 adults, $3.50 ages 5 to 15, free under 5. Cars (reservations required): Extra charge. Bicycles: $2 extra each way. Phone: 508–540–2022 or 1–800–352–7104.

To Nantucket

Greyhound (page 10) provides bus connections from Boston to all boats. The **Steamship Authority** services the island year-round. Its boats operate out of Hyannis and Woods Hole. It's a 2½- to 3-hour trip each way. Same-day round-trip fare: $15 adults, $7.50 ages 5 to 15, free under 5. Cars (reservations required): Extra charge. Bicycles: $3.50 extra each way. Phone: 508–540–2022 or 1–800–352–7104.

Horse-drawn **canal boat rides** some summer Sundays in Woburn at the junction of Routes 128 and 38. It's a 20-minute ride along the Old Middlesex Canal in a replica of the 1803 passenger boats that ran from Boston to Lowell. For information, call the Woburn Historical Commission at 935-3561.

Free rides on Lowell's canals are part of the tours at Lowell National Historical Park (page 67).

Hy-Line sails from Hyannis spring through fall. It's a 1¾-hour trip each way. Round-trip cruises (4 hours on the island): $15 adults, $8 under 16. Bicycles: $8 extra. Phone: 508–775–7185.

To Star Island
ONE HOUR EACH WAY

A treeless, rocky (no swimming) island, with birds, plants, and places to think. Bring lunch or eat at the boat's snack bar. **Viking of Yarmouth** leaves from Portsmouth, New Hampshire (page 80). Phone: 603–431–5500.

Bowling

Most alleys that are members of the Massachusetts Bowling Association (and most large alleys are) have junior candlepin leagues from September through March. Special prices and free instruction for boys and girls ages 6 to 18. Check the Yellow Pages for an alley near you.

Other programs, offered at many places: arrangements for youngsters with special needs, Sunday morning specials, lessons, and packages that include lunch. Most alleys reduce rates for senior citizens, and some participate in senior citizen leagues.

Clam Digging

Every coastal city and town has its own shellfish regulations. Check with town hall for license and contamination information before you dig. Nonresidents pay more for a season pass (the only kind available). . . . Children can help, and add excitement to the quest. . . . Bring a digging fork, sneakers, a strong back — and patience.

Farm Vacations

A relatively inexpensive vacation, for flexible families. Most farms offer little or no planned activity. Swimming may be possible on the property or a few miles down the road. Plenty of day-trip possibilities. . . . Food (lunch may not be included) is usually home cooked. . . . "Help" with farm chores varies. . . . Reservations strongly recommended.

Farm, Ranch & Country Vacations, 36 East 57th Street, New York, New York 10022, sells ($9.45) a national compilation. The only list of nearby places ($8 up a night) is available from the **New Hampshire Department of Agriculture,** 85 Manchester Street, Concord 03301.

Fishing
SALTWATER

REGULATIONS: No licenses needed by individuals.

At **Castle Island** (page 180), in South Boston, a 250-foot pier juts out into the ocean. Less-patient folk can watch fishermen and passing freighters from nearby benches. A 435-foot bridge projects from **Lynn Harbor** at the mouth of the Saugus River (off Route 1A below General Edwards Bridge).

Quincy Bay Flounder Fleet's deep-sea fishing trips leave from 57 Taylor Street (off Neponset Circle) in Dorchester. A full day is $15; a half day (morning or afternoon) is $7.50 for adults, $6.75 for senior citizens, and $6.25 for children under 12 (not *too* young, please). Rates include rod, reel, and bait. Reservations recommended for weekends. Ⓣ: North Quincy on the Red Line. Season: April through October. Phone: 773–9020.

Check the Yellow Pages for listings in outlying communities.

FRESHWATER

SEASON: Late April–February.
REGULATIONS: Licenses needed for ages 15 up. Available from city or town halls or directly from the State Division of Fisheries and Wildlife, 100 Cambridge Street, Boston 02202 (727-3151). Fee charged.

A good clearinghouse for "wheres," "how-tos," and publications (most free) is the Division of Fisheries and Wildlife, Westboro 01581. Send a self-addressed, stamped envelope for *Stocked Trout Waters in Massachusetts,* a free pamphlet.

There are several stocked ponds within a 15-mile radius of Boston:

- **Horn Pond** in Woburn.
- **Houghton's Pond** (page 215) in Milton.
- **Jamaica Pond** (page 184) in Jamaica Plain. Rowboats for rent.
- **Upper Mystic Lake** (off the Mystic Valley Parkway) in Winchester.

- **Whitman Pond** in Weymouth.

Quabbin Reservoir, an MDC property in Belchertown (65 miles west of Boston), has several designated mooring and fishing areas. Season: Mid-April through mid-October. Boat rentals: $20 a day (includes parking). Parking: $2. Phone: 413–727–5275.

Fitness Trails

ALL FREE

Illustrated signs along a running path explain sit-ups, push-ups, jumping jacks, or other exercises. Some locations:

- JAMAICA PLAIN: The path around **Jamaica Pond** (page 184) has eighteen stations.
- NEEDHAM: **Ridge Hill Reservation,** 463 Charles River Street, has twenty stations along a three-quarter-mile trail in a beautiful wooded area that's relatively flat. From Route 128 (I-95) take exit 57. Turn left on Great Plain Avenue for 3 miles, left on Central Avenue for 1.5 miles, then right on Charles River Street.
- NEWTON: **Auburndale Playground** has fifteen stations (and great play equipment for kids) in a very pretty wooded area along the Charles. Take Commonwealth Avenue (Route 30) west almost to the Marriott Hotel. Turn right at the lights on Melrose Street, then left on West Pine.
- STONEHAM: **New England Memorial Hospital,** overlooking Spot Pond, has a 1.5-mile course with eighteen stations. The trail is next to the south entrance, at 5 Woodland Road. Take I-93 north to exit 7 (Route 28), and follow the hospital signs.

Folk and Square Dancing

Thriving! Sessions — often with terrific live music — are scheduled every day of the week somewhere in the Greater Boston area. Some are for all levels, with lessons for beginners at the start; others, just for beginners, families, or experienced dancers. Rates are reasonable (about $2.50). For this week's schedule, see the *Boston Globe*'s Thursday Calendar.

Two good sources for current and long-range schedules, as well as other information about traditional dancing:

- **Folk Arts Center of New England,** 595 Massachusetts Avenue (Central Square), Room 209, Cambridge 02139 (491–6084).
- **New England Folk Festival Association,** 309 Washington Street, Wellesley Hills 02181 (235–6181).

Modern Western is done in levels, and is for couples only. The clearinghouse: **New England Square Dance Caller.** The magazine is edited by Charles Baldwin, 80 Central Street, Box NC, Norwell 02061 (659–7722). **Kramer's Hayloft** on Union Street in South Weymouth (335–9699) runs regular sessions for ages 7 to 12 and for teenagers.

Golf

COURSES

Check the Yellow Pages for a full listing. . . . Public courses are open from April through November. . . . Often a long wait on weekends.

- BOSTON: **George Wright Golf Course,** 420 West Street, Hyde Park. The 18-hole course, recently leased by the city to an outside company, is open weekends and holidays from 6:30 a.m. Rates: $4–$8. Phone: 361–8313.
- CAMBRIDGE: **Fresh Pond Golf Club,** 691 Huron Avenue. A 9-hole course, open to the public. Rates: $5 weekdays, $7 weekends and holidays. Phone: 354–9130.
- CANTON: **Ponkapoag Golf Course** (MDC), Route 138. Two 18-hole courses. Lessons. From Route 128, follow Route 138 south, toward Stoughton. Rates: $5 weekdays, $7 weekends and holidays. Phone: 828–5828 (pro shop).
- WESTON: **Leo J. Martin Memorial Golf Course,** Park Road. An 18-hole course. Lessons. From Route 16, turn right on Concord Road; from Route 30, turn left on Park Road. Ⓣ: Riverside on the Riverside–Green Line; then a 20-minute walk. Rates: $6 weekdays, $7 weekends and holidays. Phone: 894–4903.

MINIATURE GOLF

Several popular places to play with (or without) children:

- DANVERS: **Golftown,** Route 1. Rates: $.75. Phone: 508–774–9702.
- NATICK: **Fairways Sports World,** 721 Worcester Road. Rates: $1 until 7, $1.50 after. Phone: 508–653–5820.
  Golf on the Village Green, 315 Worcester Road. One of the best around. A fun house next door with electronic games. Rates: $1.25 until 7, $2 after. Phone: 508–237–0455.
- SOUTH WEYMOUTH: **Pine Meadow Miniature Golf Course,** 1431 Main Street (Route 18). Rates: $1.75. Phone: 337–5635.
- STONEHAM: **Hago Harrington's Miniature Golf,** 160 Main Street. Rate: $1.75 until 6, $2.25 after. Phone: 438–2024.

Horses

HAYRIDES AND SLEIGH RIDES

Elm Brook Farm 477 Virginia Road, Concord

PHONE: 508–369–7460.

LOCATION: 20 miles northwest of Boston.

One-hour sleigh rides and hayrides through the woods and around the farm. Reservations required.

Lazy S Ranch 300 Randolph Street, Canton

PHONE: 828–1681.

LOCATION: 14 miles south of Boston.

Hayrides through woods ($65 an hour for a wagon that holds thirty) and pony rides ($1 around a track).

Silver Ranch Route 124, Jaffrey, New Hampshire

PHONE: 603–532–7363.

LOCATION: 55 miles north of Boston.

RATES: $4 a person in groups of 10 or more for a 3-mile ride.

Hayrides, sleigh rides, and carriage rides through forest and fields. Night rides in winter by reservation only. For groups, there's a package of ride, refreshments, and country dancing in the ranch hall.

STABLES

RENTALS BY THE HOUR

The stables here are near Boston. Some give lessons. For riding in Blue Hills Reservation:

- **Belliveau Riding Academy,** 1244 Randolph Avenue, Milton. Horses ($10 an hour in a group, $12 alone) and ponies ($4 a half hour). Open: Year-round, 10 to 4. Phone: 698–9637.
- **Brookdale Stables,** 627 Willard Street, Quincy. Horses and ponies ($10 an hour, with a lead rider) for rent at the stables or on location. Pony rides (with walker): $4 for 30 minutes, $8 for an hour. Phone: 471–9547.
- **The Paddock Stables,** 1010 Hillside Street, Milton. Horses and ponies ($10 an hour, with a guide). Pony rides: $.50 once around the rink. Open: Holiday Mondays and Tuesday through Saturday. Phone: 698–1884.

For riding in Franklin Park:

- **Jamaica Plain Riding Academy,** 19 Lotus Street, Jamaica Plain. Horses and ponies ($8 an hour). Phone: 524–9739.

For riding in Middlesex Fells Reservation:

- **Stoneham Ranch,** 106 Rear Pond Street, Stoneham. Horses ($10 an hour, with a lead rider). Open: Weekdays 10 to 5, weekends 9 to 6. Night rides (in summer): 2 hours, $18 (reservations suggested). Phone: 438–9837.

Ice Skating

SKATE RENTALS

Skate rentals are available at most private rinks, at Brookline's Larz Anderson Rink (page 235), and at some MDC rinks. Figure and hockey skates "to go," in a wide range of sizes, at Charles River Outdoor Skate Company and Wheels (page 239).

YEAR-ROUND

Summer sessions (rental skates available) are usually scheduled at these indoor rinks:

- BOSTON: **Skating Club of Boston,** 1240 Soldiers Field Road, Brighton, 782–5900.
- HINGHAM: **Pilgrim Skating Arena,** 75 Recreation Park Drive, 749–6660.
- NATICK: **West Suburban Arena,** Windsor Avenue, 508–655–1014, 508–655–1013 (recorded information).
- WELLESLEY: **Babson Skating Rink,** 150 Great Plain Avenue, 235–0650, 235–0627 (recorded information).

WINTER

Rinks

For private rinks, look in the Yellow Pages (under "Skating Rinks — Ice"). Very few are limited to members. All are indoors, and almost all offer lessons and public sessions. Schedules vary from season to season, and year to year.

MDC indoor rinks are open late October through March. Call the individual rinks (Blue Pages under "Massachusetts Commonwealth of: Metropolitan District Commission") for schedule, rental, and lesson information. Rates are $.50 for adults, $.25 for senior citizens and children under 18.

Outdoors

Ponds, and flooded playgrounds and tennis courts are used in many communities.

- BOSTON: The pond in the Public Garden (page 127) is a tradition, but a fairly hazardous one.
- BROOKLINE: **Larz Anderson Rink,** at the park (page 184), is usually open mid-November through February. Different rates for residents and nonresidents, children and adults, and day and evening sessions. Phone: 232–9000 (weekdays) or 524–1220 (weekends).
- MEDFIELD: **Rocky Woods Reservation** (page 241) has an outdoor skating program on a man-made pond and a warming lodge.

The MDC operates several open-but-covered rinks:

- **Brighton-Newton** on Nonantum Road (527–1741).
- **Dorchester** on Morrissey Boulevard (436–4356).
- **Jamaica Plain** on the Jamaicaway (522–8091).
- **Roxbury** on Martin Luther King Boulevard (445–9519).
- **Saugus** on the Lynn Fells Parkway (233–9713).

Opening day is usually in mid-November. Rates are the same at all MDC rinks (see above).

LESSONS

A comprehensive list of places that give instruction is published every Saturday in the sports section of the *Boston Globe*. Some ongoing programs:

- **Bay State Ice Skating School,** 30 Ranson Road, Newton Center 02159. Group lessons for ages 4 up (adults too) — all levels — on either hockey or figure skates. At local MDC rinks. Phone: 965-0636 or 527-3517.
- **Metropolitan Figure Skating School,** 21 Regent Circle, Brookline 02146. Group lessons on weekends for boys and girls at local MDC rinks. Phone: 566-1245.
- **Northeastern Skating Association,** c/o the Charles Moores, 19 Circuit Avenue, Newton 02161. Speed-skating lessons and information about meets for registered amateurs and novices. Phone: 244-9332.

Skating Club of Boston 1240 Soldiers Field Road, Brighton

PHONE: 782-5900.

SEASON: Mid-October–March, Saturdays 2:30-4, Sundays 6-7:30.

FEES (PER SESSION): $3.50 adults, $2.50 children. It's a pay-as-you-go, advance-as-you-go arrangement. Membership isn't necessary.

Group figure-skating lessons for all ages, toddlers to adults. Groups are formed by ability, not age. Preschoolers are welcome Saturdays only; beginners, too, should come on Saturdays.

Mountain Climbing

To build stamina, many try Blue Hill (page 189) first — about an hour or so round trip depending on your route — before going on to Mount Monadnock in Jaffrey, New Hampshire, and eventually an overnight trip in the White Mountains. Reminder: May through early June is black fly season up-country (see page 282).

Mount Monadnock is a full day's adventure. It's the most-climbed mountain in the United States, so you'll find hundreds of people here enjoying the spectacular views on nice Saturdays and Sundays in spring and fall. The Dublin Trail is less crowded than White Arrow Trail, which leads from the main entrance to the park. Remember that coming down can be much harder than going up. Get an early start.

The best source for comprehensive information, guided trips, and workshops is the **Appalachian Mountain Club** (page 251). AMC has eight huts — open to nonmembers — located a day's hike apart in the White Mountains. Some have family rooms; all have plumbing and serve hot meals at 7 a.m. and 6 p.m. Reasonable rates. Reservations recommended, especially for weekends.

Orienteering

Orienteering, over sixty years old in Europe, is growing quickly in this country. The sport combines map and running skills. A course is set up in a wooded area, with flags that designate points everyone must pass. The object is to use a map and compass to locate each of the points in the shortest time. (On every control flag is a distinctive punch for marking your score card.)

The key to orienteering is more in one's decision-making ability than in running ability. It's a sport that takes you into new terrain, provides a goal or destination, and gets you out-doors — and maybe into shape!

New England Orienteering Club 57 Bent Road, Sudbury 01776
PHONE: 508–443–8502 (8 p.m.–10 p.m.).
FEES: $1–$2 entry, $5 membership (not required) for families and individuals, $.25–$.50 compass rental.

Meets are very informal. Participants of all ages range from those who leisurely tour the course to those who are competitive. Instruction is available for newcomers.

Roller Skating

Indoor rinks all rent skates. For outdoors, rentals run about $2.50 an hour, and may include pads, wrist guards, and gloves.

SKATE RENTALS

- **Charles River Outdoor Skate Company,** 121 Charles Street, Boston. Ⓣ: Charles on the Red Line. Open: 10 to dusk daily. Day rate: $6. Phone: 523–9656.
- **Roller Power,** 85 Mt. Auburn Street, Cambridge. Ⓣ: Harvard on the Red Line. Day rate: $8. Phone: 547–0695.
- **Wheels,** 270 Newbury Street (between Fairfield and Gloucester), Boston. Children's sizes too. Ⓣ: Auditorium or Copley on the Green Line. Open: Tuesday through Sunday. Day rate: $5 (group rates available). Phone 236–1566.

OUTDOORS

Where? In many open space areas (pages 175–201), including the **Charles River Reservation, Jamaica Pond,** and the **Mystic River Reservation.** On Sundays, Memorial Day through Labor

Day, **Memorial Drive** from Western Avenue to Mount Auburn Hospital is closed to traffic between 11 and 7.

INDOOR RINKS

Most have day sessions on weekends, and many offer birthday and group packages.

- MEDFORD: **Bal-A-Roue Rollaway,** 376 Mystic Avenue. Ⓣ: Sullivan Square on the Orange Line; then bus to West Medford. Open: Year-round. Phone: 396–4589.
- NATICK: **West Suburban Arena,** Windsor Avenue. Open: April through September. Phone: 508–655–1014 or 508–655–1013 (recorded information).
- NORWOOD: **Roll-Land Skating Rink,** Route 1. Open: Year-round, Wednesday through Sunday. Phone: 762–6999.
- REVERE: **Wheels Plus,** 321 Charger Street. Open: Year-round. Phone: 284–2718.
- WALTHAM: **Wal-Lex Recreation Center,** 800 Lexington Street. Open: Year-round. Phone: 894–1527.
- WEYMOUTH: **Weymouth Roller Skating Rink,** 969 Washington Street. Family night on Wednesdays ($3.75 for a family of five, including skates). Open: Year-round (not too crowded in summer). Phone: 335–1590.

Something different: **Boston Spinoff** at 145 Ipswich Street (across from Fenway Park). Waterfalls, an ongoing light show, exposed brick, and plants are part of the night club atmosphere. Live disc jockey for all sessions. Two cafes — with views of the rink — serve yogurt, pastries, and beverages. (No charge to enter the cafes only.) Weekend afternoons attract families and younger people. Friday nights are limited to those under 20; late sessions (starting around 9:30), to those over 18. Ⓣ: Kenmore on the Green Lines (except Arborway). Open: Year-round, Wednesday through Sunday, afternoons and evenings. Admission: $3 afternoons, $4 evenings, $5 late sessions. Rentals: $1. Phone: 437–0100.

SKIING

CROSS-COUNTRY

Rentals on location — or at sports stores, including the following:

- **Eastern Mountain Sports,** 1041 Commonwealth Avenue, Brighton (254–4250).
- **The Ski Market,** 860 Commonwealth Avenue, Boston (731–6100).

- **Wilderness House,** 124 Brighton Avenue, Brighton (782–5430).

Clinics

Run by many sports stores, the Sierra Club (page 201), American Youth Hostels (page 220), and the Appalachian Mountain Club (page 251).

Nearby Areas

Where to go in the Boston Area? Almost anywhere — open space areas (pages 175–201), golf courses, even the banks of the Charles River. Some suggestions:

- CANTON: **Ponkapoag Golf Course** (page 233). Lessons. A good place for varied interests: You're at an MDC skating rink (page 235) and a fantastic sledding and tobogganing area. No charge for skiing. Phone: 828-0645.
- CARLISLE: **Great Brook Farm State Park,** North Street. Rentals, groomed trails, and a warming hut. No charge for skiing. Phone: 508–369–3350 or 508–369–6312.
- CONCORD: **Walden Pond State Reservation** (page 199). Free guided tours — for all ages — on weekends.
- LINCOLN: **Lincoln Guide Service,** Lincoln Road (at the railroad tracks). Ski on nearby conservation lands. Rentals and lessons. No charge for skiing. Phone: 259-9204.
- MEDFIELD: **Rocky Woods Reservation** (Trustees of Reservations), Hartford Street. Map and rentals. From Route 109, turn on Hartford Street for 3 miles. Rates: Weekdays $2 adults, $1.50 ages 6 to 17, free under 6; weekends $2.50 adults, $2 ages 6 to 17, free under 6. Phone: 508–359–6333.
- WESTON: **Weston Ski Track,** at the Leo J. Martin Memorial Golf Course (page 233). Rentals, lessons, evening lights, and a wood stove in the cafe. Rates: $2 weekdays, $2.50 weekends (group rates available). Phone: 894-4903.
- WESTWOOD: **Hale Reservation,** 80 Carby Street. A 15-mile wooded area. Rentals first come, first served. Lessons for beginners and intermediates. Rates: $2 adults, $1 ages 7 to 14, free under 7. Phone: 326-1770.

DOWNHILL

There are many up-country areas within a 2-hour drive. Favorites depend on facilities, costs, crowds, distance, and conditions. Many areas report ski conditions and lodging information on toll-free numbers. Call 1–800–555–1212 to see if the area you're interested in has a listing.

Nearby Areas

Blue Hills Ski Area Canton
PHONE: 828-5070.
LOCATION: 14 miles south of Boston.
DIRECTIONS: I-93 south to Route 128 north, to exit 64 (Route 138 north).

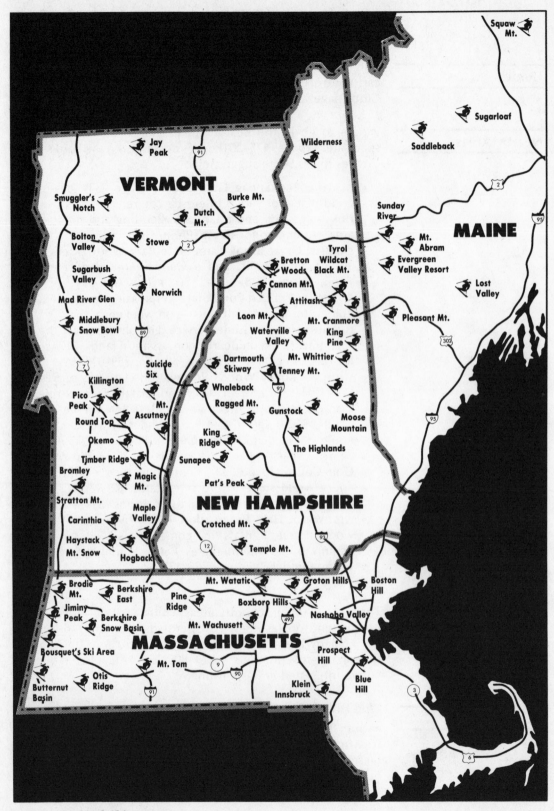

New England Ski Areas

The **Ski Train** leaves Saturdays from North Station at 8:55 and arrives in Fitchburg about 10:15. Buses ($1 each way) transport skiers to Mount Wachusett or Mount Watatic, the nearest true mountains to Boston. One-way fare: $3.50 adults, $1.75 under 12. Family fare available. Phone: 1–800–392–6099.

FACILITIES: 3 trails, 2 slopes; 1 double chair, 2 J-bars, 2 rope tows; snow making; night skiing.

Boston Hill Route 114, North Andover
PHONE: 508–683–2733.
LOCATION: 22 miles north of Boston.
DIRECTIONS: I-93 north to I-495 north, to Route 114 west.
FACILITIES: 1 trail, 5 slopes; 1 double chair, 2 rope tows; snow making; night skiing.

Mount Wachusett Princeton and Westminster
PHONE: 508–464–2355.
LOCATION: 47 miles west of Boston.
DIRECTIONS: Route 2 west to Route 140 south.
FACILITIES: 7 trails, 2 slopes; 2 T-bars, 1 rope tow; snow making.

Mount Watatic Route 119, Ashby
PHONE: 508–386–7921.
LOCATION: 60 miles northwest of Boston.
DIRECTIONS: Route 2 west to Route 13 north, to Route 119 west.
FACILITIES: 6 novice to expert trails and slopes, 1 nursery slope; 1 double chair, 2 T-bars; night skiing.

Nashoba Valley Ski Area Power Road, Westford
PHONE: 508–692–3033.
LOCATION: 25 miles west of Boston.
DIRECTIONS: Route 2 west to Route 2A. Follow Route 2A for 5 miles to Power Road (between Routes 2A and 110).
FACILITIES: 1 trail, 7 slopes; 1 triple chair, 1 double chair, 1 T-bar, 6 rope tows; snow making; night skiing.

Youth Programs

Several organizations offer membership programs for ages 9 to 18, beginners to experts. Trips to various New England ski areas include transportation, supervision, and instruction. There may be openings for adults who are willing to supervise.

- **Blizzard Ski Club,** 23 Central Street, Wellesley 02181 (235–6647).

- **Massachusetts Junior Ski Club,** 1116 Great Plain Avenue, Needham 02192 (449-3074).
- **New England Handicapped Sportsmen's Association** (page 251). For all ages.
- **Youth Enrichment Services** (page 252).

For free ski clinics, see page 277.

Sports

The *Boston Globe*'s Saturday edition lists everything, from boomerang lessons to wind surfing, and a full schedule of amateur, college, semiprofessional, and professional events.

SPECTATOR SPORTS

No phone reservations. . . . Order tickets several weeks in advance. . . . Boston Garden recorded information: 227-3200. . . . Final major league results are available 24 hours a day from the *Boston Globe*. Telephone scoreboard: 265-6600.

Baseball

Boston Red Sox 4 Yawkey Way, Boston 02215
PHONE: 267-8661 (tickets), 267-9440 (office).
Ⓣ: Fenway on the Riverside–Green Line.
TICKETS: $3–$8.50. Special group plans, some just for children, available.

Home games at Fenway Park, April through October.

Basketball

Boston Celtics 150 Causeway Street, Boston
PHONE: 523-3030 (tickets), 523-6050 (office).
Ⓣ: North Station on the Orange or Green Line.
TICKETS: $6–$12. Individual tickets go on sale in September. Group rates available for some games.

Home games are played in Boston Garden October through April. Evenings only until the first of the year; then Sunday afternoons too. Special days with giveaways for children under 14 are held a few times during the season.

Football

New England Patriots Schaefer Stadium, Foxboro 02035
PHONE: 262-1776 (Boston).
LOCATION: 25 miles south of Boston.
DIRECTIONS: I-93 south to Route 128 north, to I-95 south, toward Providence, to Route 1 south.
TICKETS: $7–$12.50, first come, first served.

Preseason in August; home games Sunday afternoons September through mid-December.

Hockey

Boston Bruins 150 Causeway Street, Boston 02214
PHONE: 227-3206.

Sports Arena Seating Plans

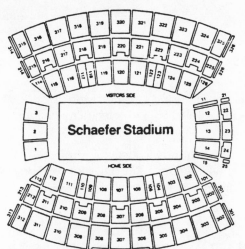

Schaefer Stadium

Sullivan Stadium

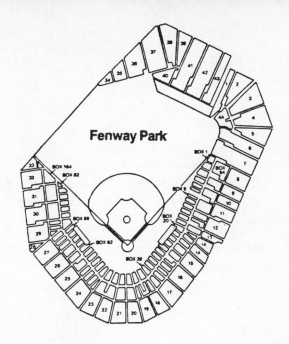

Fenway Park

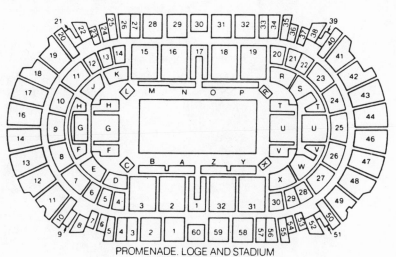

PROMENADE, LOGE AND STADIUM

Boston Garden

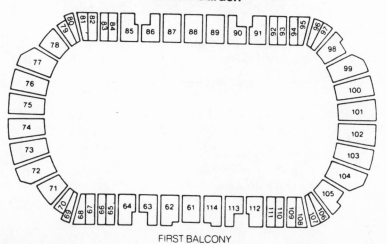

FIRST BALCONY

T: North Station on the Orange or Green Line.

TICKETS: $7–$13.50.

Games are played at Boston Garden, October through March, mostly on Thursday and Sunday evenings.

State Camping Areas

MASSACHUSETTS

SEASON: Most sites open April 15 and close October 15.

FEES: Group campsites $12, cabins $8–$10 (electricity charge $1 a day), general campsites $5–$6.

A full list of public campgrounds is available from the Department of Environmental Management, Division of Forests and Parks, 100 Cambridge Street, Boston 02202 (727-3180).

There are two public areas in or close to Boston that are not operated by the state:

- **Boston Harbor Islands (page 177):** Reservations required. Caution: Plenty of poison ivy! Bumpkin, Grape, and Great Brewster are managed by the Department of Environmental Management, Wompatuck State Park, 201 Union Street, Hingham 02043 (749-7161). Primitive camping, by permit (there's no charge) only.

  Lovells Island, the only one with supervised swimming, is managed by the MDC, 20 Somerset Street, Boston 02108 (727-5250). Permits: $3 weekdays, $5 weekends.
- **Camp Nihan:** Walnut Street (Route 129), Saugus (438-5690). The site is adjacent to Breakheart Reservation (page 186). Camping for supervised youth groups, members of nonprofit organizations. Several cabins and six camp sites. Swimming, picnicking, hiking, fishing, and cross-country skiing.

Cabins (reservations strongly recommended) are available at several places:

- **Savoy Mountain State Forest,** Savoy (413-663-8469). No electricity.
- **Mohawk Trail State Forest,** Charlemont (413–339–5504).
- **Willard Brook State Forest,** Ashby (508–597–8802).

All campsites are available on a first-come, first-served basis, and are often filled by Thursday for the weekend. Groups must make arrangements at least a week in advance.

For winter camping, check current conditions and arrangements with the regional offices:

- Berkshires Regional Supervisor, Pittsfield State Forest, Cascade Street, Pittsfield 01202 (413–442–8992).
- Northeastern Massachusetts Regional Supervisor, 817 Lowell Road, Carlisle 01741 (508–369–3350).
- Southeastern Massachusetts Regional Supervisor, Myles Standish State Forest, Box 66, South Carver 02366 (508–866–2580).

Below are several areas in eastern Massachusetts. All have showers (except Harold Parker) and toilets, and are $5 or $6 a night. Harold Parker and Wompatuck are closest to Boston.

North of Boston

Harold Parker State Forest Page 187.

DIRECTIONS: Tobin-Mystic Bridge to Route 1 north, to Route 114 north. Left on Harold Parker Road, right on Middleton, and left on Jenkins.

CAMPSITES: 120. Tent and trailer sites.

Freshwater swimming, hiking, and fishing.

Salisbury Beach State Reservation Page 213.

CAMPSITES: 500. Tent and trailer sites.

A camping and beach area. Boating, swimming, and fishing. Rest rooms are equipped for the handicapped. Weekend campers should arrive by Friday morning.

South of Boston

Horseneck Beach State Reservation Page 216.

CAMPSITES: 100.

Ocean swimming and fishing.

Massasoit State Park Taunton

PHONE: 508–822–7405.
LOCATION: 38 miles from Boston.
DIRECTIONS: I-93 south to Route 128 north, to Route 24, to Route 44 east. First right on Orchard, then left on Middleboro Road.
CAMPSITES: 130. Electrical and sewage connections for trailers.

Car-top boating. Rest rooms are equipped for the handicapped.

Myles Standish State Forest Page 216.

CAMPSITES: 475.

Not sure where the town is? Check the map on page 2.

Freshwater swimming, fishing, hiking, and cycling. Rest rooms are equipped for the handicapped.

On Cape Cod

R. C. Nickerson State Forest Route 6A, Brewster
PHONE: 508–896–3491, 508–896–3611 (winter).
LOCATION: 90 miles from Boston.
CAMPSITES: 400.

Pond and ocean swimming, hiking, fishing, and 8 miles of bicycle trails. Two-week limit. Always filled to capacity.

Beaches nearby, not in the forest

Shawme-Crowell State Forest Sandwich
PHONE: 508–888–0351.
LOCATION: 65 miles from Boston.
DIRECTIONS: I-93 south to Route 3 south, to Route 6A, to Route 130.
CAMPSITES: 260.

Nearest swimming is a 15-minute drive

Wompatuck State Park Page 192.
CAMPSITES: 400 (140 with electricity).

CONNECTICUT

A full site list is available from the Connecticut Office of Parks and Recreation, 165 Capitol Avenue, Hartford 06115 (203–566–2304). Season: April 15 to September 30, 21-day limit. Reservations allowed in most areas. Day-trippers swell the population at Hammonasset Beach in Madison and Rocky Neck in Niantic, where there's saltwater swimming.

MAINE

Sites for back-country camping (some more developed than others) are in an annual publication, *Forest Campsites,* sent free on request from the State of Maine, Department of Conservation, Station 22, Augusta 04333. A complete list of state areas is available from the Maine Department of Conservation, Bureau of Parks and Recreation, Augusta 04333 (207–289–3821). Reservations accepted only at Baxter State Park, 64 Balsam Drive, Millinocket 04462 (207–723–5140).

NEW HAMPSHIRE

An annual brochure lists all details about privately operated and public campgrounds. Write New Hampshire Vacations, Box 856, Concord 03301, or call 603–271–2343. For winter campsites contact White Mountain National Forest, Box 638, Laconia 03246 (603–524–6450).

RHODE ISLAND

An annual brochure lists private, state, and municipal campgrounds. Contact the Department of Economic Development,

Tourist Promotion Division, 7 Jackson Walkway, Providence 02093 (1–800–556–2484 or 401–277–2601). Fishermen's Memorial State Park in Narragansett is the only state site that accepts reservations.

VERMONT

A list of state-operated areas is available from the Department of Forests, Parks, and Recreation, Montpelier 05602 (802–828–3375). Advance paid reservations for 6 days or more are accepted January through April; for 3 days or more, after May 1.

Swimming

LESSONS

Try the Ys, Girls and Boys Clubs, or community pools. During the summer many towns give lessons at local beaches or ponds, and MDC pools have lessons in the morning.

Water-Babies, programs for children as young as 6 months, are given at several Ys, among them Boston, Dorchester, and Natick. They work toward adjustment to the water, not perfect form.

HANDICAPPED

Programs are offered at several MDC pools. Call 727–5250 for information.

MDC POOLS

The MDC operates sixteen outdoor swimming and wading pools. Call 727–5250 for information. Admission is $.50 for adults, $.25 for senior citizens and under 17. The enclosed Weymouth facility (335–2090) is open year-round.

Tennis

The best source for community information is the local recreation department. Boston's sixty-four courts are all on a first-come, first-served basis. Call 725–3290 for arrangements.

The MDC operates lighted courts at Charlesbank in the West

Boston youngsters, ages 6 to 17, are eligible for free tennis instruction at the **Sportsmen's Tennis Club,** 950 Blue Hill Avenue, Dorchester. Its facility, the Franklin Field Tennis Center, has seven indoor courts, five outdoor courts, and two double-sided bang-boards. The program runs from June through August, 9 to 4; from October through May, 3 to 6. Phone: 288-9092.

End. For a permit (free) apply in person at the adjacent pool. Call 782–2105 or 782–2118 for information. Other MDC courts — all on a first-come, first-served basis — are in Belmont, Dedham, Everett, Hyde Park, Mattapan, Milton, Nahant, the North End, Readville, Somerville, South Boston, and Watertown. Phone: 727–5215 or 727–5250.

Whale Watching

You really see whales. Most trips operate May through October and last 4 to 5 hours. At the moment they're about $15 for adults, a little less for children under 12. Reservations suggested.

The following lines have regularly scheduled trips:

- BARNSTABLE: **Cape Cod Seaways** half-day cruises leave from Barnstable Harbor, daily spring through October. There's a naturalist on board. Reservations are required. Fare: $17.50 adults, $15 senior citizens, $12 under 13. Phone: 508–775–7185.

- BOSTON: **AC Cruise Lines** (page 226) runs all-day trips on Saturdays, April through October. Fare: $18 adults, $12 under 13. Phone: 426–8419.

  The **New England Aquarium** (page 160) runs all-day trips from Long Wharf in the spring. Aquarium staffers give informal lectures along the way. Fare: $22.50. Phone: 742–8830.

- GLOUCESTER: **Fishermens Museum** (page 61) runs very popular trips, with a naturalist and a research crew on board. Phone: 508–283–1940.

- PROVINCETOWN: Al Avellar's **Dolphin III** and **Dolphin IV** trips were the first on the East Coast, and are among the best around. Marine biologist and research crew on board. Fare: $12 adults, $10 children. Phone: 508–487–1900.

  Ranger III's naturalist sometimes swims and photographs off the boat. Fare: $10 adults, $8 children. Phone: 487–3322.

Greenpeace New England, 286 Congress Street, Boston, has about sixty wonderful trips, spring through fall, from Plymouth and Provincetown. The fare is $20 for adults, $17 for senior citizens and students. Group rates are available for ten or more. Part of the fare supports the organization's work to end commercial whaling and the annual harp seal slaughter in eastern Canada. Phone: 542–7052.

- ROCKPORT: **Gloucester Sightseeing Cruises** is planning more trips to accommodate interest. Phone: 508–283–5110.
- SALEM: **Barnegat Boat Cruises,** one of the newer offerings. Phone: 508–745–6070.

Organizations

Local community centers, Ys, and clubs run bowling, swimming, and game programs for individuals and families. Local recreation departments offer all kinds of facilities. The Boston department is at 725-4006. (Check the phone book for local numbers.)

Many communities and organizations offer programs for children and adults with special needs. Check with local recreation departments and the organizations below. The **Thompson Center** (page 185) is a new park facility especially for the handicapped. The **Carroll Center for the Blind,** 770 Centre Street, Newton, conducts an outdoor enrichment program for blind adults. The center trains sighted volunteers as guides for cross-country and downhill skiing, ice skating, hiking, tandem cycling, sailing, and canoeing activities. Phone: 969-6200.

Appalachian Mountain Club 5 Joy Street, Boston 02108

PHONE: 523–0636.

AMC is a great resource for outdoor information. Mountain climbing, canoeing, snowshoeing, skiing, hiking, camping, or just being outside are all aspects of programming. Family trips and outings (day, weekend, or longer) are open to non-members. Details about the AMC hut system (page 239) and available AMC campgrounds (self-service and full-service facilities in beautiful areas near Boston and up-country) are published annually in March.

At headquarters, a town house on Beacon Hill, there's a knowledgeable staff, a library, extensive map and photographic collections, and guidebooks and other publications.

Explorer Posts Page 122.

For teenagers.

Metropolitan District Commission (MDC) 20 Somerset Street, Boston 02108

PHONE: 727–5250, 727–5215 (information).

Send a self-addressed, stamped envelope for a brochure complete with maps and a list of facilities. For locations and phone numbers of swimming pools, ice skating rinks, and other facilities, check the Blue Pages of the Boston phone book under "Massachusetts Commonwealth of: Metropolitan District Commission."

New England Handicapped Sportsmen's Association Box 2150, Boston 02106

PHONE: 367–8847.

Free instruction and equipment in the winter ski program. There are charges for other seasonal activities: bowling, canoeing, golf, gymnastics, hang gliding, horseback riding, karate, racquetball, sailing, scuba diving, softball, squash, swimming, tennis, waterskiing, wheelchair basketball, and yoga. Programs are for all ages.

Outward Bound 384 Field Point Road, Greenwich, Connecticut 06830

PHONE: 1–800–243–8520.

Information about all courses and programs scheduled throughout the country. Applicants must be at least 16½ years old; there is no upper age limit. Most who apply have little or no wilderness experience, but the courses aren't easy. They're intended as vehicles for personal growth. A few programs are now open to the handicapped.

Sierra Club Page 201.

Youth Enrichment Services 180 Massachusetts Avenue (between Auditorium and Symphony on the Ⓣ), Boston 02115

PHONE: 267–5877.

This private nonprofit organization started in 1968 with skiing; today, it is the largest urban program of outdoor education, vocational training, and environmental awareness in the country. In addition to skiing, activities now include bicycling, canoeing, and backpacking trips for ages 12 to 16, and summer overnight and weekend camping for ages 7 to 11. Equipment provided. Fees charged on a sliding scale. All Massachusetts residents are eligible for any of the programs.

Tours

All suggested tours are free. . . . Many of the listings don't offer a formal tour, but are happy to show you around. . . . If the day seems just right for an inside visit, call to see if your family can join an expected group (notice the minimum age; it may denote interest level). . . . Some visits are geared for people with a particular interest. If you're just looking for something to do, please shy away from those. . . . Group leaders find benefits are always greater with orientation and follow-up. . . . When parents supervise a group, it's usually better not to bring younger siblings along. . . . Often the guide makes a difference. If yours doesn't give adequate explanations, ask questions and explain details to the children. This is particularly important for those at the end of the line. . . . If a place you've suggested is among the missing, most likely it has occasional arrangements and prefers to have its name unpublished. . . . This chapter is an *In and Out of Boston* original. Please observe the restrictions and plan more than enough supervision. . . . If you have a specific interest, check the category in the Yellow Pages, and then call the public relations department. If a place hasn't been deluged with requests, it may take on a vocationally oriented group. . . . Also check tour information in Animals, Day Trips, Historic Sites, and Museums.

Local Suggestions

For almost any age, but particularly for young children. . . . Check safety regulations and double-check group size. . . . And please make an appointment.

ARCHITECT'S OFFICE: An awareness of space and how to use it.

ARTIST'S STUDIO: The medium. The time. The space.

BAKERY: Make your own before you visit. Reminder: Bakeries start early in the day.

BUS RIDE: Let a child pull the cord for a stop.

CANDY HOUSE: A small local shop.

CAR WASH: Some let children ride through the suds.

CLEANING PLANT OR LAUNDRY: Maybe one with a shirt presser.

CONSTRUCTION PROJECT: A hard-hat site.

CRAFTSPEOPLE: A home studio.

DAIRY: Find out when they milk the cows.

DOUGHNUT SHOP: Watch the holes too.

FAST-FOOD PLACES: Often with samples.

FIRE STATION: Sleeping quarters, communications system, engines and their gadgets, the firemen's gear. Some nursery school groups have found this exciting; others report that a midvisit alarm has made it a frightening experience.

GREENHOUSE: Buy a plant or bring home seeds.

HOSPITAL: Particularly for a youngster about to enter. Ask to see an X-ray reading.

KENNEL: Maybe a dog will be having a bath or a clipping.

LIBRARY: Any special programs?

LUMBERYARD: Take home an old piece from the scrap barrel.

NEWSPAPER: Does it go to press weekly?

PET SHOP: Difficult to plan just a visit, not a shopping trip.

PHOTOGRAPHER'S STUDIO: All the processes.

POLICE STATION: Its responsibilities. Is there a dog officer?

POST OFFICE: Busiest in the morning, but personnel may not be available then.

PRINTING PLANT: When do the presses roll?

RADIO STATION: Where does the voice come from?

SAVINGS BANK: What happens to the money? How is it recorded? How does a coin counter work?

THEATER: Backstage is most revealing.

Places

American Repertory Theater 64 Brattle Street, Cambridge

PHONE: 495–2668.

Ⓣ: Harvard on the Red Line.

OFFERED BY APPOINTMENT: 45-minute tours; October–May when theater schedule permits.

REQUIREMENTS: 3-week notice (call the Development Department). Group size: 10–35. Minimum age: High school.

Walk on stage and backstage. Look at the costume shop, set design department, and rehearsal area. You may even see a few minutes of a rehearsal, but the focus of the tour is more technical — an explanation of the elevator under the stage or of the lighting. Hear how everything is coordinated at showtime. How much activity you see depends on the staff at work.

Bailey's 26 Temple Place, Boston

PHONE: 426-4560.

Ⓣ: Park Street on the Green or Red Line. (Take time to look at the beautiful, intricate ceramic mural near the wide stairway.)

OFFERED BY APPOINTMENT: 30-minute tours; September–May, weekdays 9–3.

REQUIREMENTS: Group size: 5–15. No minimum age.

One of the candymakers — their average age is 65 — leads an informal tour geared to the visiting group. Different candies (caramels cooked in steam kettles, fudge, or peanut brittle) are made every day. You might see hard candy hand-pulled on a hook, chocolates hand-dipped, or cream hand-cast in starch molds. Enjoy samples at the end of the delicious visit.

Boston Edison Company Mystic Station Power Plant, Everett

PHONE: 424-2459.

OFFERED BY APPOINTMENT: 1-hour tours; Tuesday–Thursday.

REQUIREMENTS: At least 10 days' notice. Group size: Up to 35. Minimum age: 9.

Everyone wears a hard hat for a firsthand look at how electricity is generated from fuel. There's lots of interaction between visitors and staffers in the main control room, where the array of lights prompts questions. The tour includes boiler facilities, turbines, environmental control equipment, and the electrical operation control room too. Both men and women are at work here.

The Boston Globe 135 Morrissey Boulevard, Dorchester

PHONE: 929-2653.

DIRECTIONS: Southeast Expressway to exit 17.

Ⓣ: Columbia on the Red Line; then a 10-minute walk.

OFFERED BY APPOINTMENT: 1½-hour tours; year-round, weekdays.

REQUIREMENTS: Minimum age: 12.

See the editorial staff at work; reporters going, coming, and writing; news machines clicking; type being set; negatives turning into photoengravings; and mats and plates being made. The presses may be printing an edition that's on sale by the time you get home.

NEARBY: John F. Kennedy Library (page 154).

Brigham's Ice Cream 30 Mill Street, Arlington

PHONE: 648-9000.

Ⓣ: Harvard on the Red Line; then Arlington Heights bus to Central Street.

OFFERED BY APPOINTMENT: 45-minute tours; year-round, Wednesdays and Thursdays at 9:30.

REQUIREMENTS: 1-month notice. Group size: At least 10. Minimum age: 6.

A well-lit, noisy place where everything is done on a grand scale. Although you can't see the actual mixing inside the huge colorful tanks, there's a sense of the entire manufacturing process — from the receiving dock, to the lab (where all ingredients are tested), to the plant (where flavorings, fruits, nuts, and chocolate chips are added to tanks of milk and cream and 5-gallon containers are filled), to the −20 degree hardening room (where you spend a few impressionable, freezing seconds). Everyone has a taste of soft, fresh ice cream. Beyond the world of ice cream: the sights and smells in the syrup kitchen, and beefburgers turned out at the rate of one a second.

Two tours

Christian Science Center Boston

PHONE: 262-2300.

Ⓣ: Symphony or Prudential on the Arborway–Green Line.

PUBLISHING SOCIETY: 45-minute tours; year-round, weekdays (except holidays) several times daily starting at 9:30. (Young children in family groups are welcome, but the tour isn't really geared to them.) Groups: 1-week notice. Minimum age: 12.

MOTHER CHURCH: 30-minute tours; daily except Christmas and New Year's, Monday–Saturday 10-4:15, Sundays noon-4:15.

Guides at the **Christian Science Publishing Society,** One Norway Street, explain production procedures for the *Monitor* and church periodicals. You'll see the newsroom, the pressroom, and composition and shipping areas. The Mapparium (page 118) is also part of the tour.

The tour of the **Mother Church of the First Church of Christ, Scientist** focuses on architecture. Carved stone walls, stained-glass windows, and a mosaic floor are in the Romanesque Original Edifice. In the domed extension — a wide-open area with no supporting columns to block the view — is one of the largest organs in the Western Hemisphere. The latest addition is the stone-carved portico, a magnificent entrance from Massachusetts Avenue.

ALSO IN THE CENTER: The Bible Exhibit (page 118).

Coca-Cola Bottling Company of New England 9B Street, Needham Heights

PHONE: 449-4300.

OFFERED BY APPOINTMENT: ¾-hour tours; weekdays (except Wednesday afternoons) 9-3.

REQUIREMENTS: 1-week notice. No minimum age.

The only production that you actually see is the most exciting part — the canning assembly line. Then there's a 15-minute explanatory movie and a look at the collection of vintage Coca-Cola memorabilia.

Federal Reserve Bank of Boston 600 Atlantic Avenue, Boston

PHONE: 973–3464.

Ⓣ: South Station on the Red Line; then up the narrow wooden escalator — the oldest in Boston — and you're there.

PUBLIC TOURS BY APPOINTMENT: ¾ hour; year-round, two or three times a month (call for a schedule). Minimum age: 13.

GROUP TOURS BY APPOINTMENT: 1½ hours (tour and program); at 9:15. 4-week notice. Group size: 10–45. Minimum age: 6. Geared to age level and interest, and can be combined with educational programs in check writing, money and banking, and career awareness for Grades 1–12.

What happens to the bags of money collected from banks? You see bags of coins being weighed, dumped into counting and sorting machines, and then wrapped in rolls. The glass-walled corridor takes you by the computerized check clearing-house, the automated transfer department, and the data storage systems. There are plenty of opportunities for questions, and even a souvenir — some shredded currency.

The art gallery, open weekdays 10 to 4, has rotating exhibits. And there's a free performance series in the auditorium on fall and spring Thursdays at 12:30. Check with the cultural affairs coordinator to see what's scheduled.

NEARBY: Children's Museum (page 151).

Conveyor belts everywhere

General Motors Assembly Division Western Avenue, Framingham

PHONE: 508–875–7421.

OFFERED: 2-hour tours; October 15–May, weekdays at noon (at 9:30 and 6 too with advance notice).

REQUIREMENT: Minimum age: 10.

RULES: No sandals, and please wear slacks.

This is an incredible tour. It's miles of walking through the many steps of automobile assembly. The body of the car is painted (submerged in a dip tank where a primer coat is electrically adhered to the metal). The instrument panel is put together. Windows are installed. One tool puts all four tires on simultaneously. And a driver tests the finished product. Reminder: When the plant is closed, there are no tours. Call to check.

Tempting sights and smells

ITT Continental Baking Company 330 Speen Street, Natick

PHONE: 508–655–2150, 244–4647 (Newton).

OFFERED BY APPOINTMENT: 1-hour tours; September–June, Mondays, Wednesdays, and Thursdays at 9:30, 11, 2, and 3:30.

REQUIREMENTS: 1-week notice (some morning tours are booked months in advance). Group size: 1–50. Minimum age: 7.

Tons of flour are hosed from railroad cars to storage area. Miles of pipes move ingredients through the 7-acre plant —

one of the largest bakeries in the world. Everything is automated, fascinating, and noisy (the guides use bullhorns!).

Visitors follow the bread dough from first mixing to fermentation, into another mixing, before each batch (1600 pounds) is shaped into balls that turn into individual loaves of bread. Peek through the long oven to see the bread baking, a process followed by cooling, slicing and wrapping.

Depending on the schedule, you may get to see doughnuts, fruit pies, rolls, English muffins, cakes, or novelties (see how the cream filling gets inside) being made. Visits end with samples and souvenirs.

Logan International Airport East Boston

PHONE: 482–2930 (extension 418).

T: Airport on the Blue Line; then the airport bus to the tour meeting place.

OFFERED BY APPOINTMENT: 1- to 3-hour tours (by age level); year-round, weekdays at 10 and 1. (March–May is busiest.) Groups with special needs can be accommodated.

REQUIREMENTS: 3-week notice (call the Massport tour coordinator for an appointment application). Minimum age: Grade 3 (younger in summer). Groups should be well supervised.

Tours vary depending on the size and age of the group, the day, and the weather. It may be possible to include a particular interest — customs, the flight kitchen, the inside of an airplane or cockpit, the weather bureau, the fire control unit, or a hangar. Visitors take a bus right onto the inner apron of the airfield for a close-up view of ground activity.

Exotic

Margaret C. Ferguson Greenhouses Wellesley College, Wellesley

PHONE: 235–0320.

OFFERED BY APPOINTMENT: 2-hour tours; year-round.

REQUIREMENTS: 1-month notice. Group size: Up to 50. Minimum age: 12. (Casual visitors are welcome from 8:30 to 4:30 daily. See page 199.)

Plants from all over the world — a banana tree, a cotton plant, orange trees, cacti, and more — in the fascinating and beautiful collections. Plenty to see and ask about.

Just 2 miles from downtown Boston

Massachusetts Envelope Company 30 Cobble Hill Road, Somerville

PHONE: 623–8000.

T: Sullivan Square on the Orange Line; then a 5-minute walk.

OFFERED BY APPOINTMENT: ½- to 1-hour tours; year-round, weekdays 9–noon and 1:30–3.

REQUIREMENTS: 5-day notice. Group size: 6–10. Minimum age: 10.

Up to 2 million envelopes a day come through the fifteen

offset presses, but before they do, there's work to be done in the art department and darkroom. You see all that and finish up at the warehouse, where trucks are waiting at the shipping dock. The tour is geared with sensitivity to group interests and backgrounds — often with career awareness in mind.

Massachusetts General Hospital Fruit Street, Boston

PHONE: 726-2205.

Ⓣ: Charles on the Red Line.

OFFERED: 1/2-hour tours; year-round.

REQUIREMENT: Suggested minimum age: 10.

"Even if you're alone, we still run the tour."

Tours leave from the Warren Lobby to two National Historic Landmarks: the Ether Dome and the Bulfinch Building that houses it ("a shrine within a shrine"). Climb the graceful staircase and enter the Ether Dome, an operating room of the hospital from 1821 to 1867. Here was the first public use of ether in a surgical procedure. Light enters through the window in the dome (which opens with the push of a button). The amphitheater is still used for medical rounds and conferences. Around the room are cases filled with artifacts, including an operating chair, a copy of an ether inhaler, some instruments, and an Egyptian mummy. A 24-minute slide presentation gives the history of the hospital.

NEARBY: Beacon Hill (page 128) and the Esplanade, the Harrison Gray Otis House (page 130), and Government Center (page 135).

Morgan Memorial Goodwill Industries 95 Berkeley Street, Boston

PHONE: 357–9710.

Ⓣ: Arlington on the Green Line.

OFFERED BY APPOINTMENT: 1-hour tours; year-round, weekdays 9–3.

REQUIREMENTS: 1-week notice. Group size: Up to 30. Minimum age: 13.

In this rehabilitation workshop, you see handicapped adults being trained in dry cleaning, sewing, pressing, furniture repair and refinishing, radio and television repair, and pricing. Then there's a tour of Morgie's Store, where all the merchandise is sold.

National Braille Press 88 St. Stephen Street, Boston

PHONE: 266–6160.

Ⓣ: Northeastern on the Arborway–Green Line.

OFFERED BY APPOINTMENT: 1-hour tours; year-round, Tuesday–Thursday, 10–noon and 1:30–3:30.

REQUIREMENT: Group size: 5–30.

Books (for adults and children) and magazines are either manually or electronically transcribed onto braille zinc plates, printed, collated, and stitched, and then shipped around the world. Visitors go into each department, where the work is explained by staffers (disabled and nonhandicapped). There's also a brief discussion on the history of braille. Everyone leaves with samples of braille materials, including alphabet cards.

Home of Monopoly

Parker Brothers 190 Bridge Street, Salem

PHONE: 508–927–7600.

OFFERED BY APPOINTMENT: 1-hour tours; year-round at 10 and 2. (Booked months in advance.)

REQUIREMENTS: Group size: 4–20. Minimum age: 7.

How is a board game made? The printing process, the construction and folding of boards and boxes, and the assembly by hand of all the pieces into the boxes are among the steps you see on this fascinating tour through a century-old wooden factory (it's not air-conditioned).

NEARBY: Historic Salem (page 82).

Prince Company Page 68.

A small sawmill, north of Boston

Sherburne Lumber Company Coburn Road, Tyngsboro

PHONE: 508–649–7413 (Mr. Sherburne).

OFFERED BY APPOINTMENT: 1-hour visits; weekdays during reasonably warm months.

REQUIREMENTS: Group size: Up to 12. (Youngsters should be well supervised.)

See where trees are cut, and how logs are loaded and sawn into boards before they're planed. The use of a century-old waterwheel (not the kind found in gristmills) during heavy rain periods in spring and fall emphasizes the importance of the pond location.

Simpson Spring Company 719 Washington Street, South Easton

PHONE: 508–238–2741.

OFFERED BY APPOINTMENT: 1-hour tours; year-round, Wednesdays 10–3.

REQUIREMENTS: 2-week notice. Group size: 6–60. Minimum age: 7.

White tile and stained-glass windows form the setting for the spring, the source of water for this 150-year-old bottling company. Visitors also see ingredients being tested in the lab and bottling on the assembly line. In the museum are bottles dating back to the 1800s and machinery used here at the turn of the century.

Star Market Company University Avenue, Norwood 02062
PHONE: 762–8700 (Jack Battista).
OFFERED BY APPOINTMENT: 1½- to 2-hour tours (depending on group interests); year-round, Tuesday–Thursday 9–4.
REQUIREMENTS: 2-week written notice. Group size: Up to 25. Minimum age: 10.

Trains pull into the warehouse, trailers are loaded and unloaded, trucks are washed inside and out. There are dairy and flower operations, and orders from individual stores being filled. The presentation is geared to the age of the group, but generally gives a sense of the history of supermarket merchandising.

Star Market also runs **supermarket tours** that include back room operations, meat cutting, produce packaging, bread baking (from frozen dough), the deli department, stocking and receiving areas, and box baling. Here, too, visits are designed to highlight group interests. Tours are offered year-round, Tuesday and Wednesday mornings and early afternoons. Group size: Up to 18. Minimum age: 5. Contact the local store manager (written requests preferred) two weeks in advance to set a date.

Symphony Hall 301 Massachusetts Avenue (corner Huntington Avenue), Boston
PHONE: 266–1492 (Friends of the Boston Symphony Orchestra).
Ⓣ: Symphony on the Arborway–Green Line.
OFFERED BY APPOINTMENT: 1-hour tours; September–June, most weekdays. Tours for young people (page 38) too.
REQUIREMENT: Group size: At least 5 people, please.

"I stood on the stage and played my harmonica — just to say I did it here."
— A MUSICIAN

The scope of this tour is a revelation to even the most ardent symphony-goer: organ bellows, cables, and recording studio in the basement; the auditorium, the most acoustically perfect in the country; the library on the second floor. There are elevators for the larger instruments and a humidified room just for pianos. The tour is an anecdotal, historical look at the hundred-year-old orchestra and the hall that's been its home since 1900.

Trinity Church Copley Square, Boston
PHONE: 536–0944.
Ⓣ: Copley on the Green Line.
OFFERED: ½-hour tours; Sundays following the morning service at 11.

The church is open daily 9 to 4, but during the tour you hear about architect Henry Hobson Richardson and what is considered to be one of the most magnificent churches in the country. John La Farge was in charge of the interior painted decoration, and executed most of the figure painting as well as four of the beautiful stained-glass windows. Trinity's altar and chancel were extensively remodeled in 1937.

NEARBY: Other Back Bay sites (page 125).

U.S. Army Natick Research and Development Laboratories
Kansas Street, Natick 01760

OFFERED BY APPOINTMENT: 2-hour tours; year-round, Wednesdays.
REQUIREMENTS: Group size: Up to 30 (write to the public affairs officer for a reservation; individuals can join a scheduled group). Minimum age: 14.

Research here focuses on clothing, food, and protection of military personnel. Wash-and-wear shirts, freeze-dried foods, lightweight camping equipment, and crash helmets are among the items that have been developed in the laboratories.

U.S. Navy Ships Navy Office of Information, 470 Atlantic Avenue, Boston 02210

PHONE: 426–0490.

Most ships come into Commonwealth Pier. Call to check what's due in port. Public hours for tours are usually 1 to 4.

U.S. Postal Service–South Postal Annex 25 Dorchester Avenue, Boston

PHONE: 223–2457.
Ⓣ: South Station on the Red Line; then up the old wooden escalator.
OFFERED BY APPOINTMENT: 1-hour tours; January–November, Tuesday–Friday at noon.
REQUIREMENTS: 1-week notice (make appointments with the public information officer). Group size: At least 10. Minimum age: 13.

The sight of mail by the millions, an everyday scene at this highly mechanized facility, makes you wonder how anything ever gets where it's going. An optical character reader sorts letters at the rate of 37,500 an hour. Conveyor, canceling machines, and sack sorters are part of the maze where mail from seventy-three Greater Boston cities and towns is processed.

Wilson Farm 10 Pleasant Street, Lexington

PHONE: 862–3900.
OFFERED: 45-minute tours; year-round, Mondays and Wednesday–Friday 9–noon and 2–5. (Heavily booked in May and June.)
REQUIREMENTS: 1-week notice. Group size: 6–25. Minimum age: 4.

The greenhouse is always open and the vegetable farm can be seen May through October, but the poultry area is the big attraction. (Yes, you see and hear thousands of chickens!) As soon as eggs are laid, they're automatically collected in a tray and then graded. Although the grading machine (which requires four men) is operated at varying hours, it's sometimes turned on for visiting groups.

Commercial wineries are relatively new to New England. Some grow their own grapes; others make small batches of fruit wines. **Nashoba Valley Winery** (page 56) in Concord and **Commonwealth Winery** in Plymouth (page 80) are two nearby places that offer tours.

More

With apologies for not providing an encyclopedia, here's a potpourri of some other resources requested through the years of revising this book: Information and referral services ... Government ... Family ... Older citizens ... Special needs ... Health ... Horticulture ... Volunteering ... Summer camps ... International understanding.

Information and Referral Services

Where to turn with a problem? Here are two services — both free and confidential.

CALL FOR ACTION: 787-2300, weekdays 11 to 1. Ombudsman service, too, when appropriate.

UNITED WAY OF MASSACHUSETTS BAY: 482-1454, weekdays 9 to 5. Over three thousand services and programs listed.

Government

CITIZEN INFORMATION SERVICE: 727-7030 or 1-800-392-6090 (outside Boston), weekdays 9 to 5. Information about and by the Commonwealth of Massachusetts.

FEDERAL INFORMATION CENTER: John F. Kennedy Federal Building, Government Center, Boston 02203 (223-7121). Open weekdays 8 to 4:50.

VOTER INFORMATION PHONE: 357-5800 or 1-800-882-1649 (outside Boston), weekdays 9 to 3. All aspects of local, state, and federal government, provided by the League of Women Voters of Massachusetts.

Family

CHILD CARE RESOURCE CENTER: 187 Hampshire Street, Cambridge 02139 (547-9861). A broad service with computerized information.

CHILDREN IN HOSPITALS: 31 Wilshire Park, Needham 02192 (482-2915). The emotional needs and rights of hospitalized children.

CHILD STUDY ASSOCIATION OF MASSACHUSETTS: 145 Yarmouth Road, Chestnut Hill 02167 (969–8885). Parent discussion groups.

HELP FOR CHILDREN: Office for Children, 120 Boylston Street, Boston 02114 (727–8912). Where to go for services.

LA LECHE LEAGUE OF MASSACHUSETTS: Support and information on the phone and at meetings for women who are interested in, or are, breastfeeding their babies. Check the Boston phone book for the current secretary's number.

MASSACHUSETTS ADOPTION RESOURCE EXCHANGE: 25 West Street, Boston 02111 (451–1460). A clearinghouse.

PARENTAL STRESS HOT LINE: 1–800–632–8188. For parents and children.

Older Citizens

ELDERHOSTEL: 100 Boylston Street, Suite 200, Boston 02116 (426–7788). Short-term (usually one week) residential academic programs at over five hundred colleges and universities in the United States, Canada, Great Britain, and Scandinavia. The minimal charge covers room, board, classes, and extracurricular activities. Catalogs, published three times a year, describe the institutions and the wide variety of courses. There are no prerequisites, grades, tests, or credits. Minimum age: 60 (unless you attend with someone 60 or over).

SENIOR HOT LINE: 722–4646 (Boston), weekdays 9 to 5.

Special Needs

ACCESS TO BOSTON COMMITTEE: Box 501, Boston 02134. Write for information about *Access to Boston: A Guide for Disabled Persons,* two hundred pages of detailed access information for everything from fast-food places to historical sites, from shopping areas to theaters. Compiled by lots of volunteers from university, city, state, and federal organizations.

DEPARTMENT OF MENTAL HEALTH: Walter E. Fernald State School Recreation Services, Box 158, Belmont 02178 (894–3600). Planning activities for a special population? The special services coordinator has extensive experience. If time permits, she'll share that experience with you.

FEDERATION FOR CHILDREN WITH SPECIAL NEEDS: 312 Stuart Street, Boston 02116 (482–2915). Advocacy and training for parents of children with disabilities.

INFORMATION CENTER FOR INDIVIDUALS WITH DISABILITIES: Statler Office Building, 20 Park Plaza, Boston 02116 (727–5540). For all ages with disabilities, computerized statewide information about organizations, employment, transportation, housing, funding, travel — and more.

Health

LEAD POISONING HOT LINE: 1–800–532–9571.

NUTRITION HOT LINE: 727-7173, weekdays 10 to 2. Sponsored by the Massachusetts Nutrition Resource Center, Massachusetts Department of Public Health.

POISON INFORMATION: 232-2120.

Horticulture

ARNOLD ARBORETUM PLANT INFORMATION: 524-1718, weekdays 1 to 2.

COUNTY EXTENSION OFFICES: Provide soil testing, educational services, formal and informal workshops, and information about plants and insects, 4-H Clubs, home economics, commercial agriculture, and community resource development.

- **Essex Agricultural and Technical Institute,** 562 Maple Street, Hathorne 01937 (508–774–0050).
- **Middlesex County Extension Service,** 105 Everett Street, Concord 01742 (508–369–4845 or 862–2380, Lexington).
- **Norfolk County Agricultural High School,** 460 Main Street, Walpole 02081 (508–668–0268).

MASSACHUSETTS HORTICULTURAL SOCIETY GARDEN INFORMATION HOT LINE: 536-9635, weekdays.

UNIVERSITY OF MASSACHUSETTS SUBURBAN EXPERIMENT STATION: 240 Beaver Street, Waltham 02254 (891-0650). Provides soil testing (fee charged); and plant clinics and information about insect pests (inside and out) on Mondays, Wednesdays, and Fridays from 8:30 to noon and 1 to 5. The magnificent formal gardens are open daily.

Volunteering

Three clearinghouses:

CAREER AND VOLUNTARY ADVISORY SERVICE: 14 Beacon Street, Boston 02108 (227-1762).

COMMONWEALTH OF MASSACHUSETTS INTERNSHIP OFFICE: State House, Room 109, Boston 02133 (727-8688).

VOLUNTARY ACTION CENTER OF THE UNITED WAY OF MASSACHUSETTS BAY: 87 Kilby Street, Boston 02109 (482-8370).

Summer Camps

NEW ENGLAND CAMPING ASSOCIATION: 643 Moody Street, Waltham 02154 (899-2042). Publishes a directory ($4.50, $5.95 by mail) of resident camps in New England accredited by the American Camping Association. Counselor placement service too.

STUDENT CAMP AND TRIP ADVISORY SERVICE: 244 Bonad Road, Chestnut Hill 02167 (469-0681, 469-0031). This personal referral service (free to the family) visits each of the suggested private camps. Recommendations are made according to the child's needs (competitive or low-keyed, for example). Wilderness trips and international experiences are also on the list of about three hundred and fifty.

UNITED COMMUNITY PLANNING CORPORATION: 87 Kilby Street, Boston 02109 (482-9090). Its annual publication, *Campfinder* ($5), lists close to three hundred camps operated by social agencies and other organizations serving children, youth, and adults in Greater Boston.

International Understanding

BOSTON COUNCIL FOR INTERNATIONAL VISITORS: 55 Mt. Vernon Street, Boston 02108 (742-0460). New members are always welcome to act as guides for foreign visitors (usually government sponsored).

COUNCIL ON INTERNATIONAL EDUCATIONAL EXCHANGE: 1278 Massachusetts Avenue, Cambridge 02138 (497-1497). A good clearinghouse for work, study, and travel information. Free annual catalog. This New England office, located in Harvard Square, issues (for $6) international student ID cards (no minimum age) that are useful for discounts. Open weekdays 10 to 6.

INTERNATIONAL FRIENDSHIP LEAGUE: 22 Batterymarch Street, Boston 02109 (523-4273). There's a nominal charge for matching Americans (ages 8 up) with pen pals in other countries.

Exchange Programs

Possibilities include a summer or a semester. Programs are usually for high-schoolers, but there are adult opportunities too. Arrangements aren't always an exchange; ask about "just going" or "just hosting." Boston area host families — with or without children — are always needed.

- **American Field Service,** 313 East 43d Street, New York, New York 10017 (212-661-4550).
- **The Experiment in International Living,** Kipling Road, Brattleboro, Vermont 05301 (802-257-7751).
- **North Atlantic Cultural Exchange League,** c/o David Phelan, Regional Coordinator, Box 422, Marlborough 01752.
- **Youth for Understanding,** 581 Boylston Street, Room 666, Boston 02116 (267-1141).

INTERNATIONAL INSTITUTE OF BOSTON: 287 Commonwealth Avenue, Boston 02115 (536–1081). Its main purpose: social service needs.

UNITED NATIONS CHILDREN'S FUND (UNICEF): Greater Boston Committee, 99 Bishop Allen Drive, Cambridge 02139 (492–0029). This is where you'll find Trick-or-Treat projects, greeting cards, books, games, educational programs for schools, films and slides, and records and sheet music.

U.S. SERVAS: International Institute, 287 Commonwealth Avenue, Boston 02115 (536–1081). An international cooperative system of travelers and volunteer hosts established to help build world peace, goodwill, and understanding. Arrangements can be made for a meal, sightseeing, shared community experiences, or overnight stays (usually two nights).

Calendar

Comprehensive weekly newspaper listings (page 6) show exact times and fees of the myriad activities and performances in the Boston area. . . . When the media highlight a particular place, it's "discovered" by everyone that weekend. Go the following week!

January

FIRST NIGHT: New Year's Eve finds professional entertainment — folk dancing, classical music, poetry, theater, mime, kites, a parade, something for all ages — in dozens of locations throughout the city. Phone: 725–3000.

SKI CLINICS: Free, for adults, on Boston Hill slopes. Phone: 929–2637.

OUTSIDE: Feed hungry ducks (page 28). Or walk along a beach, perhaps one you don't get to during the summer.

INSIDE PLACES: To perk up what can be a dull month.

- **A GREENHOUSE VISIT:** Have you ever been to Wellesley's **Ferguson greenhouses?** What a treat. (See page 199.) Combine with the Jewett Art Museum on campus.
- **FLEA MARKETS:** Dozens are close by; check the Sunday papers. Good luck with the hunt for a treasure at a bargain price.
- **BOOKSTORES:** Particularly popular on lousy days. Browse through the endless supply of new books at **New England Mobile Book Fair,** 82 Needham Street, Newton, where it's hard to "run in" or to leave with just one book. The selection, price, and helpful staff make the warehouse atmosphere most attractive.

February

BLACK HISTORY MONTH: Abundant special programming.

SCHOOL VACATION WEEK: Call museum recorded-information numbers (page 147) for special plans, and watch for vacation columns in the newspapers.

LOGAN AIRPORT: Where not to go the Friday at the start of school vacation or the Sunday when it ends. If you plan to use the expressway, change your route. You'll spend all your time in a massive backup.

SLEIGH RIDES: At **Old Sturbridge Village** (page 75), weather permitting, on weekends and during Washington's Birthday week. For other sleigh rides, see page 233.

GUIDED WALKS AND SKI TOURS: Free and good, at **Walden Pond** (page 199).

DOG SLED RACES: In New Hampshire. (Never been? It's usually cold — and fairly passive for observers.)

ICE FOLLIES: Alternates with **Disney on Ice** every other year at Boston Garden. Group rates available. Phone: 227–3200.

CHINESE NEW YEAR: Ushered in with a dragon dance (driving the devil out to let good luck in) and firecrackers. Held at Beach and Tyler streets on a Sunday afternoon from 2 to 4. For the exact date call 426–8681.

March

NEW ENGLAND SPRING GARDEN AND FLOWER SHOW: New Englanders are starved for greenery by this time of year. Lines start forming first thing in the morning for the magnificent displays and ideas. The show isn't really child oriented. Admission charged; children under 12 (with an adult) free. Phone: 536–9280.

ST. PATRICK'S DAY PARADE: Close to or on March 17, in the afternoon, in South Boston. Floats, bands, and politicians galore in the 1½-hour procession. The date has reason for double celebration in Boston. On March 17, 1776, the British left the town. This first major success in the Revolution is noted by a monument at South Boston's Dorchester Heights (page 155).

March–April

BIRD WALKS: This is the time of year, before trees bloom, that birds are easy to find. Take your own walk in an open space area (pages 175–201) or contact the Massachusetts Audubon Society (page 200) for scheduled walks. Beginners — and children — are welcome in many groups, but keep in mind that quiet is essential.

SUGARING-OFF: The season depends on the weather. Ideal running days are cold nights followed by warm (40 degrees) days. There are about four hundred sugarhouses within a 3-hour ride of Boston, and they vary in methods and facilities. Progress means that not all farmers go from tree to tree. Some use plastic lines that connect the trees from the top to the bottom of the hill. But everywhere you'll see sap collected and boiled down into maple syrup. (It takes 40 pints of sap to make 1 pint of syrup.) There's no charge for watching, but tasting may have a price. Sugar-on-snow, the chewy product of boiled-down maple syrup poured on snow, is often served.

Visitors are usually welcome at the sugarhouses anytime, but it's a good idea to check the situation before leaving home. Dress in warm clothing and boots for the hike in the orchard.

Local demonstrations are scheduled at many places, including several Massachusetts Audubon Society sanctuaries (page 200). Elsewhere in Massachusetts:

- **PEPPERELL (40 MILES NORTH OF BOSTON):** The **Ritchies** at Boggastowe Farm on Shattuck Street, off Route 113 or Route 119, are open weekends. Many of their 330 buckets are emptied by hand into tanks on a truck. The wood-fired evaporator is in a converted shed. Free samples. Phone: 508–433–9987.

- **SUNDERLAND (2 HOURS WEST OF BOSTON):** At the **Williamses,** on Route 47, members of the family explain the process. They use oil for boiling the sap. The evaporators are right above the eating area, where sugar-on-snow and doughnuts are served. Located 6 miles from twelve historic homes in Deerfield Village. Phone: 413–665–3127 or 413–773–8301.

In New Hampshire:

"Come up on a clear day. You can see about 70 miles away."

- **ALSTEAD (100 MILES NORTH OF BOSTON):** The biggest operation in New England, second largest in the country, is at **Bascom's Sugar House,** a 2-hour drive from the city. You'll see some of the 20,000 taps on plastic tubing, and watch sap and syrup testing. The boiling and evaporation (in energy-saving equipment) are in the same room where maple pecan pie, sugar-on-snow, fried dough with maple syrup, and pickles are served. Located about 20 miles north of Keene, with a covered bridge along the way. Phone: 603–835–2230.

    Just down the road is **Clark's Sugar House,** where a wood-fired evaporator is still used.

- **MASON (60 MILES NORTH OF BOSTON): Raymond Parker** uses a tractor and pickup trucks to collect from his orchards in six nearby towns. Visitors see the tapped trees, the sugarhouse, and the 5- by 16-foot evaporator — and enjoy sugar-on-snow and pickles outdoors for $.50. Open weekends during the season. From Route 3 in Nashua take Route 130 toward Brookline, and follow the signs to Mason for about 3 miles. You'll see signs to the Parkers'. The restaurant, decorated with antique sugaring items, serves pancakes and syrup right up to Thanksgiving. It's open 8 to 6 Saturdays (not too crowded) and Sundays (up to an hour's wait) during sugaring-off season. Horse and buggy rides ($.50) for children on Saturday and Sunday mornings. Phone: 603-878-2308.

April

NATIONAL LIBRARY WEEK: Watch for special programs.

FENWAY PARK: Opening day.

MIT OPEN HOUSE: Each department — engineering, science, architecture, humanities, and industrial management — plans programs and demonstrations. Over two hundred exhibits — all free — geared for several levels. Held on a Saturday afternoon every two years, in odd-numbered years.

NEW ENGLAND FOLK FESTIVAL: Usually at Natick High School on a weekend. All ages come from miles around for dance and music performances, participation in folk, square, and contra dancing (beginner to expert), and homemade ethnic foods. Activities inside and out. Lots to choose from. For information, contact the New England Folk Festival Association, 309 Washington Street, Wellesley Hills 02181 (235-6181).

HERRING RUNS: This is the time (usually late in the month) when the fish spawn in lakes and ponds. Many do not survive the difficult, long journey. Those that do, come back year after year. (Survivors eventually go back to the ocean; young ones swim down in late summer or fall.) Watching fish by the thousands accept the challenge of the ladder is a memorable sight. To check if the season is on or for a nearby ladder, call the Division of Marine Fisheries at 727-3193.

- BOURNEDALE: One of the best and largest runs in the state is along **Cape Cod Canal.** Take Route 3 south to Route 6 at the Sagamore Bridge; then travel less than a mile to the parking lot. The herring come from the canal up the steps, then go under the road on their way to the herring pond. Later they retrace their swim. (See page 88 for nearby activities and sights.)
- BREWSTER: The prettiest productive run, about a 2-hour ride from Boston on Cape Cod, at the **Old Grist Mill** on Stony Brook Road.
- EAST WEYMOUTH: Take Route 18 off the Southeast Expressway. Left at the first light onto Middle Street, into East Weymouth. The herring come in from the ocean to freshwater **Whitman Pond.**
- PLYMOUTH: A good run (page 77) in a setting with lots of other attractions.
- WATERTOWN SQUARE: Follow Storrow Drive. About a half mile before the square, on **California Street,** on the south side of the Charles River, is the ladder used by fish that come from Boston Harbor.

PATRIOTS DAY: Although the holiday's been moved to the third Monday of the month, Concord and several nearby towns still celebrate on April 19.

- **REENACTMENTS AND CELEBRATIONS:** In many towns. Activities at dawn in Littleton and Sudbury; ceremonies and a march in Carlisle; a morning parade in Jamaica Plain; a sunrise pilgrimage from Acton to Concord; minutemen and a reenacted battle at the Old North Bridge.
- **THE FAMOUS RIDE:** William Dawes leaves from John Eliot Square in Roxbury; Paul Revere, from Hanover Street in the North End for a ride "through every Middlesex village and farm." A uniformed horseman arrives near the Minuteman Statue in Lexington about 1, and a long wonderful parade — often in freezing rain — starts at 2. While you're searching for a parking place, keep in mind that it takes about an hour for the parade to reach the Green from the official starting point.
- **THE BOSTON MARATHON:** The 26-mile race (first held in 1892) starts in Hopkinton at noon and ends in downtown Boston (usually between 2 and 2:30). Much of the route includes Commonwealth Avenue, lined with cheering spectators.

April–May

REGATTAS ON THE CHARLES: Crew races are held Saturday afternoons, April through mid-May. The crews, from Boston University, Harvard, and Northeastern, race courses of varying lengths, all between Longfellow Bridge and the MIT Boat House. Depending on the number of races scheduled for the day, they start at 2 or 3 and end at 6 or 7.

May

MAGNOLIAS: Blooming on Commonwealth Avenue near the Public Garden. Nature's performance is difficult to time, but the spectacle is unforgettable.

SHEEP SHEARING: Demonstrations at many places, including **Merrimack Valley Textile Museum** (page 165) on the third Sunday of the month, **Old Sturbridge Village** (page 75), and **Macomber Farm** (page 25).

LILAC SUNDAY: At **Arnold Arboretum** (page 179). Over four hundred kinds of lilacs — in seven color groupings, with single- and double-flowering trees in each. Well publicized. Well attended. Go just before or after to avoid the throng.

ART FESTIVALS, SHOWS, AND FAIRS: Everywhere! Many outdoors. Some are free. Some are for fund raising.

SCIENCE FAIR: Held on a weekend at MIT. High school students explain their projects, all of which have a central theme and answer a specific question. Open to the public. For information, call the *Boston Globe* Science Fair office at 929-2654.

APPLE BLOSSOMS: Late in the month. Drive through Stow (Routes 117 and 62) and Harvard (Route 110), or around Littleton and Groton (Routes 2A and 119). The countryside is a little hilly for young or inexperienced cyclists.

CHARLES RIVER FESTIVAL: A week of hands-on activities, performances, and workshops — morning, noon, and night — all free. Starts on Cambridge Common on Sunday; ends on the river the last Saturday of the month.

MEMORIAL DAY PARADES: The last Monday in May. Many short processions in several areas of Boston.

May–June

BOSTON POPS: For this Boston tradition, tables and chairs replace first-floor seats in Symphony Hall. Programs are a mix of classics, popular favorites, hit parade numbers, and novelties. Refreshments sold. The first floor is more social (and expensive); audio is better upstairs. Tickets can be reserved by phone (266-1492) with three weeks' notice.

June

MILITIA DAY: On the first Monday of the month, visiting delegations from the eastern seaboard join the Ancient and Honorable Artillery Company for a full-dress parade from Faneuil Hall to the Common. The parade starts at 1, stops for a memorial service, and arrives about 3 at the Common for ceremonies that last until about 4:30. The spectacle, which seems to attract mostly passersby, includes a drumhead election — where each ballot is cast on a huge, centuries-old drum. A booming cannon announces the governor has commissioned the new officers, and then the companies parade on the Common. Phone: 227-1638.

NEIGHBORHOOD STREET FAIRS: Almost every weekend.

DAIRY OPEN HOUSES: Very popular with families. On one Sunday, several dairy farms welcome visitors to see cows, barns, and pastures. A few are open during early-morning milking hours, but most schedule the open house in the afternoon. The list of this year's locations is usually published in the newspapers; or check with the Massachusetts Farm Bureau Federation, 85 Central Street, Waltham (893-2600).

MOUNTAIN CLIMBING NOTE: Black flies come to life in May, are at their worst in June, and supposedly taper off in July. They flourish in 72- to 94-degree temperatures. Recommended clothing: Long-sleeved heavy shirts, slacks, wool socks, and hats.

BOSTON COMMON DAIRY FESTIVAL: Upholding an old law, still on the books, that says cows must appear annually on the Common. There's a variety of dairy breeds and some ducks, chickens, goats, and calves. Staffers answer questions, and let some onlookers try milking — usually about 5 in the afternoon. Admission is free. Arrangements for schools may include a program. Call the New England Dairy and Food Council in early May at 734-6750.

DRAGON BOAT FESTIVAL: On a Saturday, midmonth, on the Esplanade. Observed by the Chinese community and shared with everyone. A highlight: rowing races on the river in lifeboats with decorated heads and tails — a reminder to all finned things to let Ch'u Yuan, poet and patriot, rest in peace. All performances and activities are free.

BUNKER HILL DAY: June 17, at 2, a 1½-hour parade to commemorate the fortification of Breed's Hill (although Bunker Hill was the original site selected by the colonists).

SUMMER PREVIEW ISSUE: A special section worth looking for. Published about the third week of the month in the *Boston Phoenix* (page 6).

KITE FLYING: A good time, before summer crowds come, to use the open space at area beaches. See pages 210–218.

June–September

MEMORIAL DRIVE: Closed to traffic on Sundays for roller skating (page 239) and parklike activities.

AGRICULTURAL FAIRS: Several of the big fairs are so much like carnivals that you have to look for the agricultural exhibits. Still, there are horse and oxen pulls, handcraft exhibits, garden prizes, duck-calling contests, ecology exhibits, and cattle and sheep judging. For a list of fairs — major, community, youth, and grange — check with the Massachusetts Department of Agriculture, Division of Fairs, 100 Cambridge Street, Boston 02202 (727-3037).

PICK-YOUR-OWN: Plans change from year to year. For a current list of places, send a self-addressed, stamped envelope to the Massachusetts Department of Agriculture, Division of Markets, 100 Cambridge Street, Boston 02202.

It's always a good idea to call before you go. Weather and supply influence schedules. Places close to Boston sell out early. Children may or may not be welcome. You may find savings are small, but produce is fresh and picking is fun.

- **APPLES:** Page 288.
- **A VARIETY:** Likely places include **Lookout Farm** and **Red Pine Acres** (page 288).
- **STRAWBERRIES:** Usually available late June into July. The

beds are hotter than you think; bring a hat. Possibilities include three places in Concord: **Verrill Farm,** 415 Wheeler Road (369-5952); **Hutchins Farm,** 806 Monument Street (369-5041); and **Brigham's,** 82 Fitchburg Turnpike (369-2219). In Chelmsford, try **Parlee's** at 135 Pine Hill Road (256-2859). In Peabody, **Brooksby Farm,** Felton Street (531-1631).

- BLUEBERRIES: Mid-July through mid-August. It's slow going (it takes up to an hour to fill a quart). Pickers of the wild variety aren't eager to share their sources, but a sure giveaway is cars lined up along the roadside. Some suggestions: the **Route 128-Trapelo Road interchange** and **Prospect Hill Park** (page 198), both in Waltham, and the Milton side of **Blue Hills Reservation** (page 189). It's a good idea to have buckets for berries, and insect repellent for you, in the car, so that you're ready for action.

  Cultivated berries are sold by the pound or quart. Again, call first to see about arrangements and availability. Try **Balboni's** at 70 Church Street, East Bridgewater (508–387–3996), where the minimum age is 16, or **Alger Farm** on Pleasant Street, West Bridgewater (508–580–1565).

FARMERS' MARKETS: Held weekly, all over. Local produce, picked that day. For a schedule, call the Massachusetts Department of Agriculture, Division of Food and Agriculture, 727-3018.

July

JULY 4 ON THE ESPLANADE: The Boston Pops and fireworks. Spectacular. Come the last minute and you'll hear; come very early (with blanket and picnic) and you'll hear and see. Free.

U.S. PRO TENNIS CHAMPIONSHIPS: The oldest professional tennis tournament in the country. At Longwood Cricket Club, 564 Hammond Street, Brookline. Day and evening sessions. Admission charged. Ⓣ: Chestnut Hill on the Riverside–Green Line. Phone: 731-4500 or 731-2900.

POPS CONCERTS FOR CHILDREN: On the Esplanade, two weekday mornings. For the schedule call 266-1492 or 727-5215.

July–August

SUMMER CAMP CLEARINGHOUSES: See page 271.

ESPLANADE CONCERTS: At the Hatch Shell since 1929, when Arthur Fiedler, then a violinist with the Boston Symphony Orchestra, dreamed up the idea of playing classical music in a band concert setting. The Boston Pops continues to play here about twelve times during the summer, to enthusiastic crowds. Other 8 p.m. performances are given by local and internationally known dance, opera, and music groups. For a complete schedule call 727–5215. Ⓣ: Charles on the Red Line or Arlington on the Green Line.

TANGLEWOOD: This 200-acre estate in Lenox, where Nathaniel Hawthorne lived and wrote, is the summer home of the Boston Symphony Orchestra. With children along, you may be more comfortable with the informal atmosphere on the lawn outside the music shed. In addition to scheduled evening performances, open rehearsals are held Saturday mornings at 10:30. Picnicking (sometimes it's lavish) allowed.

Lenox is 140 miles west of Boston via the Mass. Pike. Ticket sales and information from Symphony Hall, 266–1492.

CHILDREN'S THEATER: It thrives in the summer at universities, community and arts centers, and on tour. Check the newspapers. The **Boston Children's Theatre Stagemobile** (page 38) performs at area sites.

ICE SKATING: At several indoor rinks. See page 235.

BOSTON PUBLIC LIBRARY COURTYARD: A cool, peaceful retreat right in the city. See page 126.

WALK IN THE CITY: On your own (pages 125–143) or on a conducted tour (page 123).

GARDEN CONCERTS: At 3 on Sunday afternoons at the **Longfellow National Historic Site** (page 111), near Harvard Square. Free. Parking is limited; take the Ⓣ.

DE CORDOVA MUSEUM (PAGE 170): Performing arts presentations — some specifically for children — weekends in the lovely outdoor amphitheater. Charge includes museum admission.

CITY HALL PLAZA: Free entertainment, some evenings and most weekdays at noon. Everything from local talent to internationally recognized companies.

FOLK DANCING: In Copley Square with the Taylors, who have a special talent for getting large crowds involved. All ages come with or without partners and with or without experience. Free. Phone: 491–6084.

NORTH END FESTIVALS: Just about every weekend on a different block of the small area (see page 138). Look for lighted arches and garland-strung poles where celebrations carry out Italian customs dating back hundreds of years. One of the largest is Saint Anthony's. The Fisherman's Feast (page 286) schedules a unique event. Time has brought changes — more vendors and people. But you can still see a statue of the Madonna being carried through the streets. The money taped to it goes toward expenses and neighborhood charities. Roma Band concerts can be heard from 8 to 11. Stands, most active from dusk on, sell stuffed quahogs, Italian sausages, fried dough, hot corn on the cob, slush, and pizza. Visitors feel that they're at a well-attended neighborhood party.

August

MOON FESTIVAL: In Chinatown when the moon is full. It's the Chinese Thanksgiving, with songs and dances, a parade, and traditional chicken dishes and moon cakes. The streets are closed off for activity from noon to 6.

SANDCASTLE COMPETITION: At **Steep Hill Beach,** next to Crane's Beach (page 211), in Ipswich, always on a Saturday late in the month (rain date: Sunday). Plenty of publicity. Huge atten-, dance. Entertainment. Bring your own shovels, spatulas, and spray bottles. Registration begins at 10 (no preregistration); the day is over at 5. Judging is based on age and profession. Admission is included in the parking fee.

FISHERMAN'S FEAST: In the North End (page 138), the festival of Madonna del Soccorso (Our Lady of Perpetual Help). A highlight: Late Sunday afternoon, young girls are dressed as angels on the balconies of North Street. One girl is lowered (by a pulley) into the street, where she gives a speech in Italian. Then pigeons are released from a decorated cage, and the air and street are filled with confetti. Arrive before 5 so you don't miss it.

CAT SHOW: At the Copley Plaza for a weekend. Sponsored by Cats Plain and Fancy. Phone: 267–5300.

September

WHALE WATCHING: Ever been? See page 250.

COURSE ENROLLMENT: Whatever you're interested in is offered in at least a dozen places in the area. Many offerings for young children (Grades K through 3) fill quickly.

PERFORMANCE SCHEDULES: The season lineup is announced. Everyone is pushing for subscriptions, the lifeline to survival.

September–October

CRANBERRY HARVEST: Late September through early October — a magnificent, colorful sight. And it's the best time to take a ride on the Edaville Railroad (page 58).

FRUIT STANDS: Many, all colorful with full displays of pumpkins. Try **Bolton Orchards** at the junction of Routes 110 and 117 in Bolton, where a push on a wall spigot produces a glass of fresh cider, just a nickel. A good September combination with Fruitlands Museums (page 172). Phone: 508–779–2773. In Lincoln, not far from Drumlin Farm (page 24), right on busy Route 2, is **Lawson's,** a traditional fall stop for many, with cider press in full view. Phone: 259–877. There are two places near Broadmoor Wildlife Sanctuary (page 193): **C. A. Dowse** in Sherborn usually presses on Sundays and one other day. Phone: 508–653–2639. **Williamson's Cider Mill** in Natick welcomes visitors on Rockland Street, off Route 16. Phone: 508–655–4521.

PICK-YOUR-OWN APPLES: At many orchards, from Labor Day through early October. It's very popular, more for fun than for savings. If the weather's been unkind, drops may be for sale. Always call to check picking dates. The following orchards are no more than an hour's drive from Boston. Send for a full list of pick-your-own places (see page 283).

- **CHELMSFORD: Red Pine Acres,** 89 High Street. Apples, peaches, plums, grapes, and tomatoes — and, if the winter has been right, almonds, walnuts, and pecans. Picnicking allowed. Small place. Limited supply. Phone: 508–256–3801. Near Lowell (page 66).

- **DUNSTABLE: Apple Hill Farm,** a small place on Valley Road, is open weekends only. Plan to wait in line and bring your own containers if you want to make your own cider on the motorized press. A few farm animals for watching (no touching). Picnicking allowed. Phone: 508–649–6831.

- **LANCASTER: Deershorn,** 205 Chase Hill Road, Sterling Junction, off Route 62 at Four Ponds (follow the signs). On gorgeous fall weekends, thousands show up at this well-organized place. A flatbed trailer takes everyone from the parking lot to the picking areas. Open fields for Frisbees and football. Picnicking allowed; refreshment and farm stands. Groups by appointment during the week. All handicaps accommodated on the trailer and in the orchard. Phone: 508–365–3691.

- **NORTH BROOKFIELD: Brookfield Orchards** on Orchard Road, off Route 9, is a biggie, where you can see a grading machine and packing in process. Picnic tables, a playground, and a country store. The snack bar (open weekends) serves apple dumplings, pies, and cakes. Phone: 508–867–6858.

- **SOUTH NATICK: Lookout Farm,** the oldest operating farm in eastern Massachusetts, is at 97 Pleasant Street. You'll have plenty of weekend company for picking apples, and raspberries, pears, beans, tomatoes, eggplants, peppers, and pumpkins too. Phone: 508–655–6651 or 508–655–4294 (recorded crop information). Very near Broadmoor Wildlife Sanctuary (page 193) and a pretty picnic area at the Charles River Dam.

- **STOW-HARVARD:** The area has at least six places. In Stow, **Shelburne Farms,** West Acton Road, offers apple picking and a shop in the barn. Phone: 897–9287. **Honey Pot Orchards,** on Sudbury and Boon roads, has a pretty orchard with ponds, and a very busy store. Phone: 508–562–5225.

A little lost? Check the map on pages xviii–xix.

Carlson's Orchards on Route 110 in Harvard, near Route 2, usually opens for picking daily, 10 to 5, after Labor Day. Several times a week, the rack-and-cloth hydraulic press is in action making cider. Phone: 508–456–8263. Nearby, many patient ice cream lovers join the long lines at Kimball Farms on Route 110 at the Littleton-Westford line. The stand usually closes for the season on Columbus Day weekend.

October

FOLIAGE: As soon as up-country peak is announced, weekend traffic is bumper to bumper. Think about a back road, or wait until the peak reaches Boston, usually a couple of weeks later, and visit Arnold Arboretum (page 179).

COLUMBUS DAY WEEKEND: More up-country traffic, starting by 3 Friday afternoon. It's the busiest weekend of the year for inns in historic Concord (page 54) and in New Hampshire and Vermont.

CANADA GEESE MIGRATION: Drive to **Plum Island** (page 188) to see hundreds of geese. It's almost as though they can read the signs reserving places for them. Dozens of photographers here on weekends.

HEAD OF THE CHARLES: The largest single-day rowing event in the world. Several thousand rowers in over seven hundred shells cover the 3-mile route, which starts at BU Bridge. A spectator sport for the cheering crowds on the shore. Most gather at the finish line, opposite WBZ, on Soldiers Field Road in Brighton.

HARVEST FESTIVALS: Country crafts, farm exhibits, and demonstrations — from bread making to cider pressing to wool dyeing (using native plants). Held weekends everywhere.

HAUNTED HOUSES: In schools, museums, churches, or community centers. Nominal fees, often for fund raising. Not recommended for children under 5.

BOSTON GLOBE BOOK FESTIVAL: Hynes Auditorium at the Prudential Center, Friday through Sunday. Books and more — hear and meet an author, watch one of the many films (some come just for these), or take advantage of the special events for children. Admission charged. (Check Thursday's *Boston Globe* or libraries for discount coupons.)

CHILDREN'S BOOKS INTERNATIONAL: For adults. Always multicultural. Held for three days at the **Boston Public Library** (page 126). Talks and films by authors, publishers, illustrators, and researchers. Free.

THE GREATEST SHOW ON EARTH: The **Ringling Bros. & Barnum and Bailey Circus** arrives at Boston Garden late in the month. Discounts for children under 12 at some performances. Phone:

227-3200. Call the publicity department at 227-3206 for the exact time of the circus parade, a tradition that's carried out shortly after the circus train pulls into town. Twenty elephants march from the garden to either Faneuil Hall or Downtown Crossing for a performance and banquet.

FAMILY HALLOWEEN NIGHT: Special programs and demonstrations at the **Museum of Science** (page 158) on a Friday evening.

November

TICKETS: Christmas Revels and **The Nutcracker** (page 292), and holiday-week performances of **"Le Grand David"** (page 43) sell out early. It's time to order.

THANKSGIVING DAY: In **Plymouth** (page 76), Plimoth Plantation and Cranberry World are open. The buffet dinner (just fair) at Memorial Hall (first come, first served) is not expensive.

Old Sturbridge Village (page 75) is very active today. Dinner reservations fill long before the holiday. Cooking is done in open-hearth fireplaces and brick ovens. Services at the meetinghouse. A turkey shoot. Dinner (includes admission to the village): $26.50 adults, $16.50 under 16.

THE DAY AFTER THANKSGIVING: A warning: This is a banner day for stores and some intown museums. Plan to do half of what you would like to do — it's crowded everywhere. (Only those with unusual stamina should plan to visit Toyland.) And don't drive into the city!

November–December

ASHUMET HOLLY RESERVATION (PAGE 189): At its best, with scarlet, orange, and yellow berries on the trees. Guided tours may be available. Admission: $1 adults, $.50 children.

CHOOSE A TREE: Johnson's Tree Farm, in North Beverly at 292 and 296 Dodge Street (508–774–6518), offers free memberships, open to anyone, the weekend after Thanksgiving. You sign up and select a tree, then come back weeks later to cut. (See below too.)

December

FIREWOOD: Chop or saw your own in a state forest. Arrangements vary from year to year. Check with the Department of Environmental Management, Division of Forests and Parks, at 727-3180.

CHRISTMAS TREES: Cut down, or even dig up, your own tree. A list of farms is available from the Department of Natural Resources, 100 Cambridge Street, Boston 02202 (737-3184).

It's a good idea to check with the farm before setting out. (Some run out of trees.) You may have to bring your own ax or saw, and rope to tie the tree in or on the car. And a tarpaulin to prevent scratches or dropped pitch from marring the finish. Bundle up, and wear heavy shoes or boots.

You can dig or cut your own tree in Westford, 30 miles northwest of Boston, at **Chelmsford Nurseries.** Early tagging is allowed. Phone: 508–251–7240.

The **Nottingham Tree Farm,** Wood Avenue, East Rindge, New Hampshire (50 miles north of Boston), has a three-state view, 100 acres of woodland to walk through, and a pond for skating. Rain in Boston often means snow in New Hampshire. Bring sleds and a picnic. It's not necessary to call ahead. Someone — and the trees — are always there in season.

SUMMER CAMP: It's not too early to look into private camps or organized trips for next summer. See page 271.

TEA PARTY REENACTMENT: Every December 16 the **Boston Tea Party Ship** (page 148) is free. Local minutemen march from Old South Meeting House to the Tea Party site and toss tea chests overboard. The public's invited to create its own protest after the reenactment. It's cold and often rainy, but you can say you were here.

EASTERN DOG SHOW: On a Saturday at Hynes Auditorium in the Prudential Center. More than two thousand dogs are benched by breeds; you can see them before or after they're shown. There are handling classes for children as well as adults, and obedience tests. Dogs and owners are fun to watch. Admission charged. For a schedule call 267–8488.

FREE-FOR-ALL: Several days of wonderful free programming at the **Museum of Fine Arts** (page 156).

MUSIC: Everywhere. Check the newspapers.

MUSEUM GIFT SHOPS: Usually open without museum admission.

PLANETARIUM: The **Museum of Science** (page 158) adds a special children's program — a fairy-tale adventure among the stars — Friday and Saturday afternoons at 4. Free for children under 5.

SKI CLINICS: For children on the Boston Hill ski slopes during school vacation week. Phone: 929–2637.

ICE CAPADES: A fully staged ice show at Boston Garden for the holiday period.

FAMILY PERFORMANCES: Represent a broad scope of the arts. Casts change, but among Boston's traditions:

- **BLACK NATIVITY:** A gospel song–play by Langston Hughes that tells the Christmas story from a Black perspective. For all ages. Presented by the National Center of Afro-American Artists at several locations in the Boston area. Call 442–8820 for this year's schedule.

- **CHRISTMAS REVELS:** A celebration of the winter solstice, the shortest day of the year. Join in song and dance, and watch Highland pipers, a brass ensemble, sword dancers, children (who steal the show), mummers, Saint George and the dragon with slapstick and invective, and much more. Held in a perfect setting—Harvard's Sanders Theater. Phone: 864-9183.
- **THE NUTCRACKER:** A lavish production by the **Boston Ballet** (page 35), with exquisite sets and beautiful costumes. Highly recommended for all ages.

Newer offerings, all in downtown theaters:

- **A CHRISTMAS CAROL:** At the Charles Playhouse.
- **HANSEL AND GRETEL:** By the **Opera Company of Boston** (page 43).
- **WHERE THE WILD THINGS ARE:** By the New England Dinosaur Dance Company.

And, for a visual treat that's usually available free through January 1:

- **THE TWELVE DAYS OF CHRISTMAS:** A blend of technology and art shows what "my true love gave to me." In the rotunda (second level) of Quincy Market.

NEW YEAR'S EVE: Starts with **First Night** (page 277). Events for children before dark, then hours more of good entertainment throughout the city.

Free: 151 Things to Do and Places to See

Read a **newspaper published the day of your birthday** / pages 126 and 98

Encircle the only **outdoor observation tower** in Boston / page 117

Visit an **art gallery** / page 125

See a **herring run** / page 280

Listen to a **harbor seal talk** / page 161

Step inside a **glass globe** / page 118

Enjoy **outdoor entertainment** / pages 131 and 135

Watch **hot-air ballooning** / page 209

Feed ducks / pages 28 and 120

See a **rain forest** / page 23

Attend **live performances, lectures, or films** / page 33

Go **bird watching** with a guide / page 221

People watch / pages 131 and 135

Bicycle with a group / page 220

Fish / page 231

Take a **guided walk** around a famous pond / page 199

Meet a **children's book author or illustrator** / page 40

Browse in an **antiquarian book shop** / pages 101 and 138

See a **river otter** in action / page 165

Picnic and watch **harbor activity** / page 180

Window-shop / pages 125, 131, and 135

Watch **maple sugaring** / page 278

Tour a **Boston Harbor island** / page 177

Fill a picnic jug from a **natural spring** / pages 89 and 192

Go to a **fish hatchery** / page 29

Look through a **telescope** in a university observatory / page 120

Meet a miller at work in a **gristmill** / page 91

Visit a **national park,** and hear a ranger's talk, see an audiovisual program, or try on colonial clothing / page 54

Take an out-of-season **walk on a beach** / page 215

Try a **fitness trail** / page 232

Visit **greenhouses** to see cacti, orange and lemon trees, orchids, ferns, and birds of paradise / page 199

Check Calendar (pages 274–292) for annual event suggestions.

Comb the Thursday Calendar of the *Boston Globe* or this week's edition of the *Boston Phoenix* for one-time events, free and open to the public.

Host a foreign traveler / page 272

Steady your footing in a half-mile-long **chasm** / page 198

Take a **company tour:** candy, cars, newspaper, bakery, printing / pages 256–265

Go to a **museum.** Some are always free; some are sometimes free; some have free programs. Culled list / page 148

Walk around Boston:

- BACK BAY: Architecture, art galleries, church tours, a publishing tour, the Mapparium and the Boston Public Library, exhibits, and complimentary postcards / page 125
- BEACON HILL: Close-ups of architectural details, dramatic views of the city, and the Black Heritage Trail / page 128
- FREEDOM TRAIL: Most sites are free, and so is an outdoor guided tour / page 95
- FANEUIL HALL MARKETPLACE: Browsing, street entertainment, Faneuil Hall, and, nearby, the Blackstone Block, Government Center, and City Hall / page 131
- HARVARD SQUARE: Museums, browsing, campus and architectural tours, street and other entertainment, and a riverside walk or one along Brattle Street / page 135
- NORTH END: Old North Church, an old burying ground, an ethnic neighborhood, food-oriented sights, a good library, and festivals / page 138
- THE WATERFRONT: Custom House tour, the Aquarium plaza and walkway, and Waterfront Park / page 140

Custom-design your own freebie:

- PLAQUE READING: Look for plaques everywhere—on fences, embedded in buildings, and on statues too.
- COURTHOUSE ACTIVITY: Local or state. Small-claims hearings or a trial. Check with the clerk for a schedule of open hearings.
- JOHN HANCOCK TOWER: Focus on it from different points in the city. Does it ever have the same reflection?
- GOVERNMENT IN PROCESS: Attend an open meeting at City Hall or at the State House.
- COMBINE FAMILIAR AND UNFAMILIAR: Bring a visitor to a place you know well and see it with new eyes.

- **IDENTIFICATION GAME:** Use one of the many photographic collections of Boston, and find the weathervane, doorway, or steeple.
- **MEET PEOPLE:** Shopkeepers, zookeepers, curators, politicians, artists, firemen, bankers, road builders, and more may be available for interviews with advance arrangements.

Explore a new (to you) open space area. Some have programs and guided walks.

- **BEACHES:** Out of season more are available to nonresidents and are free / pages 210–218
- **PLACES IN OR VERY NEAR BOSTON:** Arnold Arboretum, Boston Public Garden, MDC reservations, Mount Auburn Cemetery, and local parks / pages 179–185
- **BOSTON HARBOR ISLANDS:** Free admission and tours. A charge for the ferry but not for island-hopping by water taxi / page 177
- **CAPE COD NATIONAL SEASHORE:** Parking fee at beach areas in summer / page 190
- **DE CORDOVA AND DANA MUSEUM PARK** / page 170
- **GREAT MEADOWS NATIONAL WILDLIFE REFUGE** / page 195
- **HARVARD FOREST** / page 197
- **PARKER RIVER NATIONAL WILDLIFE REFUGE (PLUM ISLAND)** / page 188
- **PHILLIPS ACADEMY BIRD SANCTUARY** / page 165
- **PURGATORY CHASM** / page 198
- **RAVENSWOOD PARK** / page 61
- **SOUTH SHORE NATURAL SCIENCE CENTER** / page 190
- **WOMPATUCK STATE PARK** / page 192

Take a day trip. All these cities and towns have museums, shops, food, and historical sites and homes, but there's no charge for the following suggestions:

- **CONCORD:** Old North Bridge, Sleepy Hollow Cemetery, Walden Pond State Reservation (parking's free in winter), and a winery tour / page 54
- **GLOUCESTER:** Harbor activity, a coastal drive, Dog Bar Breakwater, and Ravenswood Park / page 59
- **LEXINGTON:** A farm with chickens, Visitors Center, Museum of Our National Heritage, picnic sites, and a walking trail / page 63
- **LOWELL:** Guided walking tours (many), canal boat rides, and a company tour / page 66
- **MARBLEHEAD:** Ocean view dotted with sailboats and yachts, picnic sites, Old Town, an old burying ground, architecture, and charm / page 68
- **NEWPORT:** Walking in town and along the cliff, a ride along Ocean Drive, and cycling / page 73
- **PLYMOUTH:** Cranberry World (a museum), a walk along the

Phone Directory

Here's a thumbnail outline of frequently called local numbers. Looking for a category? Check the index.

American Youth Hostels / 731-6692, 731-5430 (recorded)
Amtrak (South Station) / 482-3660, 1-800-523-5720
Animal Rescue League of Boston / 426-9170
Appalachian Mountain Club / 523-0636
Arnold Arboretum / 524-1718, 524-1717 (recorded)

Blue Hills Trailside Museum / 333-0690
BOSTIX / 723-5181 (recorded)
Boston & Maine Railroad (North Station) / 227-5070, 1-800-392-6099
Boston Ballet / 542-3945 (tickets)
Boston Bruins / 227-3206
Boston by Foot / 367-2345
Boston Celtics / 523-6050, 523-3030 (recorded)
Boston Children's Theatre / 277-3277
Boston City Hall / 725-4000 (Check the Blue Pages in the Boston phone book for specific departments.)
Boston Garden / 227-3200 (events)
Boston Globe / 929-2000
Boston Harbor Islands / 727-3180 (weekdays), 749-7161 (weekends)
Boston Herald American / 426-3000
Boston National Historical Park Visitor Center / 223-0058
Boston Phoenix / 536-5390
Boston Public Library / 536-5400
Boston Red Sox / 267-9440, 267-8661 (tickets)
Boston Tea Party Ship and Museum / 338-1773

Charlestown Navy Yard / 242-5601
Children's Museum / 426-6500, 426-8855 (recorded)
Christian Science Monitor / 262-2300

DeCordova and Dana Museum / 259-8355
Drumlin Farm Nature Center / 259-9807

Faneuil Hall Marketplace / 523-2980
Fogg Art Museum / 495-2387 (recorded)
Franklin Park Zoo / 442-2002

Garden in the Woods / 877-7630, 877-6574 (recorded), 237-4924 (Wellesley)
Gardner Museum / 566-1401, 734-1359 (recorded concert information)

Gray Line / 426-8805
Greyhound / 423-5810

John Hancock Observatory / 247-1976
Harvard University / 495-1000
    Events / 495-1718 (school year), 495-2939 (summers)
    Information Center / 495-1573
    Museums / 495-1910 (recorded)
Historic Neighborhoods Foundation / 426-1898
Horse and Carriage Tours / 247-9310

Institute of Contemporary Art / 266-5152, 266-5151 (recorded)

John F. Kennedy Library / 929-4584, 929-4567 (recorded)

Macomber Farm / 879-5345, 237-0543 or 237-2310 (Wellesley)
Massachusetts Audubon Society / 259-9500
Massachusetts Cultural Alliance / 482-9393
Massachusetts Society for the Prevention of Cruelty to Animals / 522-5055
Massachusetts State Parks and Forests / 727-3180
Massachusetts Turnpike winter conditions / 237-5210
MBTA (Massachusetts Bay Transportation Authority) / 722-3200 (weekdays), 722-5657 (evenings and weekends), 722-5050 (recorded)
MDC (Metropolitan District Commission) / 727-5250, 727-5215 (public information)
Metropolitan Center / 542-3600
Minute Man National Historical Park / Headquarters: 369-6993, 484-6192 or 484-6156 (Belmont); Battle Road Visitors Center: 862-7753
Museum of Afro American History / 445-7400
Museum of American China Trade / 696-1815
Museum of Fine Arts / 267-9300, 267-9377 (recorded)
Museum of Our National Heritage / 861-6559
Museum of Science / 723-2505, 742-6088 (recorded)
Museum of the National Center of Afro-American Artists / 442-8614

National Park Service / 223-0058
New England Aquarium / 742-8830, 742-8870 (recorded)
New England Patriots / 262-1776

Opera Company of Boston / 426-2786 (tickets)

Poison Information / 232-2120
Puppet Show Place / 731-6400

Radio stations / Dozens are listed at the beginning of the Ws in the White Pages of the Boston phone book.

Skywalk (Prudential) / 236-3318
State House / 727-3676 (All department numbers are listed under "Mass Commonwealth of" in the Blue Pages of the Boston phone book.)

Steamship Authority / 508–540–2022, 1–800–352–7104
Walter D. Stone Memorial Zoo / 438-3662 (recorded)
Swan boats / 323-2700
Symphony Hall / 266-1492

Time and temperature / 637-1234 (recorded)
Trailways / 482-6620
Trolley Tours of Boston / 269-7010

USS *Constitution* / 242-5670
USS Constitution Museum / 426-1812

Victorian Society / 267-6338

WBZ-TV, Channel 4 / 787-7000
WCVB-TV, Channel 5 / 449-0400
Weather (Boston) / 936-1212 (recorded)
WGBH-TV, Channel 2 / 492-2777
Where's Boston / 367-6090, 661-2425 (recorded)
WLVI-TV, Channel 56 / 288-3200
WNEV-TV, Channel 7 / 725-2700
WSBK-TV, Channel 38 / 783-3838

Index

Want to share your impressions? Discovered a new place? A combination of places? A new activity? A new resource?

Readers' comments and suggestions are welcome. Send them to Bernice Chesler, The Globe Pequot Press, 138 West Main Street, Chester, Connecticut 06412.

**Also of interest from
The Globe Pequot Press:**

Boston's Freedom Trail: A Souvenir Guide
Historic Walks in Old Boston
Historic Walks in Cambridge
Guide to Martha's Vineyard
Guide to Nantucket
Guide to Cape Cod
Special Museums of the Northeast
The Boston Society of Architects' A.I.A. Guide to Boston
Greater Boston Park and Recreation Guide
Budget Dining & Lodging in New England
Daytrips, Getaway Weekends, and Budget Vacations in New England
Bed and Breakfast in New England
Bed and Breakfast in the Mid-Atlantic States
Guide to the Recommended Country Inns of New England
*Guide to the Recommended Country Inns of
the Mid-Atlantic States and Chesapeake Region*
Factory Store Guide to All New England
Factory Store Guide to All New York, Pennsylvania, and New Jersey
Guide to New England's Landscape

Available at your bookstore or direct from the publisher.
For a free catalogue or to place an order, call 1-800-243-0495
(in Connecticut, call 1-800-962-0973) or write to
The Globe Pequot Press, 138 West Main Street, Chester, Connecticut 06412.